THEIR HEADS IN HEAVEN

THEIR HEADS IN HEAVEN

Unfamiliar Aspects of Hasidism

LOUIS JACOBS

VALLENTINE MITCHELL
LONDON • PORTLAND, OR

First published in 2005 in Great Britain by
VALLENTINE MITCHELL & CO. LTD
Premier House, 112–114 Station Road, Edgware, Middlesex HA8 7BJ

and in the United States of America by
VALLENTINE MITCHELL
c/o ISBS,
920 NE 58th Avenue, Suite 300, Portland, OR 97213-3786 USA

British Library Cataloguing in Publication Data
have been applied for

Library of Congress Cataloging in Publication Data
have been applied for

ISBN 0 85303 562 8 (cloth)
0 85303 566 0 (paper)

Printed in Great Britain by
MPG Books Ltd, Bodmin, Cornwall

Contents

*For my granddaughter Ziva
and her husband Mark Green*

Preface

Although this book covers various aspects of Hasidic life and thought, the particular emphasis is on the relationship between the Rebbe as charismatic teacher and his followers. Chapter 2 on Hasidic Attitudes to the Study of the Torah is a reworking of my shorter article 'Study' in *The Encyclopedia of Hasidism*, ed. Tvi M. Rabinowicz, Northvale, New Jersey and London, 1996, pp. 472–74. Chapter 2 on Hasidic 'Torah' is a reworking of my shorter article 'Exegesis' in Rabinowicz, op. cit., pp. 121–3. Chapter 7 on the Zaddik in the thought of R. Elimelech was originally delivered as a Rabbi Louis Feinberg Memorial Lecture at the University of Cincinnati and published in February, 1978, ed. Benny Kraut, but has been brought up to date in order to take into account more recent scholarship. Chapter 8 on Discipleship is a reworked version of an article which appeared in *The Melton Journal*, ed. Barry W. Holtz and Eduardo Rauch, New York, Winter, 1983, pp. 2 and 28. Small sections of Chapters 9, on the *Pitka*, and Chapter 10 on the book *Rahamey Ha-Av*, appeared in the Introduction to the new, paperback, edition of my *Hasidic Prayer*, The Littman Library of Jewish Civilization, London and Washington, 1993, but here the two subjects receive far greater elaboration. A very unsatisfactory version of Chapter 12 appeared in *Cambridge Opinion* 30, February, 1965 and is here thoroughly recast. My gratitude and thanks are due to the editors and publications mentioned. Chapter 13 on Eating as an Act of Worship in Hasidism first appeared in *Studies in Jewish Religious and Intellectual History Presented to Alexander Altmann On the Occasion of his Seventieth Birthday*, ed. Sigfried Stein and Raphael Loewe, Alabama, 1979, pp. 157–65.

Introduction

'The difference between the philosopher and the poet is that the philosopher tries to get the heavens into his head while the poet tries to get his head into the heavens.' This saying, attributed to G. K. Chesterton, can be adapted to describe the difference between the great medieval philosophers and the Kabbalists and Hasidic masters. The basic aim of the philosophers was to interpret the Torah by the light of reason, that is, according to the canons of Greek philosophy in its Arabic garb. They believed, of course, that the Torah was revealed truth, but they also believed that in order to understand the transcendent Torah fully, human reason was the indispensable tool. They made many a mighty effort at getting the heavens into their head. The Kabbalists, on the other hand – and they were followed in this by the Hasidic masters – believed that their theosophical system was not only part of the revealed Torah but the supreme part. The divine mysteries had been revealed and so far as these were concerned human reason was powerless except as a tool to apprehend what the tremendous, secret lore was saying. They, unlike the philosophers, were trying to get their heads in heaven, hence the title of this book.

The essays that make up the book were written at different times so that, although they have the above unifying theme, that of heaven-stormers of diverse kinds, each essay (each chapter of the book) can be read on its own. For this reason, the same ideas recur occasionally, though too much duplication has been avoided. It hardly needs stating that my approach throughout is purely phenomenological. I am neither a Kabbalist nor a Hasid but try to be an objective student of mystical phenomena and the mystical approach in traditional Judaism.

The following is a run-through of the themes of the chapters. Chapter 1 provides a brief outline of the mystical movement of Hasidism. Chapter 2 considers the specific attitudes of Hasidism to the study of the Torah. Chapter 3 shows that the Hasidic masters had their own specific Torah. Chapter 4 considers the role of the

Rabbinic *pilpul* in Habad, the intellectual school in Hasidism. Chapter 5 provides an illustration of how Hasidic 'Torah' operates, as does Chapter 6 with Hasidic 'Torah' on the dream of Jacob. The role of the Zaddik in the influential work of the early master, Elimelech of Lizansk, is the subject of Chapter 7. Chapter 8 takes up the question of the relationship of the Hasid to his Rebbe and Chapter 9 illustrates this by providing a translation with notes of an actual petition presented by a Hasid of the Gerer Rebbe. Chapter 10 treats of a late Hasidic classic which throws light on Hasidic life as it was actually lived by the more devoted Hasidim. Chapter 11 describes a fascinating pen portrait of a Rebbe by his Hasid. Chapter 12 treats of the tensions in early Hasidism between the obligation to obey the fifth commandment and the equally strong obligation to follow the Rebbe. Chapter 13 treats of eating as a special category of worship in Hasidism. Chapter 14 seeks to demonstrate that, for the Hasidim and in certain Talmudic sources, the holy man can be a source of danger as well as goodwill. The final chapter, 15, demonstrates how a very unconventional Rebbe confronted Christianity.

Hasidism: Outline

The following brief account of the Hasidic movement attempts to cover only those features required for the understanding of the following chapters of the book by readers not too familiar with this trend in Judaism, fascinating for some, irritating for others. It is certainly not my aim to offer a guide to Hasidism. Such guides are readily available and will be referred to in the notes whenever necessary.

The founder of the movement is usually said to be Israel ben Eliezer (1698–1760), known as the Baal Shem Tov (often abbreviated to 'Besht' in English but rarely by the Hasidim themselve, for whom he is 'Baal Shem Tov Ha-Kadosh', 'The Holy Baal Shem Tov'). There is no need to waste time in rebutting the ridiculous notion of some Maskilim that there was no such person as the Baal Shem Tov, who was, in their view, a purely legendary figure. The Baal Shem Tov had known children, grandchildren and great-grandchildren. Murray Jay Rosman has examined the archives of the town of Medziboz to find there recorded the name of Israel ben Eliezer, 'Kabbalist and Doctor'. It is also recorded there that, as a respected holy man, he was provided with a stipend by the community. Despite the obviously legendary nature of the *Shivhey Ha-Besht*, 'The Praises of the Baal Shem Tov', published some fifty years after his death, the charismatic figure, hero of the Legends, is a historical person. The questions needing an answer are: What is the meaning of Baal Shem Tov? What does it mean to say that he was the founder of the Hasidic movement? What was the role of Dov Baer the Maggid of Mesirech, clearly a pivotal personality in early Hasidism?

The name Baal Shem Tov was given to Israel ben Eliezer as a folk-healer in his early career where he communed with his Maker in the pure and elevated air of the Carpathian mountains. There were many *baaley shem* in the early eighteenth century in that part of the world, men believed to be skilful in the manipulation of Kabbalistic formulae consisting of various mystical combinations of divine names, which they used, together with herbal remedies and the like, to heal villagers who came to them for the purpose. These men were called *baaley shem*, 'masters of the name', because they claimed to be adept in the application of these combinations of the names of God. Incidentally, it is incorrect to apply the word 'good' as an adjective qualifying Israel ben Eliezer, as if to imply that he was a 'good' master of the name, whereas the others were charlatans. The adjective *tov* ('good') qualifies the word *shem*, ('name'), so that Israel was described as 'The Master of the Good Name' and for that matter the other *baaley shem* were also masters of 'the good name'. The Hasidim, in fact, downplay the role of the Baal Shem Tov as a vulgar miracle worker, preferring to dwell on his role as a great spiritual teacher.

From the Biblical period down through the Talmudic, medieval and immediately pre-modern periods right up to the rise of the Hasidic movement, there were groups of especially pious or saintly men known as *hasidim*. These could occasionally have as their leader a spiritual mentor, known, in our period quite early on, as a Zaddik (originally meaning simply a righteous man but now a saintly master). The 'company', as they called themselves, of young enthusiasts around the Baal Shem Tov was, at first, one of a number of such companies, but eventually these either merged with the Baal Shem Tov's group or vanished entirely from the scene. Rabbi Dov Baer, Maggid ('Preacher') of Mesirech, did not belong to the early company of the Baal Shem Tov's associates, of which, in fact, we know little that is factual. But when fairly advanced in years he became known as the Baal Shem Tov's disciple (historically, the Maggid's relationship to the Baal Shem Tov is rather shaky), and gathered around him a galaxy of learned and saintly young men, whom he later encouraged to become Zaddikim in their own right in various towns in Podolia Galicia, Russia, Poland and the Ukraine. In point of fact, while it is not entirely incorrect to speak of the Baal Shem Tov as the founder of the Hasidic movement – he was, after all, the movement's inspiration – the real founder, or, at least, the true organizer of Hasidism, the man who turned it into a movement, was Dov Baer of Mesirech. When the movement spread and encountered the opposition of the traditional Rabbis, the name Rebbe was given to the Zaddik to distinguish him from the traditional Rabbi.

Among the reasons for the opposition on the part of the traditional Rabbis to Hasidism – some of these will be discussed later in the book – was the suspicion – largely unwarranted – that the members of the new movement were crypto-followers of the false Messiah Shabbetai Zevi, who, as is well-known, believed in him even after his apostasy and even after his death. The Sabbetians called themselves Maaminim – 'believers' – because they believed in Shabbetai Zevi as the Messiah, in reaction to which their opponents called themselves Mitnaggedim, 'opponents' or 'unbelievers'. Suspicious of Hasidism, they referred to it as the *kat*, 'sect'. The Rabbis and communal leaders stuck to the name Mitnaggedim. Indeed, the Mitnaggedim pointed to sectarian Christian movements of the time, by which, it was claimed, the Hasidim were influenced. The Mitnaggedim refer specifically to the Quakers and the Mennonites, and the Maskilim compared the Hasidic writings to those of Emanuel Swedenborg. Such is the mystery of the *Zeitgeist* that certain ideas stressed in Hasidism were paralleled in the non-Jewish revivalist movements of the time, Methodism and the sects among the Russian Orthodox. Revivalism was mysteriously in the air. There is certainly no evidence of any direct influence. It would seem that when spiritual men challenge, rightly or wrongly, the religious establishment, their minds tend to come up with similar ideas even though their religious background is quite different.

THE ZADDIK

Hasidism, despite the fierce opposition and bans of the Mitnaggedim, spread rapidly. Towards the end of the eighteenth century there were scores, perhaps hundreds, of Zaddikim, each with his own followers. In earlier times, the name Zaddik was often that given to an ordinary good man, the term Hasid being used for the man of superior piety. But now the names were reversed. The Hasid was a follower of the charismatic Zaddik or Rebbe. The Zaddik's role was to act as a spiritual mentor to his Hasidim, but also, in some instances especially, to pray on their behalf and bring down the divine blessing from above. In the writings of early Hasidism the Zaddik is the 'channel' through which the divine grace flows from heaven to earth. He can work miracles through his spiritual powers. When a Zaddik died, in the early days of the movement, his place was taken by a chosen disciple, usually one elected by the other disciples or else nominated by the Zaddik while he was alive. Later on, however, the successor to the Zaddik was a close relative, usually one of his sons. This was based on the idea that the Zaddik had such holy thoughts when he was with his wife that he could bring down from heaven a specially elevated soul. In this way there developed the notion, which eventually became the norm of Hasidic dynasties, that the Hasidim saw the Zaddik as a king with a 'court' (in some Hasidic 'courts' there was even a court jester) in a noble palace built for him by his followers, all to the chagrin of the Mitnaggedim, who saw Zaddikism as tending towards Zaddik worship, dubbing it idolatry. It is obviously true that the Zaddik was an innovation in Jewish life. There were fierce rivalries among the dynasties, sometimes among the sons of the Zaddik, who vied with one another with claims to the succession. It was not unknown for a Hasid to journey to a number of Zaddikim, sitting at the table of each and imbibing his wisdom, but rejecting all until he discovered a Zaddik with the same 'root of soul', to whom he then attached himself with bonds of spiritual steel. The usual procedure in the pre-Holocaust period, when there were many towns containing large numbers of Hasidim who owed their allegiance to different Rebbes, was for each group to worship in a small conventicle ('steibel') of its own. Thus in a large town such as Warsaw there would be one or more Gerer steibels or Alexander steibels and so on. The Rebbe himself usually lived in a town or village in which he or his forebears had established his 'court', his particular Hasidim paying him a visit to ask his advice in spiritual and material matters. The large town itself would appoint a Rabbi to administer Jewish law, and teach and preach like any other Rabbi appointed by the townsfolk. The Rebbe operated on an entirely different plane, but naturally preferred that a town Rabbi be appointed who was in line with his particular outlook even if not one of his Hasidim. Since, in the large towns, there were Hasidim owing allegiance to different Rebbes, each of these would try to have the vote sway in favour of his candidate. The result often was, where the Rebbes were divided, that the Hasidim preferred to appoint a Mitnagged as the Rabbi rather than tolerate the appointment of a Rabbi belonging to an opposing Hasidic camp. A very few Rebbes were appointed town Rabbis as well –

the Belzer Rebbe and the Munkacer Rebbe, for example – but this only meant that he had a dual role; that of Rebbe never encroached on that of Rabbi nor vice versa.

HASIDIC THEOLOGY

It is a little precarious to speak of the Hasidic theology since very many of the theological ideas found in the movement are not peculiar to Hasidism at all, nor are Hasidic ideas worked out by the masters in any real systematic form. Moreover, each Hasidic school had its own particular way of thinking, as it had of practice. It is really a matter of emphasis; the best way of studying Hasidic theology is to see what it was in Hasidic thought that was held to be offensive or heretical by the Mitnaggedim. A particular cause of offence was the idea, shared with varying emphases in every branch of Hasidism, that God pervades all creation. This is known in philosophical language – a language the Hasidim themselves could not use – as panentheism ('all is in God') or acosmism ('there is no universe' from the absolute view of God).

In the anathema hurled against the Hasidim in the Mitnaggedic town of Vilna at the end of the eighteenth century it is stated that the Hasidim render in a heretical manner the verse: 'the whole earth is full of His glory' (Isaiah 6:3). For the Mitnaggedim, the verse has to be understood in the conventional, traditional sense, that the divine Providence extends over all. But the Hasidim take the verse literally to mean that the whole universe enjoys no independent reality but is contained in God. Other verses laid under tribute by the Hasidim to convey the same idea are: 'Unto thee it was shown, that, that thou mightest know that the Lord, He is God; there is none else beside Him' (Deuteronomy 4:35) and: 'Know this day, and lay it to thy heart, that the Lord, He is God in heaven above and upon the earth beneath; there is none else' (Deuteronomy 4:39). The words 'There is none else' in both of these verses means, for the Hasidim, that, in reality, there is only God and no universe at all. How can this be? The Hasidic reply, at least in the Habad school, is that while from our point of view the universe is real enough, from God's point of view, there is no universe. The Kabbalist doctrine of *Tzimtzum*, that God withdrew from Himself into Himself before becoming manifest in the *Sefirot* and in all Creation, does not mean that there is really a divine withdrawal. *Tzimtzum* only appears to have taken place. It is no more than a screening of the divine light so that creatures may enjoy existence in its apparent existence. The Hasidim admit that it is impossible to spell this out. It is the greatest mystery of all, upon which it is permissible to dwell only for the purpose of divine worship. When human beings consider the implications of the idea that all is in God the worshipful heart leaps in rapture as the veil between God and man is not exactly ripped asunder but is, at least, moved aside.

The panentheistic idea is not the invention of the Hasidim. To some degree it was shared by some of the Mitnaggedim, who, however, urged that the idea should be used only 'to inflame the heart' during prayers. The Moroccan Kabbalist, Hayyim Ibn Atar (1696–1743) writes, in his Commentary *Or Ha-Hayyim* (to Genesis 2:1): 'The world is in its Creator and the light of the Creator is in the whole world';, this idea is, in fact, much older. The Hasidim find it in the Zohar which speaks of God both 'surrounding all worlds' and 'filling all worlds'. The Hasidim of Germany in the thirteenth century composed the *Shir Ha-Yihud* ('Song of Unity', which, though originally attacked as heretical, has been incorporated into the standard Prayer Book. In the section of this hymn for recital on the third day of the week the words are found: 'All of them are in Thee and Thou art in all of them', and 'Thou surroundest all and fillest all and when all exists Thou art in all'. Yet panentheism has practical consequences for Hasidic life.

Because God's presence is all-pervasive the Hasidim refuse to accept Maimonides' view that there is only divine Providence for species, not for individuals, except for choice human beings. For Maimonides God's Providence guarantees, for instance, that the species of spiders and flies endure, but why a particular spider catches a particular fly is due to pure chance. Hasidism denies that chance operates in the universe. For the Hasidim, every blade of grass lies where it does because of the divine wisdom. The Hasidim tell of a Rebbe walking in the field with his son and discussing Hasidic teachings. The son, engrossed in the ideas his father was imparting to him, absentmindedly plucked a leaf from a tree and twirled it in his hands. The father rebuked him: 'The leaf was put where it is. It grew by the wisdom of the Creator. How were you able to pluck it from the tree!'

This is why the Hasidic doctrine of *avodah be-gashmiut*, 'worship in corporeality', developed. Although a few of the Hasidic masters were ascetics, the Baal Shem Tov is reported to have introduced a new, anti-ascetic mode of divine worship. Instead of man rejecting worldly things, he should engage in them in a spirit of holiness, restoring the 'holy sparks' inherent in all creation to their source in God. Ideally, the Hasid should eat and drink, have legitimate sex, be an artisan or a businessman, but all with God in the mind, as we shall see in Chapter 13 on eating as an act of worship. It should be said, however, that in matters of sex Hasidism is very reserved, always on the lookout for sexual thoughts and temptations. Yet, even here, the disciple of the Maggid, the Seer of Lublin, taught that if the Hasid enjoys sex with his wife, albeit not engaging in the act for that express purpose, he should later give thanks to God for the pleasure, 'in any language available to him', even though no Hebrew benediction has been ordained by the Rabbis as they did for eating and drinking.

Akin to this is the Hasidic doctrine of *devekut*, 'attachment' to God in the mind at all times. The Hasidim admit that realisticaly such an ideal is possible only for the Zaddik, and even he has his ups and downs. But the Hasidim can also try to approximate to the ideal, and by being attached to the Zaddik, can through him be led to a degree of *devekut*. A further ideal is to aspire to the state known as *bittul ha-yesh*, 'annihilation of selfhood'. This means that, especially at his prayers, the Hasid should overcome the very existence of his individual self as he is in contemplation of the divine energy which pervades all. In their doctrine of 'the elevation of strange thoughts', the early masters carried *avodah be-gashmiut* to the extreme; when worldly things enter the mind they should not be rejected but lifted in the mind to God. For example, when a Hasid has a sensation of pride at his achievements, he should not try to get rid of it but should rather reflect that human pride has its Source in God and should bring this thought to bear on experience. Or when the Hasid inadvertently sees a pretty woman he should not, as do the Mitnaggedim, try to set his mind on more worthy matters. On the contrary, he should reflect that God has sent him this vision of beauty in order for him to reflect on God as the Source of all beauty. This idea, a subject of scorn by the Mitnaggedim, was eventually abandoned as too dangerous by the later masters. In Israel Zangwill's story 'The Master of the Name' (in Zangwill's collection, *Dreamers of the Ghetto*) the narrator is given a ride in a carriage driven by the Baal Shem Tov. To the narrator's surprise, the coachman, the Baal Shem Tov, stops for a moment to remark on the beauty of a passing maiden, not exactly the sort of thing expected of a saint. But then he witnessed the coachman's fervent prayer and realized that his mind was entirely on God. Yet while the application of the doctrine to sex was, as stated, abandoned, in other worldly matters it was retained. It was not unusual to see Hasidic businessmen conducting their affairs with success but with their minds on God. There are analogies in Quakerism and Methodism. There is a medieval legend quoted in Hasidic literature to this effect. Regarding the Biblical hero who 'walked with God and was not but was taken by God' (Genesis 5:24), Enoch, the legend states, was a cobbler by trade, but when he stitched the upper part of the shoes he repaired to the lower part he united the lower worlds to the higher worlds.

Two other Hasidic terms should be mentioned in this connection – *simhah*, 'joy', and *hitlahavut*, 'burning enthusiasm', from *lahav'*, 'flame'. *Simhah* in Hasidic thought goes much further than the Rabbinic idea of *simhah shel mitzvah*, 'taking joy in the performance of the precepts of the Torah'. Hasidic *simhah* denotes that the true Hasid who perceives God's glory pervading the universe can never be miserable, since he is always with his Father in heaven. Hasidic joy is not a facile optimism that all is well. The Hasid, like other human beings, had his worries and frustrations and his lot could be miserable. Yet he was able to rise above his sorrows in his belief that God is always present to set his feet right. The great historian of Hasidism, Simon Dubnow, though sympathetic to many of the ideas of the movement, saw in this Hasidic optimism a form of escapism, and a refusal to meet life's demands. It is hard to generalize. No doubt, for many Hasidim, joy was an evasion of life's duties but for others it was a powerful spur to noble living. The Maskilim, the enlightened foes of Hasidism, many of them physicians, accused the Hasidic masters of encouraging their followers, when ill, to go to the Zaddik to pray on their behalf rather than consult physicians. However, with few exceptions, the Zaddikim themselves did not see prayer as a substitute for natural methods of healing, which latter they also saw as God's gift to humanity. Tensions existed, of course. It is said that when R. Shneur Zalman of Liady, founder of the Habad branch of Hasidism, was imprisoned by the Czar, the Hasidim declared that in order to free their master they must adopt both a natural and a supernatural method. The natural method was to recite prayers on the master's behalf. The supernatural method was to bribe the Czarist officials!

HASIDIC LIFE

As Hasidism developed it took on outward forms of its own. The Hasidic masters believed that the Prayer Book which followed the liturgy as preferred by the great Kabbalist, Isaac Luria, the Ari, was the one the Hasidim ought to adopt, even though they belonged to communities which followed the traditional Ashkenazi rite, resulting in the separation of the Hasidim from the general community. There were Halakhic reasons why Ashkenazim should not depart from their custom. Nevertheless, the Hasidic steibel with its own liturgy became the norm everywhere. One of the liturgical differences between the Ashkenazi and the Lurianic liturgy is that in the Kaddish of the latter there is a reference to the hope for the coming of the Messiah. Hasidim relate that a little boy asked his father whether God is a Hasid or a Mitnagged. A Mitnagged, the father replied, for if He is a Hasid He would have said the Kaddish with the reference to the Messianic hope and the Messiah would have come! In another tale, a Rebbe was the son of a fierce Mitnagged. The father ordered his son, the Rebbe, not to say the Kaddish for him when he died since he would be saying the Kaddish in accordance with the Hasidic rite. When the father died, the Rebbe asked his Rebbe, the Seer of Lublin, whether he was allowed to say the Kaddish in accordance with the Hasidic rite despite the father's objection. Say it, replied the Seer, he knows now that ours is the correct version!

Although there is a lifestyle common to all Hasidim there are variations according to the patterns and traditions of particular dynasties. All Hasidim wear a girdle around the waist for prayer, to divide the upper part of the body from the lower. The majority of Hasidim wear on the Sabbath and the festivals the squat fur-trimmed hat known as the *streimel*. The Hasidim of Ger substitute for the *streimel* the tall fur hat known as the *spodik*, while the Hasidim of Lubavitch wear neither, only plain black hats. It has often been noted that the Hasidic fur hats were those worn by the Polish aristocrats in the eighteenth century, as can be seen in prints of Polish noblemen, and were adopted by the Hasidim as a dignified head covering suitable for special festive occasions. Eventually the *streimel* became the most typical form of headgear, into which various; mystical ideas were read, for example, the thirteen tails of which it is composed represent the thirteen attributes of divine mercy. A *streimel* can be made of sable and can be quite costly. It is the practice for the bride's father to provide a *streimel* for his son-in-law. Some Hasidim wear white socks on the Sabbath and festivals as a symbol of purity, but among others this is allowed only for the most distinguished, while still others do not know of the custom at all. Hasidim usually sport beards and cultivate long *peot* (ear locks) but these, among some Hasidic groups, are of the 'corkscrew' variety.

When a Hasid pays his regular visit to his Rebbe's court, he presents a written petition, the *kvittel*, to the Rebbe, in which he requests the Rebbe to pray for his needs and those of his family to be satisfied. (Despite the wilder accusations of the early Mitnaggedim, prayers are never offered to the Rebbe himself. The petition is for the Rebbe to pray on the Hasid's behalf.) In return, the Hasid donates a sum of money known as a *pidyon* ('redemption'). The Rebbe uses the money he receives from the *pidyon*, and from collections made in the various towns, not only for his own needs and the costly upkeep of his court but also, perhaps primarily, for charitable purposes, the wealthier Hasidim contributing in this way to the maintenance of their poor associates. The Rebbe is usually consulted before the Hasid arranges marriages for his children and whenever he is about to undertake an important business transaction. The Rebbe acts as a spiritual guide to his followers and, if possible, will advise in private audiences on the more intimate aspects of their religious life. Although some writers have overplayed the role of women in Hasidism, it remains true that Hasidic women are allowed access to the Rebbe for him to offer guidance.

The Hasid's access to his Rebbe is through the Gabbaim ('factotums', 'retainers', 'supervisors'). These paid officials are often the real power behind the throne; the Hasidim hate the Gabbaim in proportion to their love for the Rebbe. The Gabbaim control the queues waiting to be received by the Rebbe, see to it that proper decorum is observed, and protect the Rebbe from too many intrusions on his privacy. Some Hasidic courts are run on comparatively frugal lines, but others are conducted with great opulence. Nowadays, for instance, the Rebbes often travel in extravagant style, in chauffeur-driven limousines and in first-class seats on trains and planes, and with an entourage.

At the sacred meal on the Sabbath the Hasidim sit in awed silence around the Rebbe's *tish* (table) until he gives them the signal to sing the traditional Sabbath songs. Some Rebbes are themselves gifted composers. Others have Hasidim who compose melodies which then form the repertoire for all the Hasidim of that particular group and often for other Hasidim as well. After the Rebbe has tasted a little from the dish placed before him, the 'left-overs' (*shirayim*) are distributed among the Hasidim in the belief that to eat of the food blessed by the holy man brings spiritual and material blessings. At the *tish* the Rebbe delivers a homily on the portion of the Torah read in the Synagogue on that week. In the early days of Hasidism, to a lesser degree even later, it was believed that when the Rebbe 'says Torah', it is the Shekhinah which takes over and 'speaks through his throat', so that it was said that afterwards the Rebbe himself was unaware of what he had said. Some Rebbes used to wear only white garments on the Sabbath but this is nowadays looked upon as religious ostentation and is very unusual.

The dance is a regular feature of Hasidic life. In the Hasidic dance the Hasidim place their arms around their neighbour's shoulders to whirl around in a circle in obedience to the Psalmist's call to 'serve the Lord with gladness' (Psalms 100:2). For the same reason, on festive occasions no Hasidic gathering is complete without a generous supply of strong drink; hence the taunts of the Mitnaggedim that Hasidim are drunkards.

After the Holocaust, Hasidism has succeeded in re-establishing itself, winning the admiration even of non-Hasidic Jews, enamoured of its optmism, its colour and its joy. There are still Mitnaggedic opponents, but the majority of Jews find the revival of Hasidism a good thing.

2

Hasidic Attitudes to the Study of the Torah

To study the Torah is as much a sublime obligation in Hasidism as it is in every version of traditional Judaism, but certain nuances in the Hasidic understanding of the ideal met with strong opposition among the Mitnaggedim, the foes of the new movement. For one thing, the early Hasidic masters substituted prayer for study as the highest aim of the religious life. In the older tradition, study is far more important than all other religious obligations, including prayer. According to the Talmudic sources (*Berakhot* 21a; *Shabbat* 38a) the obligation to pray three times a day is Rabbinic, not Biblical, unlike the obligation to study the Torah, which is held to be Biblical. In the first of these sources, this distinction is stated explicitly. In another Talmudic passage (*Shabbat* 10a) a Rabbi rebukes his colleague who prolonged his prayers unduly, by protesting: 'They leave aside eternal life [= the study of the Torah] to engage in temporal life [= prayer]'. That is, prayer addresses itself mainly to the satisfaction of worldly needs, health, sustenance and so forth, whereas the Torah brings eternal life to its students and this is beyond all temporal concerns. Scholars such as Rabbi Simeon ben Yohai, we are told (*Shabbat* 11a), whose sole occupation was the study of the Torah, would not pray at all, considering prayer to be an interruption in the much more significant occupation of studying God's word.

In Hasidism, a complete transformation took place, in which prayer becomes a more elevated duty even than the study of the Torah. As a typical, early Hasidic text[1] puts it: 'The soul declared to the Rabbi [the Baal Shem Tov], may his memory be for a blessing for the life of the World to Come, that the reason why all the supernal mysteries were revealed to him was not because he had studied many Talmudic tractates and Codes of Law but because of

his prayer. For at all times he recited his prayers with great concentration. It was as a result of this that he attained to his elevated
stage.' In the older tradition it was not only that study is far more
significant than prayer but, in that tradition, neither prayer nor
study should be engaged in order to reach an 'elevated stage'. Both
are to be engaged in because they are religious duties irrespective
of whether or not they will result in high degrees of spirituality.
The Hasidic masters, acutely aware that their attitude in this matter involved a radical departure from the tradition, tried to justify
it in various ways,[2] often by stating that in our 'inferior generation'
devotional prayer is the only effective way of bringing man nearer
to God. These masters did not, of course, reject entirely the ideal of
study. It was all a question of where the emphasis was to be placed.

In another early Hasidic text[3] it is suggested that while time
should be given for reflection on God even during the study of the
Torah, a man must never actually give up his studies in order to
have more time for reflection:

> When he studies he should pause from time to time in order to attach
> himself to God. For all that, he must engage in study even though it is
> impossible to attach himself to God during the time of study. Yet study
> he must, for the Torah purifies his soul and is a tree of life to those who
> hold fast to it so that if he will refrain from study he will cease [in any
> event] from his attachment to God. He should think to himself that he
> is unable to be attached to God during the time he sleeps or at a time of
> smallness of soul and the time he spends in study is not worse than
> these times. Nevertheless, it is essential for him to settle himself from
> hour to hour and moment to moment so as to have an attachment to
> the Creator, blessed be He, as stated above.

In this passage is to be found all the tensions in Hasidic life
between the need to study the Torah and the need for constant
attachment to God in the mind (*devekut*).[4] If, according to the
Hasidic ideal, one has to have God in mind all the time, how can
the Hasid allow his mind to be diverted from thought on God by
engaging in profound study of the difficult Talmudic texts which
require all his powers of concentration? In this text, study of the
Torah, sublime an aim though it is, appears as a kind of concession
to human frailty. Ideally, the text implies, *devekut* ought to be the
state of the Hasid at all times, but since this is impossible in any
event – a man has to sleep and he is not always in the mood (his
soul is 'small' at times) – he might as well study the Torah and
cease from his attachment by carrying out a great religious duty.

Furthermore, the text implies, only a pure soul can attain to *devekut*, and the study of the Torah has the capacity to purify the soul. The real end then for Hasidism is the attainment of *devekut*, study being the means to this end in that it is the only way to equip the soul for its spiritual journey on high. Here lies the essential difference between the Hasidic and the Mitnaggedic ideal of study. For the Mitnaggedim, the study of the Torah is a sublime end in itself, whereas for the Hasidim it is only a means – albeit a very important one – to the true end of *devekut*.

This difference between the Hasidim and the Mitnaggedim expressed itself also in different attitudes on the question of motivation for the study of the Torah. The Rabbinic ideal, as stated in the Talmud (*Berakhot* 50b and throughout) is to study the Torah *lishmah*, 'for its own sake', that is, without ulterior motivation. To study with an ulterior motive, *shelo lishmah*, is held in some Talmudic passages to be unworthy and, in some instances, even sinful. There is considerable ambiguity in the matter in the Talmudic sources. For instance, it is stated in one Talmudic passage (*Berakhot* 17a) that for one who studies *shelo lishmah* it were better for him never to have been born. But against this is the statement (*Pesahim* 50b) of Rav Judah in the name of Rav (early third cenury), 'Let a man study the Torah even if it is *shelo lishmah* for out of the study *shelo lishmah* will come study *lishmah*'. The commentators try to resolve the contradiction in various ways, e.g. it all depends on which kind of ulterior motivation is present. One kind is sinful, the other kind can be tolerated since it can lead to sincere motivation. The Tosafot,[5] for example, suggest that if the motivation for study is to win fame as a scholar, such motivation, though hardly ideal, is not sinful and can be tolerated. But where a scholar studies simply because he wants to use his learning to score over others and humiliate them, such offensive motivation is positively sinful. The debate between the Hasidim and the Mitnaggedim revolves around the correct application of these Talmudic texts. For the Hasidim any kind of impure motivation is bound to be a hindrance to the ideal of *devekut* since even the study of the Torah is only a means to the attainment of this state. How, then, can a scholar allow himself to overlook the ultimate aim of study by being self-motivated? Such a scholar, far from treating his studies as a means to *devekut*, is consciously using his studies to achieve his own ends, desires and ambitions. As for Rav's saying, this can only mean, declare the Hasidic masters, that the impure motivation is tolerated but only for the weak in soul and even then only because it will eventually lead to *lishmah*. The strong in soul ought to be beyond impure motivation in the first instance. R. Jacob Joseph of Pulonnoye, in the first Hasidic book to be published, is so severe in this matter[6] as to declare that study with the aim of meriting eternal bliss in the hereafter is still considered to be study with an ulterior motive, *shelo lishmah*.

In addition to the strong emphasis on the ideal of Torah *lishmah* the early masters tended to understand the whole concept to mean not study for the sake of the Torah (Torah *lishmah* meaning 'Torah for its own sake') but study for the sake of God, i.e. study as a devotional rather than an intellectual exercise. This idea is expressed in various ways. In one of the earliest references to the teachings of the Baal Shem Tov, R. Meir Margalliouth of Ostrog (d. 1790) understands 'Torah *lishmah*' to mean both study of the Torah in order to carry out its laws and study as a novel mystical exercise. This author writes:[7]

> For the main aim of Torah study is for it to be *lishmah*, namely, to study the Torah in order to obey the laws, to keep them and carry them out. It all depends on the right intention, and this alone is the perfect manner of fulfilling this precept [of Torah study]. This is hinted at in the verse: 'they shall prepare that which they bring in' [Exodus 14:15]. This means that before a man begins his studies he should think to himself clearly and honestly that he is making himself ready to study *lishmah*, without any alien thought. As my great teachers in Torah and Hasidut have taught me, among them my dear friend, the Rabbi and Hasid, marvel of his generation, our master, Israel Baal Shem Tov, of blessed memory, that the correct intention for the study of Torah *lishmah* is for the student to attach himself [*ledabek et atzmo*], in holiness and purity, to the letters [of the Torah] actual as well as potential, in speech as well as in thought, so as to bind the portion of his *nefesh, ruah, neshamah, hayyah* and *yehidah* [the five parts of the soul according to the Kabbalah] to the sanctity of the lamp that is the precept and the light that is the Torah, the letters which make a man wise and through which there is an influx of illuminations and true and eternal vitality.

The meaning of this somewhat cryptic passage appears to be that, in addition to the conventional understanding of Torah for its own sake, which this author mentions at the beginning, a mystical nuance is introduced, in which the student attaches himself in the deepest recesses of his psyche to the spiritual energy and vitality contained in the very letters of the Torah. This author continues that such attachment to the letters enables the student to penetrate the essence of the letters, that he becomes empowered to forecast the future. R. Meir Margalliouth wrote this when he had become a very learned Rabbi, probably little involved in Hasidic life. It is not surprising, therefore, that he first records the conventional understanding of Torah for its own sake and only introduces the mystical understanding in the name of the Baal Shem Tov, the 'dear friend' of his youth. In this latter R. Meir Margalliouth is very unusual among Hasidic teachers, if he can be considered a Hasidic teacher at all, since all we have in connection with Hasidism are reminiscences of his youth. The majority of the early Hasidic masters do understand the doctrine of Torah *lishmah* in terms of *devekut*, but not in the sense of attachment to the letters but attachment to God. Yet R. Meir's report is substantiated by the statement in the writings of R. Jacob Joseph of Polonnoyer:[8] 'I have heard from my teacher in the matter of *lishmah* that this means for the sake of the letter.' But R. Jacob Joseph says nothing about the quasi-magical ability to forecast future events through the energy inherent in the letters. It would seem that, indeed, the Baal Shem Tov did understand the doctrine of Torah *lishmah* in the manner stated by R. Jacob Joseph and R. Meir Margalliouth)[9] but, as Hasidic thought developed, Torah *lishmah* came to mean Torah for the sake of God, i.e. study as serving the ideal of *devekut*. Such an understanding was totally different from the conventional view, which was the view of the Mitnaggedim, for whom the study of the Torah, especially the complicated Talmudic dialectics, was not for any other end but solely for the sake of the Torah itself. The Mitnaggedim argued that study with God in mind is no study at all. The mind of the student has to be on the subjects he studies if he is to have any success. The Hasidim retorted that study without *devekut* could not be considered study *lishmah* and that to study for the sake of the Torah could be self-seeking in that for a man to be a scholar enhanced his reputation.

A problem for the Hasidic masters was how can the study of the Torah be purely for the sake of God since the student obtains intense intellectual pleasure from his studies; a problem that did not exist for the Mitnaggedim, in whose view Torah *lishmah* means study of the Torah for its own sake, of which the intellectual pleasure derived is an integral part. The usual Hasidic reply was that, indeed, the motivation for study should be for the sake of God, with any pleasure derived from the study only an incidental by-product. The early Hasidic master, R. Meshullan Feivish of

Zhbarazh (d. c. 1795), a notable exponent of Torah *lishmah* according to the Hasidic understanding, deals explicitly with this problem.[10] 'It is true', observes this author, 'that it is impossible not to obtain pleasure from [the study of] the Torah, for it is sweeter than honey. This [pleasure] is only permitted to us but we must not study for this purpose [to obtain pleasure from the study].' R. Meshullam Feivish quotes the verse: 'Say unto wisdom: Thou art my sister' (Proverbs 7:4). Man's attitude to the Torah should be one of pure, disinterested love, like that of a brother for his sister, not like that of a husband for his wife. R. Meshullam Feivish goes so far as to say that one who studies the Torah out of motives of self-interest, *shelo lishmah*, commits spiritual prostitution.

The Mitnaggedim, for their part, argued that because of the Hasidic emphasis on *devekut*, the Hasidim were unable to study adequately and never became true scholars proficient in Talmudic learning.[11] This kind of polemic is obviously biased. For all their emphasis on *devekut*, many Hasidim did manage to acquire great proficiency in Talmudic learning, and hardly any of the masters discouraged their followers from pursuing the traditional ideal of intense concentration on the subjects studied. Like all other traditional Jews, the Hasidim believed that to study the Torah in the traditional sense was to study the very word of God, although it is likely that a minority of Hasidim did neglect their studies because of the *devekut* ideal and some of the Mitnaggedic critique may have been justified.

We can now turn to R. Hayyim of Volozhyn (1749–1821), disciple of the Gaon of Vilna, the arch opponent of Hasidism. R. Hayyim composed his *Nefesh Ha-Hayyim* in defence of the Mitnaggedic view. R. Hayyim, in this work, stoutly maintains that the doctrine of Torah *lishmah* does not imply *devekut* but means that the Torah should be studied for its own sake. Moreover, R. Hayyim refuses to admit that study of the Torah with ulterior motivation is valueless. Even study *shelo lishmah* is still study of the Torah and even scholars whose motivation is impure are still to be respected as men learned in the Torah should be. Rav, in the Talmudic passage, allows study with ulterior motivation because, as he says, this will eventually lead to study *lishmah*. R. Hayyim is very realistic. It must not be supposed, says R. Hayyim, that Rav means the insincere scholar will wake up suddenly one morning to find that he wants to study from now onwards only *lishmah*. Human nature does not change overnight. Rav means that when a scholar immerses himself in study of the Torah, whatever his original intention, in the course of his studies he will forget his self-seeking motivation and enjoy his studies in themselves and this, for R. Hayyim, is the study of the Torah for its own sake.[12]

It should be appreciated that the *Nefesh Ha-Hayyim* was first published in Vilna-Grodno in 1824, a time when the more fierce opposition to Hasidism had abated, but the actual writing of the book took place at an earlier date when the battle was still enjoined in all its ferocity. Yet R. Hayyim, even in the earlier period, was less than whole-hearted in his opposition to Hasidism. He generally refers to the Hasidim as 'those who desire the nearness of God' and throughout the book his debate is conducted on the theoretical level and with a degree of courtesy. The *Nefesh Ha-Hayyim* is more of a calm theological treatise than an unbridled polemic.

R. Hayyim, without actually mentioning the Hasidim, is obviously referring to them when he writes:[13] 'With regard to the matter of studying the Torah *lishmah* it is clear and true that *lishmah* does not mean *devekut*, as most people in the world [*rov ha-olam*] now understand it'. R. Hayyim's reference to 'most people' is astonishing. It looks as if the Hasidic view had become the accepted view of the majority of Lithuanian Jews, including the Mitnaggedim. If, continues R. Hayyim, *lishmah* means *devekut*, how is it possible to study adequately such topics as rival claims to property, of which the Talmud is full, with the mind on God? Talmudic studies, in all their complexity, demand complete absorption in the arguments presented. To have the state of *devekut* at the same time is virtually impossible. It follows[14] that *lishmah* must mean for the sake of the Torah, that is, to study the Torah and all the topics treated therein for its own sake, not out of ulterior motives. It goes without saying, observes R. Hayyim,[15] that the student of the Torah must be a God-fearing person, otherwise, indeed, the studies are of no religious value. The Talmud (*Shabbat* 31a) compares the fear of heaven to a storehouse in which is preserved the produce that is the fruit of study. On this R. Hayyim writes:

> Scripture [as interpreted in the Talmud] compares the Torah to an abun-
> dance of produce and the fear of Heaven to a storehouse to contain the
> wisdom of the holy Torah by means of which it will be preserved.
> Unless a man has first prepared the storehouse of fear, the abundance
> of Torah produce is as if it were left in the field to be trampled on by the
> feet of the ox and the ass and nothing will be remain.

For all that, R. Hayyim pointedly remarks,[16] the very comparison of the fear of heaven to a storehouse implies 'the very opposite of the mistaken opinion among many of the children of our people who devote all their studies to books dealing solely with the topics of fear and ethical conduct'. Who would be so stupid as to spend all his time in constructing a storehouse while never bringing his produce into the storehouse?

On the Hasidic side, R. Meshullam Feivish (mentioned above) had argued[17] in the name of R. Menahem Mendel of Peremyshlani (d. 1728), an associate of the Baal Shem Tov, that the conventional distinction between *nigleh*, the revealed part of the Torah, and *nistar*, the secret part of the Torah, is false.

> *Nistar* refers to something it is impossible to communicate to another, the taste of food, for example, which cannot be conveyed to one who has never tasted that particular food. It is impossible to convey to another the how and the what of the matter. This is called a secret thing. So it is with regard to the love and fear of the Creator, blessed be He. It is impossible to convey to another how such love is in the heart. This is called *nistar*. But how can it be correct to call the science of the Kabbalah *nistar*? Whoever desires to study [Kabbalah] the book is open for him. If he cannot understand the book he is simply an ignoramus for whom the Talmud and the Tosafot would equally be *nistar*. But the meaning of *nistarot* ['the secrets'] in the whole of the Zohar and the writings of the Ari of blessed memory, is that these are all constructed on the idea of *devekut* to the Creator for whomsoever is privileged to become attached to the Chariot on High and to gaze at it, like the Ari of blessed memory for whom the Heavenly Paths were clearly illumined so that he was able to walk constantly in them guided by the eyes of his intellect.

It is obvious that R. Hayyim is reacting to R. Meshullam Feivish when he defends the traditional understanding of *nigleh* and *nistar*.[18]

> Therefore the statement occurs frequently in the Zohar that the whole of the Torah is both closed and open, a statement which obviously refers, for anyone who understands it, to the hidden aspect of the holy Torah, to that which is not written explicitly and clearly but is secreted and concealed behind the words. And the revealed aspect is the simple meaning of Scripture, that which is recorded in writing and clearly explicit. (Not as I have seen it written by someone who had gone into the topic: 'Why do we call the Kabbalistic science by the name *nistar*? For one who understands it is revealed and for one who does not know and understand, there are simple matters of Scripture which for one who cannot explain are hidden.' And he gives whatever reply he give.)

Undoubtedly, R. Hayyim is correct in his understanding of the traditional view, namely, that *nistar* means the secret things, the mysteries of the Torah, as found in the Kabbalah, while *nigleh* means those matters that can be understood at once, provided the student has the ability to master the texts. R. Meshullam Feivish was surely aware that he, or rather Menahem Mendel whom he quotes, was an innovator. The terms *nistar* and *nigleh* are now given an entirely new interpretation in line with Hasidic ideas. *Nistar* is not the name for a body of texts – the Kabbalah – but for a mystical experience. What R. Meshullam Feivish is saying is that study without *devekut* is a study of *nigleh*, a mere surface study, even if the texts studied are about the Kabbalistic mysteries. Conversely, study with *devekut*, with the mind on God, is a *nistar* type of study, because it involves mystical awareness, even if the texts studied belong to the 'revealed' things such as the Talmud and the Tosafot. It was thus not which texts were studied that mattered but how the Hasid studied them. And it was precisely here that the Mitnaggedic view saw Hasidism as a threat to the traditional view since, for the Mitnaggedim, such study was self-defeating.

R. Hayyim, speaking on behalf of the Mitnaggedim, also stresses the need for the student to be God-fearing. Yet, for him, fear is only the storehouse in which the produce of learning is preserved. For the Hasidim, on the other hand, fear, in the sense of *devekut*, is an essential ingredient in study itself. It has to be said, however, that many of the Hasidic masters were extremely proficient in Talmudic learning and refused to see the *devekut* ideal as a hindrance to their acquisition of proficiency.

At a later stage in the history of Hasidism, a number of Hasidic masters took the Mitnaggedic critique sufficiently seriously to deal with it frankly and consciously. R. Yizthak Isaac Safrin of Komarno (1806–74), for example, comments[19] on the statement in the Mishnah (*Avot* 1:13): 'He who does not study deserves to die and one who uses the [royal] crown will pass away.' R. Yitzhak Eisik writes:

> In this statement he [the teacher mentioned in the Mishnah] warns against stupid saintliness [*hasidut shel shtut*]. Since the main thing is to study *lishmah* and with *devekut* and such is a very lofty stage, it is impossible to attain immediately this category of *lishmah*. It is perforce necessary to engage in the study of the Torah even *shelo lishmah*. For as long as the student has not become sufficiently refined to desire the delights of the Torah, since out of the inwardness present in *shelo*

lishmah the light of the Torah will restore him to the good. The stupid seize hold immediately of this inner light but, since they do not have the merit, they leave aside completely the study of the Torah. They do not want [to study] *shelo lishmah* since they are Hasidim and they do not have as yet the merit of attaining to *lishmah*. To counter this folly – for the main thing is the study of the Torah and nothing is more precious than the Torah – the Tanna states: 'He who does not study deserves to die' by the hands of Heaven. He has no portion in eternal life. [The Tanna continues:] 'And one who uses the crown', namely, one who studies *shelo lishmah*, using the royal sceptre for his own benefit, 'will pass away'; for those who wait on the Lord will renew their strength [i.e. taking the word *halaf* to mean not 'will pass away' but 'will suffer change'] and out of *shelo lishmah* they will attain *lishmah* and the stage of holiness. But one who does not study at all will have nothing by which he can renew himself and will remain in a state of great embarrassment on high.

In this remarkable passage, R. Yitzhak Eisik advocates the ideal of study *lishmah* and with *devekut* but urges the Hasid not to be so stupid as to give up the study of the Torah entirely because, at the stage at which he finds himself, he is unable to reach that lofty stage. Let him persist, says R. Yitzhak Eisik, and the light of the Torah he studies, even if the study is *shelo lishmah*, will lead him to the higher stage. R. Yitzhak Eisik has certainly departed from the older Hasidic ideal according to which study with ulterior motives is valueless. He even implies that, at first, the stance of *shelo lishmah* is the only one possible and is certainly preferable to giving up the study of the Torah because of inferior motivation.

Another later Hasidic master, R. Abraham Bornstein of Sochaczew (1839–1910), son-in-law of the famous Rebbe of Kotzk and, like his father-in-law, a very learned Talmudist, is aware of the problem, discussed earlier by R. Meshullam Feivish, of how delight in study can be compatible with the ideal of *lishmah*. R, Abraham writes:[20]

In the course of my remarks, I must mention that which I have heard said by a few people, who depart from the intelligent way in the matter of the study of our holy Torah. They say that one who studies and creates new ideas and is happy and finds delight, his studies are not as much *lishmah* as are those of one who simply studies without any delight in his studies but only because it is a *mitzvah* [a religious obligation]. In one who studies and enjoys his studies there is an admixture of selfhood. Truth be told this is obviously a mistaken view. On the contrary, it belongs to the main methodological principle of the *mitzvah* of Torah study that one rejoices and is happy and takes delight in his studies for then the words of the Torah become absorbed in his blood and through his enjoyment of the words of the Torah he becomes attached [*davuk*] to the Torah ... admit that one who studies not for the sake of the *mitzvah* but only because he enjoys his studies, his study is considered to be *shelo lishmah*, like one who eats *matzah* not for the sake of the *mitzvah* but simply because he likes eating *matzah*. It is with regard to this that the Rabbis say that a man should study even if it is *shelo lishmah* because it will lead to *lishmah*. But where one studies because it is a *mitzvah* and enjoys his studies, this is study *lishmah* and all of it is holy for the enjoyment itself constitutes a *mitzvah*.

Not only does R. Abraham hold that where the study is for the sake of the *mitzvah*, that is, as a religious duty, enjoyment of the studies is essential and hence the study is *lishmah*, but he holds that even if the study is simply because one enjoys studying, it is still considered to be Torah study, albeit of an inferior kind, and it will lead to study *lishmah*. Here this Hasidic master comes very close to the approach of R. Hayyim of Volozhyn and the other Mitnaggedim.

Another still later Hasidic master, R. Hayyim Eleazar Shapira (1872–1937) of Munkacs went even further in the matter. According to a reliable report,[21] R. Hayyim Eleazar would urge his students to study particularly out of self-seeking motivation provided they would have the intention that it should lead eventually to study *lishmah*. R. Hayyim Eleazar would also urge his students to immerse themselves in the complex dialectics of the Talmud and to try to clarify the subject by means of keen *pilpul*.

Here and there, but sparsely, one finds a reversal to the older Hasidic attitude prevailing well into the twentieth century. Many Hasidic young men in the post-war years adopted the methods of study of the Lithuanian Yeshivot. The teachers in these Yeshivot were not usually hostile to Hasidism. On the contrary, the 'Litvaks' had long made common cause with the Hasidim against the Maskilim. And yet the keen analytical methodology in the Lithuanian-type Yeshivot was poles apart from the study with *devekut* advocated in early Hasidism. The majority of Hasidim, even when they founded Hasidic Yeshivot, were content on the whole to study in the Lithuanian way. Yet R. Zevi Hirsch Rosenbaum of Kiryat Ata in Israel, in his introduction to a book about his grandfather, R. Eliezer Zeev of Kretchnif (1882–1944), can still quote the extremely severe view of R. Meshullam Feivish when he writes:[22]

For it is a tradition that we have from all the Zaddikim, our fathers and teachers, the Torah and fear that is in the way of the light of our eyes, the Baal Shem Tov, of blessed memory, from whose lips we live, will bring near our true redemption, speedily to come before our eyes. (Not like those who err and are envious of ordinary scholars. This brings about daily an increase of speakers and guides in Hasidic Yeshivot, those who do not follow the way of elevated *hasidut*.) As the words uttered in truth by that holy divine, our master R. Meshullam Feivish of Zbarazh, of blessed memory, in his book *Derekh Emet*.

Evidently R. Meshullam Feivish's views were still alive in some Hasidic circles 200 years after his death.

In the matter of how the Torah was studied in Hasidism a common pattern developed among the majority of Hasidic Jews wherever they lived. Until the post-war years Hasidic young men were married at an early age. Before marriage they studied the Talmud and Codes on their own in the Bet Ha-Midrash or in the Hasidic *steibel*, the more affluent in their own homes with a private tutor. After marriage, it was the norm for a young Hasid to be supported by his father-in-law for some years, depending, naturally, on the father-in-law's means. Young Hasidim with an ambition to becoming Rabbis studied the portions in the Codes required for them to be ordained, such ordination (*semikhah*) being given to them by a famous Rabbi after he had examined them to see if they were proficient. With the exception of the Tomekhey Temimim Yeshivah of Lubavitch and the Yeshivat Hakhmey Lublin, established by Rabbi Meir Shapiro of Lublin, there were hardly any specific Hasidic Yeshivot,[23] although a number of bright Hasidic youths made their way into the Lithuanian Yeshivot, where they were usually encouraged to persist in the Hasidic way of their fathers, for instance, by wearing the traditional Hasidic garb.

Following the general pattern of Eastern European religious life, the Hasidim studied the Talmud and Codes.[24] From infancy, the Hasidic youngsters, like non-Hasidic youngsters in Eastern Europe, studied in the cheder the weekly portion of the Torah together with Rashi's commentary ('Chumash and Rashi'). The study of the other portions of the Bible was not generally encouraged by the Hasidim in the belief that concentration on the Bible itself tended to obscure the Rabbinic interpretation, the Oral Torah, the real source of traditional Jewish religious life. Since the Haskalah, which Hasidism generally believed to be detrimental to pure religious thought, Mendelssohn's Biur was taboo in Hasidic circles as tending to replace Rabbinic Midrash with the plain meaning of Scripture. To this day, Hasidim do not read the

Haftarah, the prophetic reading, aloud in the synagogue but recite it quietly to themselves. For the same reason the Hasidim ignored the study of Hebrew grammar.[25] Jewish history was not studied at all by the Hasidim, many of the Hasidic masters having only a scant knowledge of the Jewish past apart from the history of Hasidism itself. The study of the Kabbalah was discouraged, especially for young men, but a reliable report has it that R. Hayyim Eleazar Shapira of Munkacs, mentioned above, did encourage this study by young men attracted to it.[26] The study of the Rabbinic Midrash was highly prized by the Hasidim probably because it lent itself easily to a Hasidic interpretation. Naturally, the Hasidim studied, especially on the Sabbath and Festivals, the classical Hasidic works as well as other devotional works of a mystical character such as Elijah de Vidas's *Reshit Hokhmah*, Eliezer Azkiri's *Sefer Haredim*, Isaiah Horowitz's *Shney Luhot Ha-Berit* (known by the Hasidim as 'The Holy Shelah') and the Commentaries to the Torah of Moshe Alsheik and Hayyim Ibn Atar. Some few Hasidic masters such as R. Hayyim of Zanz, R. Zevi Hirsh Eichenstein of Zhydachov and R. Menahem Mendel of Lubavitch, were fairly proficient in Jewish philosophical works. But the Hasidim in general were discouraged from studying works like Maimonides' *Guide for the Perplexed*.

It is difficult, however, to pin down any specific Hasidic course of studies in view of the proliferation of Hasidic dynasties each with its own way of worship. It might also be noted that in the nineteenth and twentieth centuries there emerged a host of Hasidic masters and Hasidic followers who managed to combine in their person the Hasidic ideal and Talmudic and Halakhic expertise, as did many of the eighteenth-century masters.[27]

NOTES

1. *Keter Shem Tov*, ed. Jerusalem, 1968, p. 22b; the same statement appears in the other early Hasidic collection: *Tzavaat Ha-Ribash*, no. 41, ed. Brooklyn, New York, 1975, p. 6b.
2. See my *Hasidic Prayer*, paperback edition, The Littman Library of Jewish Civilization, Londonand Washington, 1993, pp. 17–21.
3. *Tzavaat Ha-Ribash*, no. 29, ed. Brooklyn, New York, p. 4b.
4. On *devekut* see the famous essay by Gershom Scholem, '*Devekut*, or Communion with God', in *The Messianic Idea in Judaism*, New York,1971, pp. 203–27.
5. *Berakhot* 17a *s.v. ha-oseh* and *Pesahim* 50b *s.v. ve-khan*.
6. *Toledot Yaakov Yosef*, Koretz, 1780, p. 131b.
7. *Sod Yakhin U-Voaz*, Jerusalem, 1990, pp. 41a–b.
8. *Toledot Yaakov Yosef*, p. 3b. For the severe criticisms of the Rabbis by this author see Samuel H. Dresner, *The Zaddik*, London, New York and Toronto, 1960, Chapter 4, pp. 63–74.

9. See the careful analysis of R. Meir's view by J. G. Weiss, 'Study of the Torah in Israel Baal Shem Tov's Doctrine' (Heb.), in, *Essays Presented to Chief Rabbi Israel Brodie on the Occasion of his Seventieth Birthday*, ed. H. J. Zimmels, J. Rabbinowitz and I. Finestein, London, 1967, Hebrew section, pp. 151–69 (on R. Meir in particular see pp. 162–7).

10. *Yosher Divrey Emet*, no. 9, in, *Likkutim Yekarim*, Jerusalem, 1974, pp. 113b–114a.

11. See M. Wilensky, *Hasidim U-Mitnaggedim*, Jerusalem, 1970, Index *s.v. bittul torah*.

12. On R. Hayyim of Volozhyn and his attitude towards Hasidism see Nahum Lamm, *Torah Lishmah*, Jerusalem, 1972 and D. Eliach, *Avi Ha-Yeshivot*, Jerusalem, 1991, pp. 291–332, cf. Allen Nadler, *The Faith of the Mithnagdim: Rabbinic Responses to Hasidic Rapture*, Baltimore and London, 1997.

13. *Nefesh Ha-Hayyim, Shaar* 4, Chapter 2, ed. Bene Berak and Y. D. Rubin, 1989, pp. 209f.

14. Ibid., Chapter 3, pp. 211f.

15. Ibid., Chapter 4, pp. 212–14.

16. Ibid., Chapter 8, pp. 219f. cf. *Kol Ha-Katuv Le-Hayyim*, ed. Dov Eliach, Jerusalem, 1988, p. 147, where the following is quoted from an old manuscript: 'Our teacher [R. Hayyim] said to a member of his family who had a leaning towards Hasidism, keep at least these three things: a) Study the Gemara and its dialectics and let this be for you the greatest manner of worshipping God; b) Never transgress any law stated in the Gemara; c) Never speak ill of our master, the Gaon [of Vilna].'

17. *Yosher Divre Emet*, no. 22, ed. Jerusalem, p. 122.

18. *Nefesh Ha-Hayyim*, Shaar 4, Chapter 28, ed. I. D. Rubin and Bene Berak, pp. 274–7. Rubin's note 36 on p. 276 overlooks that the source which R. Hayyim criticizes is R. Meshullam Feivish. R. Hayyim, in fact, quotes R. Meshullam incorrectly. R. Meshullam refers to the Talmud and the Tosafot, as difficult subjects of study, not, as R. Hayyim says, Scripture. The point R. Meshullam is making is that Kabbalah cannot be considered *nistar* because it is hard to understand for if this were the meaning of *nistar* then it would embrace the Talmud and Tosafot, equally difficult to understand for an ignoramus.

19. *Notzer Hesed* on Mishnayot, 2nd edition, New York, n.d.

20. *Egley Tal*, Pietrikov, Jerusalem, 1905, p. 1b.

21. Y. M. Gold, *Darkhey Hayyim Ve-Shalom*, Jerusalem, 1974, no.886, p. 325.

22. *Raza De-Uvda*, Kiryat Ata, 1976.

23. See Aaron Wertheim, *Halakhot Ve-Halikhot Bahasidut*, Jerusalem, 1960, I, Chapter 4: 'The Manner of Study in the Hasidic World' (Heb.), pp. 45–8.

24. See ibid. for the quote from Aaron of Karlin (d. 1872) in his *Bet Aharon*, Brody, 1875 (photocopy, Jerusalem, 1977), *Likkutim*, p. 287, 'If you would study a page of Gemara with deep concentration on the Sabbath before the time of prayer the soul would undergo a complete change.'

25. As early as the beginning of the nineteenth century the Hasidim were attacked for their indifference to Hebrew grammar, J. B. Levinson, *Teudah Be-Yisrael*, Vilna, 1820, directs his barbs at the Hasidim for their indifference to grammar, see his remarks in the note to p. 23. Levinson claims to have heard a Hasidic master develop a whole 'Torah' on the Book of Esther based on a confusion between the masculine and feminine genders in Hebrew, and see Levinson's note on p. 28 that despite the many printing houses in Volhynia no work of Hebrew grammar has ever been published there. On Hasidic indifference to grammar see also R. Hayyim Eleazar Shapiro of Munkacs, in *Divrey Torah*, Munkacs, 1933, Part V, no. 22, p. 11a.

26. Y.M. Gold, *Darkhey Hayyim Ve-Shalom*, p. 324.

27. See A. Surasky, *Marbitzey Torah Me-Olam Ha-Hasidut*, eight volumes, ed. Bene Berak, 1980–89.

3

Hasidic 'Torah'

From the earliest beginnings of the Hasidic movement, the Hasidim ate the sacred meal on the Sabbath at the table of the Zaddik, during the course of which he would 'say Torah', namely expound a verse or verses from the current *sidra* to convey specific Hasidic ideas.[1] Solomon Maimon, in his autobiography,[2] describes, with a mixture of admiration and irony, a visit he paid to the court of Rabbi Dov Baer, the Maggid of Mesirech:

> Accordingly on the Sabbath, I went to this solemn meal, and found there a large number of respectable men who had gathered from various quarters. At length the awe-inspiring great man appeared, clothed in white satin. Even his shoes and snuffbox were white, this being among the Kabbalists the colour of grace. He gave every newcomer his greeting. We sat down to table and during the meal a solemn silence reigned. After the meal was over, the superior struck up a solemn inspiring melody, held his hand for some time upon his brow, and then began to call out, 'Z - H -, Mr - or R-', and so on. Every newcomer was thus called by his own name and the name of his residence, which excited no little astonishment. Each recited, as he was called, some verse of the Holy Scriptures. Thereupon the superior began to deliver a sermon for which the verses recited served as a text, so that although they were disconnected verses taken from different parts of the Holy Scriptures they were combined with as much skill as if they had formed a single whole.

Maimon goes on to say that he quickly came to realize that this ingenious exegesis was at bottom false and that, in any event, the verses were made to yield the doctrine of annihilation of selfhood, easy, once one had mastered it, to read into almost any verse.

The pattern described by Maimon, with variations in accordance with particular attitudes of other Hasidic masters, came to be the norm in Hasidic circles, though the 'Torah' of the Zaddik was usually delivered at the Third Meal, *Seudah Shelishit*, on Sabbath afternoon.[3] In some Hasidic circles, the idea developed, referred to obliquely in Maimon's account, that the Zaddik's 'Torah' came directly to him by divine inspiration, the Shekhinah speaking, as it was put, out of his throat.[4] Some of the Hasidic classics contain the sermons uttered by the Zaddik at the Sabbath meal, his disciples recording these from memory at the termination of the sacred day. Other Hasidic works were compiled by the Zaddikim themselves[5] but in all the Hasidic works there clearly emerges the typical form of exposition that came to be known as 'Hasidic Torah'. Maimon refers to 'Holy Scripture' in general but the usual practice was for the 'Torah' of the Zaddik to be taken from the *sidra* of the week or, on Festivals, from the reading for that particular festival. In addition verses were expounded in the Hasidic manner from the weekly Haftarah. It is rare to find Hasidic 'Torah' on other parts of the Bible with the exception of Psalms, familiar to the average Hasid. Moreover, passages from the liturgy and the Rabbinic literature are called into service during the course of the exposition. This typical Hasidic 'Torah' is found in the works of the Zaddikim. These works are usually referred to as *Sefarim Kedoshim*, 'Holy Books'.[6]

Hasidic 'Torah' can hardly be described as exegesis. The texts are taken completely out of context to yield the desired conclusions; ideas are read into the texts that by no stretch of the imagination can they possibly mean; grammar and syntax are completely ignored; there is not the slightest indication of any awareness of the historical background. Occasionally, the Hasidic masters admit that their 'Torah' is inadequate as Scriptural exegesis, as when they remark that this or that comment is only by way of *remez* ('hint'). In the work *Botzina De-Nehora*, containing the teachings of Baruch of Medziboz, the grandson of the Baal Shem Tov, there occurs this very revealing passage,[7] itself an example of Hasidic 'Torah' completely divorced from the plain meaning of Scripture: 'He [Baruch] remarked that the Zaddikim utter words of Torah and rebuke and link their ideas to Scripture by means of vague hints which barely touch the text. This is because Scripture says: "and the spirit of God hovered over the face of the water" [Genesis 1:2]. "Water" refers to the Torah, and the Rabbis [Genesis Rabbah 2:4] understand [the word "hovered" to mean] touching and yet not touching [i.e., barely touching]'. R. Baruch here suggests that the spirit of the Lord, which inspires the Zaddik to produce his 'Torah' only 'hovers' over the Scriptural verses he expounds. R. Baruch implies that the actual discourse can be derived from Scripture only by extremely far-fetched exegesis, yet, since it is inspired teaching, it becomes in itself part of the Torah. For all that, this type of exposition is so ubiquitous in Hasidic works that it does seem as if the Hasidic masters really believed that their expositions were far more than mere hints but were really contained somehow in the texts they expounded.

First, it has to be appreciated, the Hasidim believed that, over and above the conventional understanding of Scripture, there is an inner, mystical meaning. As an oft-quoted passage in the Zohar (III, 152a) has it:

> Rabbi Simeon said: Woe to the man who says that the Torah merely tells us tales in general and speaks of ordinary matters. If this were so we could make up even nowadays a Torah dealing with ordinary matters and an even better one at that. If all the Torah does is to tell us about worldly things there are far superior things told in worldly books so let us copy them and make up a Torah of them. But the truth is that all the words of the Torah have to do with lofty themes and high mysteries.

The Kabbalists read the Torah as referring chiefly to the Kabbalistic doctrines so that, for example, the stories about the patriarchs are, in this inner meaning, accounts of the various aspects of the Sefirot on high. By the time of the rise of Hasidism, this idea had long been accepted so that the Hasidic masters belonged in an old-established tradition even though, for them, the inner meaning, was, in addition, the Hasidic doctrines.

Second, this very methodology, in which verses are taken out of context and applied in a manner totally different from that of the plain meaning, is, in fact, the methodology of the Rabbinic Aggadah and Midrash, especially in its later manifestations.[8] The Hasidic masters were very fond of the Midrashic literature. Quotes from the Midrashic literature abound in the Hasidic works and, often, Midrashic texts are themselves interpreted to yield Hasidic doctrine. For instance, we find in the Talmud (*Bava Batra* 78b) a lengthy homily on the verse:

> Therefore they that speak in parables say: 'Come ye to Heshbon! Let the city of Sihon be built and established' (Numbers 21:27), a verse dealing in the context with the conquest by the Israelites of the Amorite city of Heshbon whose king was Sihon. The word *ha-moshelim* ('they that speak in parables') is read as: 'they that rule' (from *moshel*, 'a ruler') and

the meaning is: 'they who rule over their evil inclination'. The name of the city, Heshbon, is read to mean a 'reckoning' or an 'account', a meaning it has in a different context. Thus the verse reads, in this novel interpretation: 'Therefore those who rule over their evil inclination say: Come let us consider the account of the world: the loss incurred by the fulfilment of a precept against the reward secured by its observance, and the gain gotten by a transgression against the loss it involves.'

The author of this 'interpretation' knew full well that he is taking the verse completely out of context but he was applying the Midrashic method according to which there are 'seventy modes of interpreting the Torah' (Numbers Rabbah 13:15).[9]

In the following Talmudic passage (Gittin 7a) there is both an implied critique of such far-fetched exegesis and, at the same time, a justification of it when practised by skilful teachers.

> R. Huna b. Nathan asked R. Ashi: 'What is the meaning of the verse: *Kinah and Dimonah and Abdalah* [Joshua 15:22]?' He replied: 'These are cities in the Land of Israel.' Said the other: 'Do I not know that the text is enumerating cities in the Land of Israel? But I want to tell you that R. Gebihah from Argiza gave the following interpretation: "Whoever has cause for indignation [*kinah*] against his neighbour and yet keeps quiet [*domem*] about it, He that abides for all eternity [*ade ad*] shall espouse his cause."' Said the other: 'If so the verse: *Ziklag and Madmunah and Sansanah* [Joshua 15:31] also [should be interpreted in this fashion]?' He replied: 'If R. Gebihah from Argiza was here he would have indeed given an interpretation. R. Aha from Be Hozae expounded it as follows: "If a man has just cause of complaint against his neighbour for taking away his livelihood [*zaakat legima*] and yet hold his peace [*domem*], He that abides in the bush [*shokhni sneh*] will espouse his cause."'

Maimonides (Guide III, 45), fulminating against those who understand Midrash as conveying the plain meaning of Scripture instead of seeing it as poetry, quotes the interpretation of Bar Kappara in the Talmud (*Ketubot* 5a) of the verse: 'And thou shalt have a paddle [*yated*] upon thy weapon [*azenekha*]' (Deuteronomy 23:14). Bar Kappara comments: Do not read *azenekha* but *oznekha*, 'thy ear' and interprets the word *yated* not as a 'paddle' but as a finger (shaped like a peg, another meaning of *yated*). Thus Bar Kappara reads the verse as: 'You should put your peg-shaped [i.e, tapering] finger in your ear so as not to hear a reprehensible thing.' It is not suggested that the Hasidic masters always saw Midrashic niceties in the way Maimonides does. It is probable that they took the Midrashim more literally than the great philosopher of the middle ages. But for our purpose it suffices to show that the Midrashic interpretations had long been known among Jews so that there is nothing strange in the Hasidic masters' manipulation of texts to suit their own purposes. Jewish preachers throughout the ages, even those who inclined to a more plausible exegesis, still availed themselves of the Midrashic methodology in order to convey ideas they felt important for the lives of their audiences and readers.

In particular, the Moroccan Kabbalist Hayyim Ibn Atar (1696–1743) employs frequently the Midrashic/allegorical methodology in his book *Or Ha-Hayyim*, a work highly favoured by the Hasidic masters,[10] who called the author, after his book, 'The Holy *Or Ha-Hayyim*'. For instance, Ibn Atar comments on the verse 'neither shalt thou favour a poor man in his quarrel' (Exodus 23:3) that this verse has a meaning beyond its context as a warning to a judge not to decide unjustly in favour of a poor man. Every poor man has a quarrel with God for having made him poor. When the poor man is assisted and his poverty diminished his otherwise legitimate quarrel with God is removed. Similarly, and quite in what became the Hasidic vein, is Ibn Atar's comment on the injunction to restore to its rightful owner a brother's ox or ass that has gone astray (Deuteronomy 22:1–3). The 'brother' is said to be God and the lost sheep and oxen the sinners. The good man, for whom God is a Brother, should not be indifferent to sinners but should seek to restore them to the good way and hence bring them back to 'Brother God'. As a mystic Ibn Atar uses the Midrashic methodology more in order to convey teachings for the individual than the community as a whole. In this he is followed by the later Hasidic masters.

In his account Solomon Maimon refers to three examples of Hasidic 'Torah' told to him by a young man who belonged to the circle of the Maggid of Mesirech,[11] one on the doctrine of the Zaddik, the other two on that of annihilation of selfhood, which so captivated Maimon that he resolved to journey to Mesirech to see for himself. The first of these was a comment on the verse (Psalms 149:1): 'Sing unto the Lord a new song, His praise is in the congregation of His saints [*hasidav*].' Before the time of the new Hasidim, praising God consisted of relating His mighty deeds of deliverance when He intervened in human history by performing miracles. The only way humans have of praising God is to speak of those supernatural acts impossible for humans and hence the type of praise in which He is described as performing acts no human being can possibly perform. But now the Zaddikim[12] are able to work such wonders in the performance of supernatural acts, God can no longer be praised in this manner and a new song, a new way of describing the uniqueness of God, is required. Thus the verse is interpreted as: 'Sing unto the Lord a new song since the praise hitherto suitable is now found in the congregation of His Hasidim.'

Maimon, quite charmed, as he says, by this novel method of interpreting Scripture, requested the young man to give him some more of the same kind. The young Hasid proceeded to quote an interpretation of the Maggid[13] of the verse: 'When the minstrel played, the spirit of God came upon him' (2 Kings 3:15). The Hebrew for 'when the minstrel played' is: *kenaggen ha-menaggen* which, with the strong degree of homiletical licence typical of Hasidic 'Torah', can be read as 'when the minstrel [*ha-menaggem*] is like the instrument [*naggen*] on which he plays'. This yields the thought that if a man, when he plays the melody of worship, has as little of selfhood as the instrument on which he plays, then, and only then, can the spirit of the Lord rest upon him.

A third interpretation by the young man, in the name of his mentors, was of the Rabbinic saying (*Avot* 2:10): 'Let your neighbour's honour be as dear to you as your own'. Implied in this saying is that a man is entitled to the honour paid to him, but he should be concerned with his neighbour's honour just as he is concerned with his own. But in Hasidic thought the self needs to be transcended and honour of the self is a hindrance to the mystical aim. Hence the saying is turned on its head. For a man constantly to be paying himself honour is simply ridiculous. Only a lunatic keeps telling himself that he is wonderful. It is different when others pay a man honour. He takes delight in it and feels good that others recognize his worth. But the ideal is for the Hasid to be as little moved and affected by the honour another pays him as he is by the honour he pays himself. Hence the saying is understood as: 'Let your neighbour's honour [i.e. the honour your neighbour pays to you] be as dear to you [i.e. of as little significance] as the honour you pay to yourself.'[14] In all three interpretations Maimon was moved to admiration both by the refinement of the thought and the ingenious way in which it was read into the text.

The first Hasidic book to be printed was the *Toledot Yaakov Yosef* by Jacob Joseph of Polonnoye.[15] Hasidic 'Torah' is found on every page of this book in which there are similar far-fetched interpretations of both Scripture and Rabbinic literature, all for the sake of particular Hasidic ideas, especially on the doctrine of the Zaddik.[16] The Talmud (*Berakhot* 33b) quotes the verse: 'And now, O Israel, what doth the Lord thy God require of thee but to fear' (Deuteronomy 10:12), implying that all that God requires is for men to fear Him. Why 'only', asks the Talmud. Is the fear of God such a small thing? The answer is given: 'Yes, indeed, in relation to Moses [*le-gabey Moshe*] it is only a small thing.' But surely, the commentators ask, Moses was speaking to the people and for them fear was anything but a small thing? The *Toledot*,[17] developing the idea that the Zaddik is the 'channel' through which the divine grace flows, understands the words 'in relation to Moses' to mean 'those in a relationship with Moses', i.e. the people of his generation to whom Moses addressed his words. Moses opened up the 'channel' of fear and through Moses the fear of God truly became a 'small thing', easy to attain, for the people close to him. Thus the Talmudic saying is skilfully but obviously incorrectly interpreted as referring not to Moses himself but to those to whom he addressed his remarks.

A famous and oft-quoted interpretation in this vein is attributed to the Baal Shem Tov himself, which came to serve as the keynote to the ideal of Hasidic prayer.[18] This is a comment on the verse (Genesis 6:16) in which are stated the instructions to Noah regarding the construction of the ark 'A light [*tzohar*] shalt thou make to the ark [*la-tevah*].' The word *tevah* is interpreted as having the much later Hebrew meaning of a 'word', and the reference is to the 'word' uttered in prayer. This must be illumined through intense concentration on the divine so that the soul of the worshipper is elevated to the supernal realms.[19] Here, too, an apparently unpromising text – of no relevance to the life of devotion – is made relevant by using it to call attention to the Hasidic ideal of intense self-transcending concentration in prayer.

The early Hasidim followed the Rabbinic Aggadah in using names of figures in Scripture as a means of conveying their particular ideas. Uziel Meizels, a disciple of the Maggid of Mesirech, has a comment[20] on the verse (Exodus 38:30): 'the son of Uri, the son of Hur, of the tribe [*lematteh*] of Judah [*yehudah*]'. The word Uri is taken as referring to *or*, 'light'. Hur is understood as meaning 'a crevice', a meaning it has in other contexts. *Lematteh* is read as if it were written *lemattah*, meaning 'downwards', and *yehudah* is read as *hodaah*, 'praise'. Thus the verse is read as meaning: 'When one who was formerly a son of light, of high spiritual elevation, in which he illumined the world, falls into the depths of degradation, all the high praises of God he had uttered when in the state of grace are rejected and cast downwards'. Similarly, the early Hasidic master, R. Elimelech of Lizensk, comments[21] on the names of the three divisions of the Levites in the book of Numbers, chapter four. These are Kehot, Merari and Gershon. Kehot is understood as if it was connected with the word *kahal*, 'assembly'; Merari as if from *maror*, 'bitter'; and Gershon as if from *ger*, 'stranger'. This yields the thought that there are three kinds of Zaddikim. The Kehot type is the one around whom people gather in order to learn from his saintly life. The Merari type is one who engages in bitter mortification of the flesh. The Gershon type is the Zaddik who is so humble that he sees himself as a stranger on earth with no real right to exist. All three types of Zaddikim are required if the world is to endure, obviously an implied defence of the proliferation of Zaddikim, each with his own manner of worship. The grandson of the Baal Shem Tov, R. Moshe Hayyim Efraim of Sudlikov, even finds his grandfather's name[22] referred to. albeit obliquely, in the Torah. The Targum to the verse (Exodus 14:8): 'And the children of Israel went out with a high hand [*beyad ramah*]' translates the latter clause as: *beresh geley*, 'with bared head'. R. Moshe Efraim quotes R. Lippa Chmelnik, who interprets this Targumic passage in the light of the well-known letter of the Baal Shem Tov[23] in which the Messiah informs the Baal Shem Tov that he, the Messiah, will come when the Baal Shem Tov's teachings will be widespread. Thus the verse 'hints' (the author uses this word *remez* because of the obvious anachronism involved in the Torah and the Targum referring directly to the teacher of the eighteenth century) that the children of Israel will go out of their exile, when the Messiah comes, when Israel Baal Shem Tov comes into his own, that is, when his teachings become widespread. This is read into the Targum because the letters of *beresh* are the same as those of *Rabbi Israel Baal Shem*. While he does not suggest that this is in any way an exegesis of the verse and the Targum, this author does appear to believe that the Torah does contain hints of events that will take place in the remote future.

The whole of the Hasidic 'Torah' consists of an attempt to make the texts directly relevant to the life of the Hasidim. The past is of little moment unless it is seen as a call to saintly living. Nowhere is this seen more clearly than in the treatment of the Exodus in Hasidic thought. Everything in the Exodus narrative and the laws of Passover is adapted to the psychic life of the Hasid. And yet the Torah does dwell at length on the Exodus and the Passover rituals are designed as potent reminders of the tremendous historical event. Two devices were adopted by the Hasidic masters in order to make the past experiences of the group relevant to the personal religious strivings of the contemporary Hasid.

The first of these was to draw on the Kabbalistic idea that the original divine illumination at the time of the Exodus shines forth once again whenever Passover comes round, so that, on the spiritual level, there is a new Exodus each Passover, a new freedom of the spirit open to those able and willing to draw on it. In one version, there is a spark of Moses and the generation witness to the Exodus present in the soul of the Hasid as he relives Moses' confrontation with Pharaoh. In this version, the Hasid is both Moses and Pharaoh, struggling against the hardening of the heart to allow his soul to fly upwards. But the more usual device was to interpret the details recorded in the Torah as referring directly to the spiritual struggle between good and evil in the soul of the Hasid as he proceeds on his mystic quest. The very word for Egypt, *Mitzrayim*, is connected with the word *metzar*, meaning a narrow path. There is an Exodus from *Mitzrayim*, from constriction and confinement, whenever the soul is moved to transcend its finitude as it soars towards the Infinite.

The following illustrations of how the process works are taken from two Hasidic classics, one early, the other late, with regard to the interpretation of the Exodus and the Biblical injunctions to avoid leaven, *hametz*, on Passover and to eat unleavened bread, *matzah*. It goes without saying that the Hasidic authors who used *hametz* and *matzah* as symbols for their particular ideas never saw these as substitutes for the actual observance of Passover. In point of fact, the Hasidim, to this day, are exceptionally scrupulous in avoiding the slightest trace of *hametz* during Passover. The Hasidic masters regularly quote the saying of the sixteenth-century Kabbalist, R. Isaac Luria, the Ari, that whoever is careful to avoid the smallest amount of *hametz* on Passover will be spared from offending against any of the dietary laws during the whole of the coming year.[24] What the masters appear to be doing is to read the Torah at two different levels. As Orthodox Jews they understands the laws of leaven and unleaven in their plain meaning. Yet, at the same time, relying on t he Kabbalistic idea referred to above of a secret meaning of the Torah, they interpret the Passover rituals in accordance with their own mystical stance.

A theme which appears again and again in the Hasidic writings is the identification of *hametz* with the evil inclination and *matzah* with the good inclination. This identification is found in the Talmudic prayer:[25] 'Sovereign of the Universe, it is known full well to Thee that our will is to perform Thy will and what prevents us? The yeast in the dough and the subjection to foreign powers. May it be Thy will to deliver us from their hand, so that we might return to perform the statutes of Thy will with a perfect heart.' This identification is very old since it is also found in the New Testament,[26] although in this context it is in association with Christian dogma.

The Hasidic masters were able to use the idea of personal struggle against the blandishments of the evil inclination, utilizing the symbolism of *hametz* and *matzah* on Passover. R. Jacob Joseph of Polonnoye writes:[27] 'Just as the exile and the deliverance therefrom took place for the people as a whole so are these present in each individual. As I have heard the exposition of the verse [Psalms 69:19]: "Draw nigh unto my soul and redeem it" that before a man prays for the general redemption he must pray for the redemption of his individual soul.' Elsewhere[28] this master writes: 'I have heard from my teacher [the Baal Shem Tov] that a man must pray over the exile of his self, spirit and soul in [the clutches of] the evil inclination.' In his *Ben Porat Yosef*,[29] R. Jacob Joseph understands the 'new Pharaoh who knew not Joseph' (Exodus 1:8) to be the evil inclination and the wise Joseph he did not know to be the intellect which exercises control over the passions, a good example of Philo-type allegorical interpretation.

On these lines R. Jacob Joseph[30] applies the Talmudic rules regarding *hametz* and *matzah*. The search for *hametz* at night by the light of a candle denotes man's investigation into his inner self when spiritual darkness prevails there. The investigation is assisted by the insights the Torah provides to enable him to get the better of his evil inclination. According to the Talmud, *matzah* made with honey cannot be used to fulfil the precept of eating *matzah* and, obviously, when yeast is present in the dough it is no longer *matzah* but *hametz*. Yeast, which causes the dough to rise, represents pride,

which puffs up a man with an exaggerated sense of his own importance, whereas honey represents the sweet enticement of lust. The
good inclination, represented by *matzah*, containing neither yeast
nor honey, has to struggle with worldly temptations if man is to
cleave to God. But such a state can be attained only through the
purgation of suffering, represented by the bitter herbs eaten together with the *matzah* on Passover. Thus the rituals of *matzah* and the
bitter herbs have relevance not only as reminders of the Egyptian
bondage and the glorious redemption God wrought for His people;
they also represent the bitterness of suffering which brings about
personal redemption to each individual soul.

The symbolism of *hametz* and *matzah* is also applied by R. Jacob
Joseph[31]) in a rather different fashion. *Matzah* represents the virtue
of humility whereas *hametz* represents pride. Now the letters of the
word *matzah* – *mem, tzaddi, hey* – are the same as those of the word
hametz, except for the *hey* in *matzah* and the *het* in *hametz*. These two
letters differ only in the small space at the top left-hand side of the
hey. Humility is a great virtue when it is the result of a man seeing
himself as nothing in the presence of God, Such a state is known
in Hasidic thought as *bittul ha-yesh*, 'annihilation of selfhood'.
When a man is guilty of false modesty by being consciously humble, he draws attention to the self in the very attempt at self-transcendence. Such false modesty, differing by a fine hair-breadth
from true humility, turns the *matzah* of religious and ethical life
into *hametz*.

According to the Talmudic Rabbis (*Pesahim* 5b) 'you must not see
your own leaven [on Passover] but you may see leaven belonging
to others and the sacred'. In the context 'others' refers to Gentiles
and the 'sacred' to the Temple, and the meaning is, you must not
have *hametz* in the house on Passover if it belongs to you (or any
other Jew) but you may keep in your house *hametz* belonging to
Gentiles or to the Temple. But R. Jacob Joseph[32] adapts the saying
as a warning against being soft on oneself and judgemental with
regard to others. It is *your* leaven that poses a danger to the spiritual life. A man is all too ready to find fault with other human
beings or with the Zaddikim, the 'sacred' teachers, while ignoring
his own character defects.Thus the Torah complains: You do not
see your own leaven but you do seek to expose the sins of others
or the alleged faults of the Zaddikim; an obvious counterblast to
the opponents of Hasidism, the Mitnaggedim, who saw
Zaddikism as tomfoolery, charlatanism or worse.

The majority of the Hasidic masters, in their commentaries on Passover and the Passover Haggadah, generally follow the pattern set by R. Jacob Joseph. Many of their ideas are found in the great compendium on the festivals, *Beney Yisaskar*, by the later Hasidic master, R. Zevi Elimelekh of Dynov (1785–1841)[33] and in the same author's commentary to the precepts of the Torah entitled *Derekh Pikkudekha*.[34] In the first of these works, the author follows more or less in the footsteps of R. Jacob Joseph, albeit with nuances of his own. In the second work, he is rather more legalistic and closer to conventional orthodoxy. R. Zevi Elimelech was a fierce opponent of the Haskalah and he often directs his comments to an attack on the total insufficiency of human reasoning in grasping the true meaning of the Torah. Hence in the second work his thrust is more social and communal than personal, even though here, too, his thoughts are directed to the individual as well as the group.

On the precept of destroying all leaven before Passover, R. Zevi Elimelech first remarks that since the Torah states no reason for the precept there is really no need to attempt to discover the reason. The precept should be carried out in simple obedience to the divine command. Nevertheless, since the precepts were given in order to refine the soul,[35] it is worthwhile exploring how they achieve this, that is, to interpret the precepts in psychological terms as do the other Hasidic masters.

A human being is incapable, observes our author, of any love and fear unless he can grasp the object of these in his mind. This is why a little child is frightened only by trivial things and has no fear, for example, of a drawn sword – the danger of which he cannot fathom. The child will be puzzled if his father orders him not to play with a piece of broken glass since it appears attractive to him and he is totally unaware of the risk he is taking of being cut by it. It is only as the infant's mind develops that he comes to appreciate that this object is threatening while another offers no threat, or that this object is likable and the other unlikable. Before the Fall, Adam had no knowledge of any other love and fear save the love and fear of God. After Adam had eaten of the Tree of Knowledge, his love and fear were no longer pure and his descendants are now engaged in the struggle to prevent their love and fear of worldly things distracting them from serving God. From Adam onwards there began the cosmic drama in which man struggles against the evil in his own nature, an evil caused largely by man's pursuit of knowledge. At the Exodus, when God was revealed in all His power, the worship of the false gods of Egypt was seen to be sheer stupidity, and the souls of the people of Israel were purged of all their dross. But when the people worshipped the Golden Calf, the spirit of impurity rested upon them once again and their descendants are now required to rectify Adam's sin by removing all *hametz*, the symbol of human arrogance, before Passover, the anniversary of the Exodus. This is the basic difference between *hametz* and *matzah*. The former rises of its own accord, whereas the latter is baked in its original form. Leaven represents man's attempt to gain unlawful autonomy, to be independent of his Maker. Unleavened bread denotes man's total dependence on the Creator. Continuing this theme, R. Zevi Elimelech notes in passing that the numerical value (*gematria*) of *hametz* and *matzah* is the same as that of *etz ha-daat*, 'The Tree of Knowledge'. But the task of self-discipline is far from easy, hence the need for the bitter herbs, representing the obstacles a man has to overcome if he is to reach out to God.

R. Zevi Elimelech's exposition is very different from that of R. Jacob Joseph and most of the other Hasidic masters yet, essentially both the methodology and the thrust in the direction of personal experience are present in this and the other works of R. Zevi Elimelech. It is only that in the time of R. Zevi Elimelech the Haskalah presented a real challenge to Hasidism, one that, he evidently felt, required a Hasidic master to emerge from his isolation to wage the battles of the Lord.

In his battle against the Haskalah, R. Zevi Elimelech concludes:

> He who is intelligent [*Ha-Maskil!*], when he reflects on this precept, will search out in his innermost heart and in his actions to see whether he retains, Heaven forbid, any slight trace of *hametz*, and then remove it from his house and his domain. Even if it be some custom [the Maskilim attacked many Jewish customs as superstition] or some linguistic expression [probably referring to the contempt of the Maskilim for Yiddish] or some garment [i.e. a garment in the Western style] adopted by the proud who speak arrogantly. And he should investigate whether, Heaven forfend, there is found among the members of his household any trace of this and if so he should keep them far from it and train them in the ways of the Torah. And he should take upon himself and the members of his household to be of the servants of the Lord and servants of the Torah and servants of Israel. Reflect long on this!

Evidently, R. Zevi Elimelech saw no harm, only good, in observing with a critical eye the leaven of others, provided these 'others' were the Maskilim.

The 'Torah' of some Hasidic masters is presented in a different form than the arrangement of the material as comments to Scripture. The *Tanya* of R. Shneur Zalman of Liady (1745–1813), founder of the Habad school in Hasidism, consists of a fairly systematic treatment of Hasidic psychology and Hasidic panentheism together with letters by the author to his followers. R. Shneur Zalman's son, R. Dov Baer of Lubavitch, wrote his famous *Kunteros Ha-Hitpaalut*, 'Tract on Ecstasy', to provide his followers with a detailed and systematic guide on the attainment of ecstasy in prayer and warning of the dangers of uncontrolled or contrived enthusiasm. The work *Derekh Mitzvotekha* by R. Shneur Zalman's grandson, R. Menahem Mendel of Lubavitch, is an interpretation of the precepts of the Torah in the light of the Kabbalah and Hasidism. In these Habad classical works the particular philosophy of the Habad tendency in Hasidism is presented in a far more philosophical manner than is usual in Hasidic writings. An amalgam of Kabbalah and Hasidism is also found in the works: *Avodat Yisreal* by R. Israel Hapstein of Koznitz (1733–1814); *Amud Ha-Avodah* by R. Baruch of Kossov (d. 1795); *Sur Mera Vaaseh Tov* by R. Zevi Hirsch Eichenstein (1763–1831); and the *Hekhal Ha-Berakhah*, 'Palace of Blessing', by R.Yitzhak Eisik Safrin of Komarno (1806–74).

R. Pinhas Shapiro of Koretz (1726–91) is accepted by all Hasidic groups as a founding father of the movement despite his quarrel with the Maggid of Mesirech and the fact that he was more of an associate of the Baal Shem Tov than an actual disciple. R. Pinhas's 'Torah' is found largely in the form of verbal aphorisms collected by his disciple, Raphael of Bershad, and others and published in the work *Midrash Pinhas* and similar collections.

The works of R. Nahman of Bratzlav (1772–1811), great-grandson of the Baal Shem Tov, form a genre of their own in Hasidic writings. R. Nahman's *Likkutey Moharan* consists of the 'Torah' of this very unconventional Hasidic master collected by his disciple, Nathan Sternhartz. The work contains many original ideas, some of them owing much to the Haskalah, although R. Nahman became a fierce foe of the Haskalah and, indeed, of rationalism in general. An extraordinary work, not only in Hasidism but in traditional Jewish literature in general, is the collection of R. Nahman's fairy tales into which his disciples and other Hasidic groups read all sorts of mystical ideas.

The bizarre interpretations of Scripture, totally devoid of any linguistic sense, by R. Meir of Peremyshlani (d. 1850) are no more than holy jokes and were probably so intended by their author. This popular Hasidic master is reported to have commented in this way on the verse (Exodus 14:14): 'The Lord will fight [*yillahem*] for you, but ye should hold your peace [*taharishun*].' This master is reported to have taken the word *yillahem* as if it were connected with *lehem*, 'bread', and *taharishun* as if it were from the root *harash*, 'to plough', yielding the idea that God can help only when man first takes the initiative in working for his sustenance. R. Meir renders the verse: 'God will give you bread, but you must do your share by ploughing the field.'

The Hasidic 'Torah' found in the work *Mey Ha-Shiloah* by R. Mordecai Yosef of Izbica (d. 1854) consists of, at times, very radical ideas such as that of religious determinism, that all is determined by God, which leads to this author's defence of some of the Biblical villains as believing that they were compelled by their destiny to commit the sins for which Scripture blames them.

Hasidic 'Torah' is then the interpretation or adaptation of Scriptural and Rabbinic passages by the famous Hasidic masters who believed the Hasidic approach to be the authentic understanding of Judaism even while acknowledging that the Baal Shem Tov and his disciples introduced a new way to worship God. Although all the masters had basically the same general approach, naturally, each introduced nuances of his own. The classical works of Hasidic 'Torah' are venerated by the Hasidim as *Sefarim Kedoshim*, 'Holy Books'. There was no actual attempt formally to decide which Hasidic works belong in the new 'canon' of sacred works but it was arrived at by a kind of consensus among the faithful that this or that book is totally acceptable as an inspired work. In recent years over seventy volumes have been published as a huge collection,[36] each volume containing a number of smaller volumes or collections of essays by the masters.

In the last century, R. Nahman of Tcherin, a disciple of R. Nahman of Bratzlav, compiled two anthologies of Hasidic ideas arranged according to two topics: *Leshon Hasidim* ('The Language of Hasidim') containing teachings culled from the immediate disciples of the Baal Shem Tov; and *Derekh Hasidim* ('Way of Hasidim') culled from the works of their disciples. Both works were first published in Lemberg in the year 1876. In both works the topics are arranged in alphabetical order under such headings as: *emet*, 'truth'; *emunah*, 'faith'; *nevuah*, 'prophecy'; *shalom*, 'peace'; *simhah*, 'joy' and so forth. A later work, with the sub-title, *Leshon Hasidim*, is *Siah Sarfey Kodesh* ('Speech of the Holy Seraphim') by Yoetz Kayyam Kadish, and is an anthology of the 'Torah' of the Zaddikim of the Psychsa school. The work *Eser Kedushot* ('Ten Sanctities') by Israel Berger contains the 'Torah' of prominent Hasidic masters as well as much biographical material, all of which must be treated with a degree of caution since the work, while containing much useful information, is hagiographical rather than historical in its approach. A good deal of Hasidic 'Torah' is found in the voluminous work: *Beer Moshe* by R. Moshe Yehiel Epstein of Ozarov (1890–1971).[37] Among more recent works mention should be made of the commentary to the Torah, *Peniney Ha-Hasidut* ('Pearls of Hasidism'), edited by S. Kowalsky and Y. Feigenbaum.[38] Y. Hasidah compiled *Biurey Ha-Hasidut Le-Nakh* ('Hasidic Commentaries to the Prophets and the Hagiographa')[39] and *Biurey Ha-Hasidut Le-Shas* ('Hasidic Commentaries to the Talmud').[40] The works of Kowalsky/Feigenbaum and Hasidah are useful reference works but are vitiated by consisting entirely of snippets and by inadequate references to the sources on which they draw. In short, for all the references in later works, the serious student of Hasidic 'Torah' has no recourse but to study the works of the masters themselves.

NOTES

1. J. G. Weiss, *Studies in Eastern European Jewish Mysticism*, OUP, 1985, p. 41, note 22, refers to R. Jacob Joseph's *Toledot Yaakov Yosef* ed. Koretz, 1780, p. 10b, as a very early Hasidic source for the 'table' at the Third Meal. On the other hand, the same author, *Toledot*, p. 84b, states that he prefers meals to be eaten in solitude so that proper concentration on holy thoughts can better be realized. It is possible that a distinction has to be made between ordinary, weekday meals and meals on the Sabbath.
2. An English translation of this chapter in Maimon's autobiography is given in David Hundert (ed.), *Essential Papers on Hasidism*, NYU Press, 1991, 11–24.
3. Maimon, however, simply says that he was present at a Sabbath meal without specifying that it was the Third Meal.
4. For the Shekhinah speaking out of the throat of the Zaddik see Rivka Schatz Uffenheimer, *Ha-Hasidsut Kemistika*, Jerusalem, 1968, pp. 118–19.
5. See e.g. Rachel Elior, 'Between *Yesh* and *Ayin*: The Doctrine of the Zaddik in the Works of Jacob Isaac, the Seer of Lublin', in *Jewish History: Essays in Honour of Chimen Abramsky*, ed. Ada Rappoport-Albert and Steven J. Zipperstein, London, 1988, pp. 393–455, that the 'Seer' was the actual author of his works. Among other early Hasidic works composed by the Zaddikim themselves are: R. Jacob Joseph's *Toledot*, R. Moshe Hayyim Ephraim of Sudlikov's *Degel Mahaneh Efrayim* and R. Levi Yitzhak of Berditchev's *Kedushat Levi*.
6. See e.g. the title page of the Hasidic anthology, *Leshon Hasidim* by Nahman of Tcherin, Lemberg, 1876: 'collected and gathered from the holy and awesome books' (*sefarim ha-kedoshim ve-ha-noraim*).
7. *Botzina De-Nehora*, Lemberg, 1930, p. 27a.
8. On the Rabbinic Aggadah and its methodology see Yitzhak Heinemann, *Darkhey Ha-Aggadah*, Jerusalem, 1974.
9. In this very passage of the Midrash there are a number of different types of symbolism

on the gifts the Princes brought to the Tabernacle. Cf. *Sanhedrin* 34a: 'A single Biblical verse may convey several [different] meanings'.

10. See e.g. the Responsum of the Hasidic master R. Hayyim of Zanz (1793–1876) where this master (Responsa *Divrey Hayyim*, Part I, *Yoreh Deah*, No. 105) castigates a teacher who declared that Ibn Atar's work was not written through the influence of the holy spirit.

11. Hundert, *Essential Papers*, pp. 18–19

12. In Maimon 'the superiors'.

13. J. G. Weiss (*Zion* 20 [1955], pp. 107–8) has noted references to this interpretation in early Hasidic works.

14. On the Hasidic ideal of disinterestedness or equanimity see my *Holy Living: Saints and Saintliness in Judaism*, Northvale, New Jersey and London,1990, pp. 59–64.

15. R. Joseph Jacob's other works, *Tzafenat Paneah, Ketonet Pasim* and *Ben Porat Yosef*, are all in the same style as the *Toledot*.

16. See Samuel H. Dresner: *The Zaddik: The Doctrine of the Zaddik According to the Writings of Rabbi Yaakov Yosef of Polnoy*, London, New York and Toronto,1966.

17. *Toledot, bo*, p. 42b.

18. See *Sefer Baal Shem Tov*, Lodz, Vol. I, pp. 118–95.

19. On this whole subject see my: *Hasidic Prayer*, Paperback edn, Littmann Library of Jewish Civilization, London and Washington 1993.

20. *Tiferet Uziel*, Jerusalem, 1952, *vayakhel*, p.48.

21. *Noam Elimelekh, naso*, beg., ed. G. Nigal, Jerusalem, 1978, pp. 370–1.

22. *Degel Mahaney Efrayim, beshalah*, ed. Jerusalem, 1963, p. 101.

23. See my *Jewish Mystical Testimonies*, New York, 1977, 'The Mystical Epistle of the Baal Shem Tov', pp. 148–69.

24. This saying of the Ari is quoted frequently in Hasidic works on the theme of Passover e.g. in *Toledot*, p. 102d.

25. *Berakhot* 17a and found also in Zohar II, 40b.

26. I Corinthians 5:6-7.

27. *Toledot, shemini*, p. 79b.

28. *Toledot, devarim*,p. 166a.

29. *Ben Porat Yosef*, ed. Brooklyn, New York, 1976, p. 83b.

30. *Toledot*, pp. 44b–45b.

31. Ibid., p. 46a.

32. Ibid., p. 46b.

33. *Beney Yisakhar* was first published in Zolkiew in 1850 and has since gone into a number of editions.

34. *Derekh Pikkudekha*, new edition, n.d., Jerusalem, on *hametz* and *matzah*, pp. 90–106.

35. Leviticus Rabba 13:3.

36. No than 75 volumes have been published under the title: *Sefarim Ha-Kedoshim Mikol Talmidey Ha-Besht Ha-Kadosh* ('Holy Books of All the Disciples of the Holy Baal Shem Tov'). Volume 1 of this series was published in Brooklyn, New York, in 1980; Volume 75 in 1989.

37. In ten volumes, Jerusalem, 1980–87.

38. Jerusalem, 1977.

39. Jerusalem, 1980.

40. Jerusalem, 1975. This is the only work in which a running Commentary to the Talmud is provided from passages from the classical works of Hasidism.

4

The Aim of *Pilpul*
According to the Habad School

The early Kabbalists were acutely aware of the tensions that existed between their theosophical/mystical approach and the traditional methods of Torah study in which the Talmudic dialectics known as *pilpul* were the predominant factor. Already in the Zohar[1] there appears this remarkable comment on the verses: 'And the Egyptians made the children of Israel to serve with rigour. And they made their lives bitter with hard service, in mortar and in brick, and in all manner of service in the field' (Exodus 1:13–14). 'With mortar' (*homer*) refers to the *kal va-homer*, the argument from the minor to the major, the most typical form of Talmudic dialectics. 'With rigour' (*be-farekh*) is interpreted as referring to the *pirkha*, the term used for the refutation of an argument. There is undoubtedly here a veiled critique of the Talmudic-style *pilpul*, although not a complete rejection.[2] These tensions were eventually resolved, generally by postulating that there are two different levels in the Torah – the *nigleh*, 'revealed things', and the *nistar*, 'the secrets', the hidden meaning of the Torah as taught in the Kabbalah. Each of these was seen as significant in its own sphere. Each was necessary and the one complemented the other. The *Ramban*, Nahmanides (1194–1270), and the *Rashba*, Solomon Ibn Adret (*c.* 1235–*c.* 1310), were both Kabbalists and outstanding Halakhists. In sixteenth-century Safed the two fathers of the Kabbalah, Cordovero and Luria, were proficient in Talmudic/Halakhic learning.[3] The great Halakhist, R. Joseph Karo, author of the *Shulhan Arukh*, had strong mystical leanings.[4] Whether the emphasis was to be placed on the Kabbalah or the Talmudic dialectics seems to have been solved by the *Ramban*, the *Rashba* and Karo in favour of the latter, by Cordovero and Luria in favour of the former. But there was no basic incompatibility between the two subjects of study. Among some of the later Kabbalists, however, the Kabbalistic mysteries were read into the Talmudic/Halakhic dialectics[5] so that these themselves were said to have an esoteric meaning in line with the Kabbalistic doctrines. In a famous essay on the study of the Kabbalah, R. Jair Hayyim Bacharach (1638–1702) remarks[6] that he is aware of this tendency to read the words of the Talmudic sages as if these words of dialectics themselves possessed an inner, Kabbalistic meaning but refuses to accept this notion if it cannot be proven to be an authentic tradition (*kabbalah*, punning on the word), which he doubts. In *Habad* the tension was resolved in a different way. According to the founder of this intellectual tendency in Hasidism, R. Shneur Zalman of Liady (1747–1812), the very act of studying the Talmudic cases, no matter how far-fetched and impractical, is to think God's thoughts after Him so that the *nigleh* ('the revealed') becomes itself the *nistar* ('the secret') so to speak. R. Shneur Zalman writes:[7]

> Behold with regard to every kind of intellectual perception, when one understands and grasps an idea in his mind the mind seizes the idea and encompasses it in thought so that the idea is held, surrounded and enclosed in the mind in which it is comprehended. For instance, when one understands fully a rule in the Mishnah or Gemara his mind seizes the rule and encompasses it and, at the same time, the mind is encompassed by the rule. Now, behold, this rule is the wisdom and will of the Holy One, blessed be He, for it arose in His will that, for instance, when A pleads thus and B thus the the rule will be thus. And even if, in fact, a case of this kind will never come before the actual Courts, nevertheless, seeing that it rose in the will and wisdom of the Holy One, blessed be He, that this is the rule it follows that when a man knows and grasps with his mind this rule in accordance with the decision laid down in the Mishnah or the Gemara or the Codes he grasps, seizes hold of, and encompasses in his mind the will and wisdom of the Holy One, blessed be He, of whom no thought can conceive. (Not the will and wisdom in themselves but as they are enveloped in the rules set down for us.)[8] In addition man's mind is encompassed by them, a wondrous unification with which there is none to compare in material things, to be completely united and actually at one from every aspect.

R. Dov Baer of Lubavitch (1773–1827), R. Shneur Zalman's son and successor, known as the Mitteler Rebbe ('the Middle Rebbe', i.e. the leader who came between the founder of *Habad* and the third leader) developed his father's teachings and places particular emphasis on study.[9] The following is a translation of the passage[10] in which R. Dov Baer has a particular understanding of the aim of *pilpul* and where a distinction is made between the Babylonian and the Jerusalem Talmuds in this matter.

We discover a difference between the Babylonian Talmud and the Jerusalem Talmud. Our Rabbis of blessed memory say[11] that the verse: 'He hath made me to dwell in dark places' [Lamentations 3:6)] refers to the Babylonian Talmud. An amazing statement! Is it not said: 'and the Torah is light' [Proverbs 6:23] so how can it be called 'dark places'? And why the Babylonian Talmud in particular and not the Jerusalem Talmud? The matter is as follows. It is well-known that in Eretz Yisrael they used to study clearly defined rules [*halakhot pesukot*] without any deep or prolonged *pilpul*, except when this became necessary in order correctly to elucidate the rules, They simply received the tradition one from the other. Even though R. Johanan and Resh Lakish, who compiled the Jerusalem Talmud[12], did engage in *pilpul*, this was only among themselves, Resh Lakish raising difficulties and R. Johanan providing the solutions, and, afterwards his disciple R. Eleazar b. Pedat and such-like.[13] But the majority of the disciples used to study only clearly defined rules, which they had by tradition, known as *girsa*.[14]

All the disciples of the Babylonians, on the other hand, as their main activity, used to engage in *pilpul*, raising many difficulties and providing solutions in connection with every rule, all in great depth until they brought light to bear on it. Out of this *pilpul* many entirely new rules emerged. Just as there took place there the well-known debates between Abbaye and Rava[15] there also took place this kind of debate among all the disciples. This is the reason for the Rabbis saying that the 'dark places' refers to the Babylonian Talmud. Just as one who walks in darkness cannot see the light, they, too, were unable to see the correctness of the reasoning for a given law. For the main idea behind *pilpul* is that the truth of a rule or law is not attained by a superficial appreciation accessible to everyone. On the contrary, at first a man finds it exceedingly difficult to grasp the reasoning behind the law so that the harder he tries to penetrate in depth to the reasoning the less is he capable of attaining to complete understanding. And even after he has tried to grasp a meaning that is open to sound reasoning new difficulties present themselves so that the subject becomes even more opaque and unintelligible. The more he delves into the profundities of the topic the more obscure it becomes. This is called concealment after concealment.

Now there are many stages in *pilpul*. For example, many difficulties are first raised against the initial understanding of the topic and then further difficulties present themselves with regard to the more profound understanding that results from the difficulties raised against the first understanding and so on with regard to the next degree of comprehension attained after the arguments in favour of the second have been demolished. This can produce the twenty-four objections and the twenty-four solutions, which means the great effort of the intellect to rise higher and ever higher.[16] The more profound the grasp the more

opaque the topic becomes and the more dim the light of the law.
However, once a man has solved all the numerous problems and contradictions and has attained to the ultimate truth behind the profound
reasoning on which the law is based, he can be said to have engaged in
a great *pilpul*, whereas if he arrives at the truth without having to
encounter so many problems and their solution he can be said to have
engaged in a lesser *pilpul*. In any event, it can be observed that the main
aim of *pilpul* is to uncover the great concealment of the topic by means
of the difficulties to which it gives rise, all comprehension being
rendered unobtainable so that the topic becomes impenetrable to the
intellect.

For all that, if the topic were to remain opaque and without any ultimate grasp whatsoever, of what use would the *pilpul* be since the aim is
to arrive at the truth? But the matter is as follows. After all the problems
raised and after the aforementioned concealment after concealment,
one does eventually arrive at the true meaning of the topic as it is without any further difficulties or contradictions. It is like the
filtering of wine or the refining of silver from the most subtle of the
dross so that all that remains is pure silver or wine of the utmost
clarity. And so, too, one who refines flour with thirteen refinements and
so forth. And this is sufficient for the wise.

On the basis of this exposition, R. Dov Baer comes to the conclusion[17] that the light which proceeds from the darkness – i.e. as a
result of the darkness – comes from a far higher stage than the light
attained at first glance. This is on the analogy of the attempt to
have a comprehension of the divine where the Zohar[18] states that
after all searching out everything remains as opaque as it was
beforehand. But, then, to know that one does not know is itself a
major attainment of knowledge and, by the same token, the more
darkness at first the greater the eventual illumination. Thus the
Babylonian Talmud, so strong in *pilpul* is, indeed, a 'dark place' at
first but precisely because of this it is eventually the source of a
light far higher than could have been attained in the more direct
approach typical of the Jerusalem Talmud.

R. Dov Baer's treatment, while very similar to that of his father,
seems to differ slightly from it. For both R. Shneur Zalman and R.
Dov Baer the Talmudic-style *pilpul* is itself a mystical devotional
exercise, but for R. Shneur Zalman it is the decision arrived at after
the *pilpul* that brings about the desired aim of thinking God's
thoughts after Him, whereas for R. Dov Baer the *pilpul* itself is a
mystical exercise in that through it the ultimate truth is revealed
and this whole process is a mirror of the cosmic processes by
means of which the *En Sof* emerges out of concealment to become

manifest in the *Sefirot*. By such means *Habad* was able to have the best of both worlds – the world of Kabbalah and Hasidism and the world of Talmudic casuistry.

It is remarkable that R. Dov Baer's contemporary, R. Aryeh Laib Heller of Stry in Galicia (d. 1813), a strong opponent of Hasidism, has a similar defence of the high, almost mystical value of *pilpul*. Heller[19] quotes the comment of Moses Almosnino (*c*. 1515–*c*. 1580) of Salonika on the verse: 'Dead flies make the ointment of the perfumer fetid and putrid; so doth a little folly outweigh wisdom and honour' (Ecclesiastes 10:1). For Almosnino a 'little folly' outweighs wisdom in the sense that it contributes to a better understanding of the truth. That is to say, as Almosnino remarks, those with perfectly straight, uncomplicated minds are not generally very keen. Sharpness of intellect is due to the need to overcome errors and confusions which set up obstructions to the questing mind. It is *pilpul* that alone can overcome these obstacles to the truth. Heller quotes Almosnino with approval. Just as fire spurts and gains in power when a little water is poured on to it, so the mind that is obliged to grapple with problems becomes even more alert. This is the 'little folly' that acts as a spur to the scholar. Heller applies this to the moral life of man. Without temptation to sin, life would no doubt be 'good' but life can become 'very good' only as a result of man's struggle against the evil inclination. Heller and Dov Baer did not know of one another but the problem of learning versus *devekut*, 'attachment to God', was in the air as a result of the debates between the Hasidim and the Mitnaggedim[20] so it is perhaps not surprising to witness the reaction of both teachers. It is also worth remarking that while R. Dov Baer put most of his intellectual gifts at the service of Hasidic teaching, he seems to have used the Talmudic-style *pilpul* in this Hasidic activity, raising questions and supplying solutions here as if he were engaging in traditional Talmudic studies so far as methodology is concerned.[21] Further research is required on how far some Kabbalists employed similar methods of transfer from one discipline to the other.[22] For Dov Baer such transfer was quite natural and even inevitable, granted his notion that *pilpul* is indispensable for the attainment of truth.

NOTES

1. Zohar I, 27a; Tikkuney Zohar 21, ed. Reuben Margaliot, Jerusalem, 1940, p. 44a.
2. On this see I. Tishby, *Mishnat ha-Zohar*, Vol. I, Jerusalem, 1957, p. 384. The traditional commentators, naturally, understand the passage to mean that the 'hard service' of *pilpul* was required in order to bring redemption by overcoming the power of the *kelipot*, the demonic forces, or that their studies were bitter because they did not study for its own sake. See e.g. the commentary to the Zohar by Daniel Frisch, *Matok mi-Devash*, Jerusalem, 1986, Genesis, pp. 98–9.
3. For a full treatment of this subject see, 'Kabbalah and Halakhah as Rival Subjects of Study' (Heb.) in Jacob Katz, *Halakhah ve-Kabbalah*, Jerusalem, 1984, pp. 70–101; on Codovero and Halakhah see Katz, p. 93, and on Luria see Katz, p. 98.
4. Karo kept a mystical diary for 40 years in which he recorded the communications he received from 'the soul of the Mishnah', see R. J. Z. Werblowsky's penetrating study: *Joseph Karo Lawyer and Mystic*, Clarendon Press, Oxford, 1962.
5. The Hasidic master and rival to Habad, R. Zvi Hirsch of Zhydachov, especially, is fond of interpreting Talmudic passages as having the esoteric meaning of the Kabbalah, see his *Sur me-Ra va-Aseh Tov, Pest*, 1942 (pp. 77ff in my translation *Turn Aside From Evil and Do Good*, Littman Library, London, Washington, 1995).
6. Responsa *Havvot Yair*, Frankfurt, 1699, No. 210.
7. *Tanya*, Vilna, 1930, Chapter 5, pp. 17–19.
8. R. Shneur Zalman means here that the actual will is incomprehensible to the human mind but it is possible for the human mind to grasp that will when it is contained in the garments of the law given to humans.
9. See Naftali Loewenthal, *Communicating the Infinite: The Emergence of the Habad School*, University of Chicago Press, 1990, Index; *s.v.* 'Study program' for Dov Baer's programme of studies for his followers.
10. R. Dov Baer, *Shaarey Orah*, Brooklyn, New York, 1948, Nos. 54 and 55, pp. 22b–23a.
11. *Sanhedrin* 24a in a saying attributed to the early fourth-century Amora, R. Jeremiah who emigrated from Babylon to Eretz Israel. In the context, then, *talmudah shel bavel* means 'the teaching in Babylon' and is R. Jeremiah's wry comment on why he preferred to emigrate to Eretz Yisrael where the teaching provided greater illumination. In the Middle Ages the saying was applied to the Babylonian Talmud as we now have it, though, of course, this is anachronistic. See the marginal note in the Vilna, Romm edition of the Talmud to this passage for attempts to explain it as complementary to the Babylonian Talmud. R. Dov Baer has his own method of justification.
12. According to Maimonides (Introduction to *Mishneh Torah*) the Jerusalem Talmud was edited by R. Johanan (third century), which R. Dov Baer follows here. Modern scholarship departs from this since the Jerusalem Talmud as we now have it must have been edited much later; see H. L. Strack and G. Stemberger, *Introduction to the Talmud and Midrash*, Edinburgh, 1991, pp. 188–9.
13. R. Eleazar b. Pedat was R. Johanan's study companion and disciple after the death of Resh Lakish; see *Bava Metzia* 84a.
14. The *girsa* is the rehearsal of the plain text without the *sevara*, the detailed exposition of the text.
15. The *havvayot de-Abbaye ve-Rava*, 'debates of Abbaye and Rava', are given as an illustration of the typical debating activities of the Babylonian teachers; see *Sukkah* 28a.
16. See *Bava Metzia* 84a, which Resh Lakish used to raise twenty-four difficulties to every statement of R. Johanan and R. Johanan would supply twenty-four solutions.
17. No. 55, p. 23a.
18. Zohar I, 1b.
19. Heller's *Shev Shematata* has been published in many editions. Heller's remarks in praise of *pilpul* are to be found in the introduction to the work under the letters *hey* and *vav*. See my article, 'Rabbi Aryeh Laib Heller's Theological Introduction to his *Shev Shematata*', in *Modern Judaism*, Vol. I, 1981, pp. 184–216.
20. On the debate between the Hasidim and the Mitnaggedim on Torah study and *devekut* the essential work is the attack from the ranks of the Mitnaggedim by R. Hayyim of Volozhyn (1749–1821), entitled *Nefesh ha-Hayyim* (edition I. D. Rubin, Bene Berak, 1989, Gate Four, pp. 188ff). See N. Lamm, *Torah Lishmah*, Jerusalem, 1972 for a full discussion

of the subject. Cf. M.Wilensky, *Hasidim u-Mitnaggedim*, Jerusalem, 1970, Vol. 2, pp. 345–9 and, especially, the little work *Yosher Divrey Emet* by the early Galician Hasidic master, R. Meshullam Feivush Heller of Zbarazh (d.c. 1795). This work is part of the anonymous *Likkutey Yekarim* (ed. Jerusalem, 1974, pp. 110–14). Both R. Dov Baer, from the Hasidic side, and Aryeh Laib Heller, from the Mitnaggedic side, must have been keenly aware of the polemics on this matter even though neither makes any direct reference to them.

21. See the very interesting observation attributed to the famous Talmudist R. Joseph Rozin (1858–1936), the Rogachover Gaon, in *Migdol Oz*, Memorial Volume for A. Z. Slonim, ed. J. Mundstein, Kfar Habad, 1980, p. 94 that while R. Shneur Zalman was undoubtedly a 'Gaon' (in the context a genius in Talmudic learning) his son, R. Dov Baer, was 'a Gaon of Geonim'. The Rogachover explained that in R. Dov Baer's Hasidic works there is clear evidence of extreme proficiency in dialectics. Cf. S. Zevin: *Ishim Ve-Shittot*, Jerusalem, 1952, p. 21 for a similar view by the Netziv of Volohozhyn.

22. A good illustration is provided by Cordovero's Commentary to the Zohar, *Or Yakar*, Jerusalem, 1962 – where Cordovero expounds Zoharic passages by first raising a number of difficulties and then providing solutions.

5

The Derashah of the Maggid on the Two Forms

The famous exposition of the silver trumpets (Numbers 10:1–10) by R. Dov Baer, the Maggid of Mezirech (d. 1772), disciple of the Baal Shem Tov and organizer and prominent theoretician of the Hasidic movement, provides us with an excellent introduction both to Hasidic thought and to Hasidism's use of Scripture for its own purposes. The passage is in the work *Maggid Devarav Le-Yaakov*, edited by the Maggid's disciple, Solomon of Lutzk. (The edition used in this article is the critical edition, based on manuscripts, of Rivka Schatz-Uffenheimer, with an Introduction and Notes, Jerusalem, 1976. The passage is, in this edition, No. 24, pp. 38–40.) The text is given here in translation, followed by a detailed comment.

> 'Make thee two trumpets [*hatzotzerot*] of silver' [Numbers 10:2]. The meaning [of two *hatzotzerot*] is two half forms [*hatzi tzurot*], after the manner of [the verse]: 'upon the likeness of the throne [*ha-kisse*] was a likeness as the appearance of a man [*adam*] upon it above' [Ezekiel 1:26]. For man [*adam*] is only *dalet mem* [the second and third letters of *adam* forming the word *dam*, blood] with the Word resting upon him and when he is attached to the Holy One, blessed be He, the Lord of the universe, he [then] becomes man [*adam*; the expression 'Lord of the universe', *alufo shall olam*, is found in the Talmud, *Hagigah* 16a, but in the Kabbalah is understood to denote God as the *alef* of the universe]. The Holy One, blessed be He, contracted Himself through many worlds in order to be united with man who could not [otherwise] have had the capacity to endure His brightness. Man is required to separate himself from all that is corporeal, ascending through all the worlds to be united with the Holy One, blessed be He, to the extent that he loses his [separate] identity and then he is called man [*adam*]. And this is the reference to 'the likeness of the throne', where He, blessed be He, is concealed [*mekhusah*, pun on *kisse*, throne], after the manner of [the verse]: 'a cloud with a fire flashing up' [Ezekiel 1:4] – a 'cloud', since

darkness rests on man so that, at first, he is unable to pray with burning enthusiasm [*hitlahavut*] but afterwards 'a fire flashing up', denoting burning enthusiasm. This is the meaning of 'the likeness of the covering', where He, blessed be He, is concealed, is 'like the appearance of a man', that is the awakening of the Holy One, blessed be He, on high is in direct proportion to man's awakening. When love [of God] is awakened in the Zaddik love is awakened in all worlds. And so it is with regard to all the [other] qualities. This happens when he [the Zaddik], by virtue of his great [spiritual] refinement [of character] elevates himself higher than all worlds so that there He becomes united to Him. For His, blessed be He, sole intention is to bestow His goodness on man, as the saying has it [Kiddushin 82b]: 'The whole world was only created to serve me' and all the upper worlds and all the qualities are placed in his [man's] possession for him to rule over them as a king has dominion over his regiment, as King David, on whom be peace, says: 'and let Thy saints [*hasidekha*] sing Thy praises' [Psalms 132:9]. The Zohar [I, 148b] asks: 'Surely it is the Levites [not the saints] who sing God's praises?'. But [the meaning of the verse is] whatever the Zaddik wants the Holy One, blessed be He, wants. Even the sex acts of the patriarchs constitute a perfect Torah [in themselves] since they are recorded in the Torah and if the verses: 'And he went in also unto Rachel' etc. [Genesis 29:30] or: 'And Jacob loved Rachel' [Genesis 29:14] were lacking the Sefer Torah would be unfit for use. For they [the patriarchs] did everything in close attachment [*devekut*] to Him, blessed be He, and the Holy One, blessed be He, had delight in them, with the result that they became Torah and the Torah and the Holy One, blessed be He, are all One [Zohar II, 60a] so that, despite the fact that it [the sex act] is a very corporeal thing, the Holy One, blessed be He, has delight. Hence the verse says: 'Two trumpets of silver'. For man is a half form since he is only *dam* and the Holy One, blessed be He, is called: 'Lord of the universe' and when they are joined together a whole form is the result. 'Silver' [*kesef*] means 'desire', that thou shouldst constantly have a desire for the Holy One, blessed be He, and the Holy One, blessed be He, will love thee.

In this and in numerous other passages the Maggid, like the other Hasidic masters, pursues the quasi-Midrashic method in which Biblical verses are taken out of context to yield lessons for the mystical approach. The fact that the Torah ordained in the time of Moses that two silver trumpets be fashioned is seen as irrelevant unless it has a meaning for the strivings of the contemporary Hasidic mystic. For the Maggid, the Torah is addressing the Zaddik, the spiritual superman, whose task it is to transcend the limits imposed on him by his bodily instincts. While the dichotomy between body and soul exists for the Hasidim just as much as it does for the medieval thinkers, in the usual Hasidic approach the ascetic flight from the body is not advocated. The Hasidic ideal is rather that of *avodah be-gashmiut* ('worship through corporeality'), namely, engaging in worldly activities with the mind on God. For the Hasid the ideal is that of devekut ('attachment' to God), a state of mind in which everything one does is directed to God. Eating, drinking and other material needs have to be satisfied for the sake of God and, elevated in this way, become themselves acts of worship. The further, Kabbalistic idea is invoked, that human deeds have a cosmic effect. When man is benevolent he sends beneficent impulses on high and thus brings about harmony in the celestial realms with the result that the divine grace can flow unimpededly through all creation. Conversely, when man is vicious he sends baneful impulses on high and these disturb the harmony of the celestial realms and the flow of the divine grace is impeded.

The Maggid begins with a pun on the word for 'trumpets' (*hatzotzerot*), reading it, anachronistically, and with as little regard for grammar and syntax as in general Midrashic exegesis, as 'half forms' (*hatzi tzurot*).The command is for man to combine the two half forms so that they become a single whole and complete form. What are these two half forms? For the Maggid they are God, represented by the letter *alef*, the first letter of the alphabet and the first letter of the word for man, and man, represented by the letters *dalet* and *mem*, the second and third letters of the word for man. When the Maggid says that these two letters form the word *dam*, 'blood', he means that man on his own without God is only flesh and blood; earthy and earth-bound without the *alef* to raise him heavenwards. The Maggid's reference to the Word is to be understood as meaning that man could not exist, even in his aspect of flesh and blood, without the sustaining Word of God. This is the Shekhinah, the Sefirah of Malkhut ('Sovereignty'), the principle by means of which the world is governed. Moreover, in the Kabbalah, Malkhut is God's 'speech', as it were, His creative communication, hence the word *dam* is formed from the initial letters of *dibbur* ('speech') and *malkhut*.

The Maggid proceeds to expound the verse in Ezekiel, which he interprets to mean that God is concealed (pun on the words *kisse*, 'throne', and *mekhusah*, 'covered') from man, but reveals Himself in proportion ('as the likeness of') to man's efforts at self-transcendence. God, according to the Lurianic Kabbalah, 'descends' from His 'throne' – His concealment – through the contraction of His powers in successively decreasing worlds, away from His essence, in order that man might meet him, otherwise His 'brightness' would be too strong for humans to contain and they would vanish into nothingness or, rather, be totally engulfed in its splendour. When man ascends in his contemplation through all the worlds to God, losing himself in the process, he reaches to the other half of the equation where the *alef* is joined to the dam to form the word *adam*. In other words, man, paradoxically, becomes truly human – a true 'man' – only when he succeeds in rising above his individual human nature. This is the typical Hasidic doctrine of *bitul ha-yesh*, 'annihilation of selfhood', the goal of the Hasidic mystic to be attained especially in prayer. But there are stages in the mystical ascent. At first there is the 'cloud of unknowing' or the 'dark night of the soul'. But if the worshipper persists he will attain in his prayers to the state of burning enthusiasm, *hitlahavut* (from *lahav*, 'a flame'), the Hasidic ideal in the life of prayer. Since human deeds mirror forth the divine 'qualities', the powers or potencies in the Godhead such as love, power and harmony, man can awaken all the beneficent qualities in the Godhead by allowing these good qualities to enter into his own life. When man truly loves God, it will have the effect of awakening God's love and then the divine grace will flow as it is God's intention. It should be noted, however, that, in Solomon of Lutzk's rendition, the Maggid refers in this connection to the Zaddik, implying that such spiritual flights are fully possible of realization only by the spiritually elite.

This self-transcendence, the Maggid continues, was achieved by the patriarchs even when carrying out the sex act. Since the minds of these holy men, prototypes of the Zaddik, were on God even when performing such a grossly corporeal act, on the face of it totally at variance with the spiritual, God was present even in this act, and, since God and the Torah are one and the same, these acts related in the Torah become themselves divine. The patriarchal narratives, including those which tell of their sex lives, are, evidently, an essential part of the Torah, and if they were omitted the Torah would be defective.

The Maggid concludes with another pun. This is on the word for 'silver', *kesef*. The connection of silver with the word *kisufim*, 'longing', enables the Maggid to render 'two trumpets of silver' as 'two half-forms of longing' – when man longs for God, God longs for man and the two halves become one.

The Maggid here is going far beyond the idea, found in a number of ancient Rabbinic texts, that God needs man just as man needs God and beyond the Kabbalistic idea that man, by his deeds, influences the upper worlds. For the Maggid, when man rises above the confines of his human state to reach out to God, he attains to unity with the divine, the two half forms become one. It is sometimes said that in Jewish thought the abyss between the transcendent God and finite man is too vast ever to be crossed. On this view, Judaism knows nothing of the *unio mystica*. This passage in the Maggid's writings is sufficient in itself to give the lie to such a contention. For the Maggid, at least in his disciple's formulation, it is possible for the soul of the mystic in its rare flights to be completely united with its Source.

It is necessary to note that in all this we do not have the actual words of the Maggid but his teachings as recorded by Solomon of Lutzk. It is worthwhile examining a different record of the Maggid's ideas of the two half forms. R. Israel of Koznitz (1733–1814), disciple of the Maggid (he was also a Maggid and is known as the Koznitzer Maggid) writes in his *Avodat Yisrael* (Lemberg, 1858, p. 61b) in a comment to the verse containing the command to fashion the silver trumpets: 'We have received [the teaching] from our Master and Teacher, the Gaon, Rabbi Dov Baer, his memory is for a blessing for the life of the world to come, that the combination of half forms [*hatzi tzurot*] from *hatzotzerot* hints at the Community of Israel in Her relationship with Her Lover, in which each is only a half form in itself. He, blessed be He, by His tremendous will, directs all His love and attachment to His partner, the Community of Israel, and She also longs and for and attaches Herself to the Creator, blessed be He, until all is included in the unification.' The Koznitzer Maggid was a noted Kabbalist, often interpreting Scripture in its Kabbalistic meaning. His reference here to the Community of Israel is to the Sefirah *Malkhut*, the archetype of the Jewish community on earth. The Lover is the Sefirah *Tiferet*, the male principle on high, with *Malkhut* the female principle. Thus, for the Koznitzer, the Maggid does not refer to the individual soul. The two forms which become one are *Tiferet* and *Malkhut*, which become united and in harmony by the deeds of Israel on earth. As the Koznitzer goes on to say, some of the precepts such as the Lulav and Etrog represent this 'sacred marriage'.

It is obvious that the Koznitzer's interpretation is later and given in accordance with his own Kabbalistic stance. He refers to the Maggid as a departed saint and makes no claim to having heard the exposition from the Maggid himself, whereas Solomon of

Lutzk claims to be recording an authentic saying of the Maggid. As with similar oft-repeated sayings of the Hasidic masters, the Maggid's original saying was reported in different ways and may have referred only to the two half forms in his comment to the verse about the two silver trumpets. But the exact application of the saying was left to the Maggid's disciples. In any event, it is only in the interpretation of Solomon of Lutzk that we find the idea of the *unio mystica*.

6

Jacob's Dream in Hasidic Interpretation

*And he dreamed, and behold a ladder set up on the earth,
and the top of it reached to heaven: and behold the angels
of God ascending and descending on it.* (Genesis 28:12)

This dream of Jacob has received many and varied interpretations in the history of Jewish exegesis.[1] The Hasidic masters read their own interpretations into a narrative, obviously fascinating to them, of a ladder linking heaven and earth. Here are examined some of the main interpretations found in the Hasidic classics.

R. JACOB JOSEPH OF POLONNOYE (d. c. 1784)

In the writings of this seminal Hasidic author[2] the dream of Jacob receives various interpretations. Like most Hasidic authors, R. Jacob Joseph presents no systematic treatment of a theme but rather comments as the spirit moves him. In one passage in his *Toledot Yaakov Yosef*,[3] this author interprets the dream as symbolic of the Zaddik at a low stage (*madregah*) of his spiritual ascent. At this stage the Zaddik is 'set up on the earth'; he is earthbound and comparatively remote from God. Yet, precisely because he is aware of his lowly stage and is distressed at his descent from holiness, he is moved to rise higher; his head reaches heavenwards. The more a man perceives himself to be remote from God, the more God, who dwells with the contrite of spirit, is with him to help him rise higher. The *malakhim* ('angels' but here understood as 'those who are sent') are the members of the Jewish people who have been sent into the world in order to perfect their souls by living the life of holiness as ordained by the Torah. There are a number of groups (*kitot*, R. Jacob Joseph possibly uses this word because the Mitnaggedim dubbed the Hasidim as belonging to a *kat*, a 'sect'). There are those who cleave (*ledabbek et atzmam*, referring to the ideal of *devekut*, attachment to God through attachment to the Zaddik) to the Zaddik even when they perceive that he is lowly of spirit. They descend with the Zaddik and are not put off by the fact that he is at an inferior stage because they know that he will rise much higher and take them with him in his rise. The word *bo*, usually translated 'on it', is taken to mean 'because of him'. Those sent into the world who attach themselves to the Zaddik rise through him from their descent. Others (an obvious dig at the Mitnaggedim), however, ignore the Zaddik and certainly have no desire to become attached to him. On the contrary, they exalt themselves over him and feel greatly superior to him. When the Zaddik rises these people cannot rise with him since there is no cure for one who despises a *talmid hakham*.[4] In the next verse it says: 'Behold the Lord stood over him', that is to say, the Shekhinah is with the Zaddik even when he is at his lowly stage.

In another interpretation of the dream,[5] R. Jacob Joseph develops the idea that it is impossible, even for the Zaddik, to remain always in the state of *devekut*. No human being is capable of having God in mind all the time. There are ups and downs even in the spiritual life of the Zaddik. The ladder represents the *talmid hakham* (equivalent, as above, to the Zaddik) since the word for ladder, *sulam*, has the same numerical value (130) as the word Sinai, on which the Torah was given to Israel. The reason why it was divinely ordained from the beginning that the Zaddik should suffer this 'dryness of soul', was for him to have some point of contact with lesser mortals whom he can raise higher together with him in his ascent. Since man's deeds have a cosmic effect, the very angels of God (R. Jacob Joseph boldly adds, and the Shekhinah) rise and fall with the Zaddik. When the Zaddik falls from his elevated stage, they all fall with him and when he rises higher they all rise with him. However, through his descent to the comparative level of ordinary folk, the Zaddik takes the risk that he will be unduly influenced by them. This is why, after Jacob's sun had set (verse 11), that is, when the spiritual light had departed, to some extent, from his life, he was informed (verse 13) that the Lord stood above him to protect him. Since the Zaddik's descent is for the benefit of sinners, it is only right and proper that he should be protected from the sin that might result from his association with them.

Moreover, the Zaddik's descent is essential since (and here the Hasidic ideal of *avodah begshmiyut* 'serving God in corporeality', is introduced) the Zaddik must have his feet on the ground so as to be able to serve God even, or especially, when he engages in the things of the world. This is why the feet of the ladder stand firmly on 'the earth'. The Zaddik's head, the top of the ladder, must reach heavenwards even when he is on earth and in this way bring about the elevation of his earthly pursuits to God. By uniting the deed with the thought, the Zaddik brings about the unification of the Sefirot on high. As R. Jacob Joseph writes: 'We can now understand that man is a ladder standing on the earth, to engage in earthly, corporeal matters, yet his head reaches out to heaven, having his thoughts on high so as to combine the deed with the thought, through which a unification takes place on high. Hence the verse goes on to say that the angels of God, the Holy Chariot, ascend and descend through him, that is, because of his unification [of thought and deed].' This comment gives expression to all the tensions in Hasidic life in which the Zaddik is bound to come down to the level of his followers if he is to exert an influence over them and yet, in the process, he places his own spiritual life at risk.

In another of his works, *Ben Porat Yosef*,[6] R. Jacob Joseph quotes the author of *Megalle Amukot*, R. Nathan Shapiro (1585–1633), who is said to have noted that the word *sulam* (spelled with a *vav*) has the same numerical value (136) as the word for wealth, *mamon*. R. Jacob Joseph, evidently giving this only by hearsay, has confused this supposed saying of R. Nathan Shapiro, with the well-known saying, quoted in other Hasidic works, of Jacob ben Asher, the *Baal Ha-Turim* to the verse. Here the *Baal Ha-Turim* observes that the word for poverty, *oni*, also has the same numerical value as *sulam*, yielding the thought that both riches and poverty come from God. For the *Baal Ha-Turim*, the ladder of both riches and poverty reaches to heaven in the sense that it is divinely ordained which person should be rich and which poor. R. Jacob Joseph, however, quotes it as: 'I have heard in the name of the work *Megalle Amukot* that *sulam* has the same numerical value as *mamon*. For, because of their fondness for money, even the righteous [*ha-tzadikkim*], called the angels of God, ascend and descend because of it.' It is doubtful whether R. Nathan Shapiro ever made this comment (it is not found in his work), but even if he did make it and actually used the word *tzaddikim*, he meant by it simply 'righteous people' and it is R. Jacob Joseph who has applied it to the

Zaddikim in the Hasidic sense. Even the Zaddikim are liable to descend from their elevated stage if their love of money gets out of control. However, R. Jacob Joseph continues, while, indeed, the love of money can drag a man down it can do so only if he allows his physical and material nature (*homer*) to gain the upper hand of his spiritual form (*tzurah*). Then, indeed, the angels of God, human beings sent by God into this world, do fall from grace through their love of money. But when they subordinate their base desire for riches to higher things, by giving charity, for instance, their very love of money is the cause of their spiritual elevation.[7] In t his comment, the further tensions are expressed, both in the lives of the Zaddikim and of their followers. The Mitnaggedim constantly accused the Zaddikim that they were ready to sell their souls for gain; the Hasidim supporting the Zaddikim that they should pray on their behalf. And the Hasidim themselves, in the severe economic situation that obtained in Eastern Europe,[8] were often obliged to engage in unscrupulous means of earning their daily bread. R Jacob Joseph here defends both the Zaddikim and their followers. Yes, he implies, love of money is natural in the conditions in which these found themselves, but it need not result in spiritual degradation. The ladder of riches can reach to heaven if it is employed to achieve higher things.

R. MOSHE HAYYIM EPHRAIM OF SUDLIKOV (d. 1800)

R. Moshe Hayyim Ephraim, grandson of the Baal Shem Tov, was the author of *Degel Mahaney Efrayim*, after which he is known by the Hasidim as 'the Degel'. The work was first published by the author's son in Koretz in 1810.[9] The Degel's comment on Jacob's dream opens with reference to a statement of his grandfather, the Baal Shem Tov. The Degel writes:

> Contained in this passage [of the dream] is the mystery of greatness and smallness [of soul]. The saying of my master, my grandfather, his soul is in Eden, his memory is for a blessing, is well-known, that 'the living creatures run to and fro' [Ezekiel 1:14], and it is impossible for a man to remain always at the same stage but he is obliged to ascend and descend. His descent is for the purpose of further ascent. For, when a man becomes aware that he is in the state of smallness he prays to the Lord, as it is said: 'But from thence ye will seek the Lord thy God, and thou shalt find Him' [Deuteronomy 4:19]. The meaning of 'from thence'

is, from whichever place you find yourself, as my master, my grandfather, his soul is in Eden, his memory is for a blessing, has said.

The mystic's 'dark night of the soul' is described by the Degel,
using Kabbalistic terminology, as 'smallness' (*katnut*), while
enlargement of soul is described as 'greatness', *gadlut*. The application of the verse in Ezekiel about running to and fro was first
made by Cordovero[10] but this famous sixteenth-century mystic
applies the idea to human cognizance of God. Cordovero remarks
that when man engages in worship he cannot help having a
picture of God in his mind. But whatever he depicts is totally
in adequate since God is beyond all comprehension. Man must,
therefore, run to and fro in his mind; running to affirm God's existence and then immediately recoiling from the mental picture he is
bound to have. In the saying of the Baal Shem Tov quoted by the
Degel, this running to and fro is applied not to cognitive awareness but to the states of *katnut* and *gadlut*. There is an ebb and flow
in the mystical life. The typical Hasidic doctrine of *devekut*, a state
which, as R. Jacob Joseph has also observed, is impossible for man
all the time. When his mystical experience is intense, when his soul
is completely absorbed in contemplation of God, he is said to be in
the state of *gadlut*. But when he is remote from *devekut* he is in the
state of *katnut*. The word for 'living creatures' in the Ezekiel verse
is *hayyot*, but is pointed in Hasidic thought to read *hiyyut*, 'vitality'.
Man's spirit soars in rapture and is full of vitality when he is in the
gadlut state but becomes weak when he is the *katnut* state. Yet the
state of *katnut* must not be despised. On the contrary, once the
mystic appreciates that he is in that state and is severely distressed
at the diminution of his spiritual vitality, clear evidence that he has
become remote from God, this very fact is a spur for him to rise
higher. The very descent is the spur to a greater ascent. The
descent is in order to ascend and is not a descent at all but an
ascent, just as one who climbs a ladder may need to step down a
rung or two in order to rest and then continue the ascent with
renewed energy. 'From there' in the verse quoted by the Baal Shem
means from wherever the mystic finds himself, even at the *katnut*
stage. Indeed, the Baal Shem Tov implies, he can seek his God only
from that stage.

The term used by the Degel: 'a descent for the purpose of
ascent' (*yeridah le-tzorekh aliyah*), is taken from the Talmud (*Makkot*
7b). There are cases of accidental homicide for which a person is

culpable and has to go in exile to one of the refuge cities (Deuteronomy 19:1–15), but there are other cases where he is not held culpable. If a man going down a ladder falls off the ladder on to someone beneath him and kills the man upon whom he falls, he is held to be culpable. But if he falls while climbing up the ladder he is not culpable. The Talmud discusses whether he would be held culpable if he fell while descending but with his intention for the descent to be for the purpose of an ascent. This legal terminology is employed by the Degel and in other Hasidic works for the spiritual descent of the Zaddik. This is not really a descent at all, since it is for the purpose of the ascent.

The Degel continues that Jacob's ladder set up on the earth symbolizes the mystic's descent. The top of the ladder reaches to heaven since the Zaddik's soul soars higher precisely because the feet of the ladder are on the earth, close to earthly things, in the rise from which he obtains the fresh vitality by which to rise. In the passage from the *Toledot*, quoted above, the descent of the Zaddik is chiefly so that he might raise his followers to greater heights. In the Degel's analysis the Zaddik himself needs to descend to the state of *katnut*, without which he can never attain the state of *gadlut*.

In another interpretation, the Degel quotes the saying, which he attributes correctly to the *Baal Ha-Turim*, that, as above, the word *sulam* has the same numerical value as the word *mamon*. The Degel advances a further Gematria. The numerical value of the word *malakh*, 'angel' is 91 and 91 is the same as that of the combined value of the two divine names, the Tetragrammaton (26) and Adonai, 'Lord' (65). These two divine names represent, respectively, the Sefirot of *Tiferet*, the male principle, and Malkhut, the female principle. Riches, *mamon*, are, on the face of it, very worldly and earthy. The ladder of *mamon* is set firmly on the earth. But when its head reaches to heaven, when a man uses his riches to benefit others, he brings out the unification of the Sefirot on high and assists the flow of divine grace through all creation. These unifications are the angels seen in Jacob's dream. The charitable impulses from below, from the earth on which the ladder stands, send beneficent impulses on high and, in turn, the divine grace comes down to earth. These are the angels which ascend and descend on the ladder. Here, in the Degel, there is also an elaboration of the theme of the importance of charity.

R. LEVI YITZHAK OF BERDITCHEV (D.1810)

R. Levi Yitzhak provides, in his *Kedushat Levi*,[11] two different interpretations of the ladder. In the first interpretation, Jacob foresaw in
his vision the working out of the whole cosmic drama. When
Scripture says that Jacob took a stone on which to lay his head
(verse 11; in Rabbinic interpretation Jacob took only one stone) it
means that his head – i.e. his vision – embraced the cornerstone of
the whole process of human history in which Jacob's descendants,
the people of Israel, bring about the restoration of the whole
cosmos to God. (R. Levi Yitzhak adds in parenthesis that he is not
suggesting that the verse loses its plain meaning. Jacob took a real
stone upon which to lay his head and later on he poured oil over
it. Yet, at the same time, this stone hinted at the cornerstone of
history.) It should be added that in Hasidic folklore, R. Levi Yitzhak
is the mighty pleader for his people who, for him, do form the
cornerstone of history. According to this interpretation, the ladder
represents the long exile of Israel. That the ladder was set up on
earth means that Israel will suffer the downfall and degradation of
exile from its land, but the top of the ladder reached to heaven
since the ultimate purpose of the exile was the restoration of the
Kingdom of Heaven. All this is based on the Lurianic Kabbalah,
according to which there are 'holy sparks' scattered through all
creation and imprisoned by the demonic powers. Israel's task is
to restore these 'sparks' to their Source in God by means of holy
living. At the beginning of the whole cosmic process, when God
emerged out of concealment to become revealed to His creatures,
the divine light was shattered into fragments and this cosmic catastrophe, as Scholem calls it, brought about the scattering of the
sparks which now have to be rescued through the deeds of the
righteous. Thus the sparks descended and will ultimately ascend
to God. The angels of God which Jacob saw ascending and
descending are precisely the holy sparks which will receive their
ultimate ascent when the Messiah will come and Israel's exile will
be no more.

In R. Levi Yitzhak's second interpretation, the ladder is man
himself. As R. Levi Yitzhak puts it:

> *And he dreamed, and behold a ladder.* For, when he begins to worship
> man's heart becomes inflamed [*mitlahev*, a reference to the Hasidic ideal
> of worship with *hitlahavut*, burning enthusiasm] within him when he
> considers that all the upper worlds become elevated through his

worship of God. As a result his heart becomes ever stronger in worship. Afterwards, once his heart has become strong in worship, he no longer thinks at all of anything but God and God takes delight in him since he has become a Chariot of the Shekhinah. Thus the word *vayahalom* ['and he dreamed'] is an expression of strength, as in the verse: *vetahalimeni vehahayeni* ['strengthen Thou me, and make me live', Isaiah 38:16], namely, that divine worship should be strong in his heart so that he stands firm in his worship; this is when he begins to worship, when he needs to be encouraged. This encouragement is provided by the fact that man in this world is a ladder set up on earth but its head reaches to heaven and the angels of God ascend and descend through him, the angels become elevated through him. All of this because of man. But the opposite, God forbid, is also true, that he can bring about their fall. As the Rabbis say, when the Temple was destroyed the ranks of the angels were decreased, as it were. However, once he has become strong, he then considers that behold, the Lord stands above him, namely, because of his worship, for he has become a Chariot of the Shekhinah.

R. Levi Yitzhak relies here on the idea, mentioned above, that human deeds have a cosmic effect. Virtuous deeds send beneficent impulses on high and the very angels of heaven become elevated. Evil deeds send baneful influences on high and bring about a diminution of the heavenly hosts. There are fewer angels to sing God's praises. But R. Levi Yitzhak extends all this to the inner life of the mystic. In order to find encouragement to persist in his mystic quest, a man needs at first to reflect on the tremendous significance of his worship in that he holds up the very heavens, so to speak. But once he has persisted in his worship and has become a true worshipper of God, this is all that matters to him. He needs no further encouragement since he is already 'there'. He has become a Chariot of the Shekhinah.

R. ELIMELECH OF LIZANSK (1717–87)

R. Elimelech's work *Noam Elimelekh*, a foremost Hasidic classic, was first published by his son in Lemberg in 1788 and subsequently in many editions.[12] For R. Elimelech the ladder is the ladder of prayer. The Zaddik, in his prayers, must be mindful of God's tremendous majesty and his own unworthiness to address God. This is the ladder set up on the earth, representing the Zaddik's earthiness and lowliness, but its head reaches to heaven to confront the divine glory. R. Elimelech adds that the Zaddik does not delude himself that his prayers have no effect. He knows full well that, through his prayers, blessings are brought down to earth. Yet he should attribute it all not to his own worthiness but to God's grace. The words of the prayers are the angels of God seen in Jacob's dream. These ascend and descend on the ladder of prayer; first ascending to heaven and then descending to the Zaddik himself. R. Elimelech quotes 'the saying of the Rabbis':[13] 'Words that come from the heart enter the heart.' This saying is usually taken to mean that words uttered sincerely from the heart enter the hearts of others who are moved by them. But R. Elimelech understands the saying as referring to words of prayer and 'enter the heart' to mean the heart of the one who prays. There is a two-way traffic in prayer. The words the Zaddik utters in prayer ascend heavenwards and then return into the Zaddik's heart so that he becomes ever stronger in his devotions and acquires a further degree of sanctity.

This is how R. Elimelech puts it: *'And behold, a ladder set up on the earth*. This means that prayer, hinted at in the [dream of] the ladder, at first was set up on the earth, namely he [Jacob] reflected on his lowliness. *And the top of it reached to heaven*, namely to the majesty of God. As a result he achieved that *and behold the angels of God ascended*, namely, the holy words of the prayers, called angels, ascended to the upper worlds, and descended into him [taking *bo* as 'into him']. Namely, these very words came back into him for as there was an increase of holiness in himself.'

R. HAYYIM TYRER OF CHERNOWITZ (1760–1816)

R. Hayyim Tyrer's most famous work is *Beer Mayyim Hayyim*. First published in Sudlikov in 1816, it has subsequently gone into many editions.[14] R. Hayyim, as always in his work, writes with great clarity and considers every aspect of the subject with which he deals. His sources are Kabbalistic and Hasidic texts but he contributes novel ideas of his own. The ladder represents the Zaddik who is, in R. Hayyim's words, 'an intermediary' (*memutza*) between man and God. While prayer and study of the Torah influence the higher worlds they can achieve their effect only if they are engaged in the love and fear of God. Love and fear are the two wings by means of which their prayers uttered and the Torah studied fly upwards. Merely to mouth the prayers, without even the intention that they should fly upwards, is completely ineffective. Even if ordinary folk cannot be expected to have attained true love and fear and they are, in any event, ignorant of the Kabbalistic mysteries regarding prayer, they can, at least, have a desire for them to be present in the heart. The Zaddik, on the other hand, his heart full of true love and fear of God and with complete knowledge of the Kabbalah, can actually achieve whatever has to be achieved. The Zaddik's prayers really do rise to the upper world and, in the process, the Zaddik raises the prayers of his followers since they have a close attachment to him. When the Zaddik prays with love and fear he reaches to the source of blessing on high. The top of his ladder of prayer reaches to heaven. But not all Zaddikim are endowed with the same spiritual powers. Each Zaddik can achieve only that which is within his spiritual grasp. It is the top of *his* ladder that reaches to the particular heaven that it is within his capacity to reach. The reason why ordinary folk require the Zaddik's assistance and cannot rise to heaven by their own efforts, is because their ladder is set up all too obviously on earth. Their souls are earthbound either because they have not been given a lofty soul or because, more usually, they are immersed in earthly, worldly concerns. The angels in the dream are the cosmic forces, which ascend through worship in love and fear and then descend to bring down the flow of the divine grace.

R. Hayyim elaborates on all this by drawing on the doctrine of the Sefirot. In the Sefirotic realm when *Tiferet*, the male principle, is united with the female principle *Malkhut* (the Shekhinah) harmony is produced on high, reaching back to the even higher Sefirot, where there are only mercies and no judgments, and blessing flows down to all creatures The unification of *Tiferet* and *Malkhut* is effected by *Yesod*, 'Foundation', represented in the human body by the organ of generation. (All this is, of course, a highly charged mythology which R. Hayyim does his best to demythologize.) Now *Malkhut*, the lowest of the Sefirot, and through which all things below grow and flourish, is the 'earth' of the whole Sefirotic realm. On the analogy of the Biblical heroes, *Yesod* is called the Zaddik ('The Zaddik is the *foundation* of the world', Proverbs 10:25) so that Joseph the Zaddik (because he resisted the blandishments of Potiphar's wife) represents *Yesod*. The patriarch Jacob represents *Tiferet* and Joseph was Jacob's favourite son. Thus Jacob, through Joseph (*Tiferet* through *Yesod*), is the ladder which connects earthly things to heaven, to the Sefirotic realm. This causes, in turn, the Earth (*Malkhut*) on high to be united with *Tiferet* and, in turn, this reaches to the even higher Sefirot. From these higher Sefirot, where there are only pure mercies, the divine grace flows back into the lower Sefirot and, through the unification of *Tiferet* and *Malkhut*, the divine grace flows freely to all creatures through the human Zaddik who is on the earth. Thus the dream (R. Hayyim adds that it was far more than a mere dream but a prophetic vision) represented Jacob's personal role in promoting cosmic harmony as well as the role of the Zaddikim descended from him. R. Hayyim adds an interesting note. Jacob knew that the ladder he witnessed in his dream represented the supernal illuminations, but he perceived them only as forming a real, physical ladder. Jacob, unmarried at the time, had not reached the stage at which he could see the supernal illuminations 'without their garments'. In a further addition R. Hayyim writes that the 'earth' on which the ladder was set up refers, also, to the Land of Israel (Eretz Israel); all prayer ascends through the Holy Land and the divine grace flows down there first.

In a less esoteric vein, R. Hayyim offers, 'by way of hint', a different interpretation. Like the Degel, mentioned earlier, R. Hayyim holds that spiritual vitality is often lacking even in the Zaddik, who is, after all, only a human being prone to temptation because of his earthly concerns. But when the Zaddik reflects on his lowly stage this, in itself, provides the spur for him to overcome his earthly nature to rise to a far greater degree of spirituality. This is why the repentant sinner is greater than the righteous man who has never sinned. The penitent, hitherto immersed in sin, has been obliged to struggle with the earthiness in which he has been immersed and such struggle is the fruit of a more powerful love and fear than the more routine love and fear of the perfectly righteous. The ladder of the penitent reaches higher precisely because it had stood all too firmly on earth. Yet R. Hayyim, eager to apply all this to the Zaddik as well, is obliged to postulate that the Zaddik, too, has to struggle with his earthy nature and he, too, rises even higher as a result of the struggle.

R. NAFTALI OF ROPSHITZ (1760–1827)

R. Naftali comments on Jacob's dream in his work *Zera Kodesh*.[15] R. Naftali is renowned in Hasidic lore for his wit and intellectual brilliance. His comments are usually quite brilliant but more fanciful than those of most other Hasidic masters. R. Naftali notes that the word *sulam* (spelled with a *vav*) has the same numerical value (136) as the word for 'voice', *kol*. The ladder reaching from earth to heaven is the voice of prayer, as when God is entreated to hear our 'voice'. Now in the famous Midrash in the Zohar[16] on the letters of the alphabet each letter entreats God to use that letter in the creation of the word, but each is rejected in turn until the letter *bet* is chosen. The letters *shin* and *resh* are rejected since, together with the letter *kuf* they form the word *sheker*, 'falsehood', even though when combined with the letter *alef* they form the word *rosh*, 'head'. Moreover, the leg of the letter *kuf* extends downwards beneath all the other letters. Furthermore this letter hints at the demonic side, the Sitra Ahara, since the word *kuf* means an ape, the unholy aping the holy, the Sitra Ahara being an unholy parody of the Sefirotic realm. Thus the letter *kuf* is a 'bad' letter but is still a letter of the holy alphabet by means of which the whole world and the Torah were created. The word for 'voice' is *kol* and this is formed from the letters *kuf*, *vav* and *lamed*. Just as the leg of the *kuf* extends below all other letters so does the point of the *lamed*, its *yod*, extend higher than all the other letters. The *vav* (= six) represents the six rings of the windpipe, which mirror the six Sefirot from *Hesed* to *Yesod*. When a man despairs of ever really reaching out to God in prayer, he should reflect that the lowly *kuf*, when combined with *vav* and *lamed*, forms the word *kol*, that is, the voice of prayer. Furthermore, the *yod* of the *lamed* represents the higher Sefirot. The ladder seen in Jacob's dream is the 'voice' of prayer, which, indeed, is set up on the earth but which for all that reaches to the highest heavens. Again the letter *kuf* has the same numerical value (186) as the word for 'place', *makom*, which according to the Rabbis is one of the names of God who is the Place of the world. Thus even in the depths of degradation man must never despair since his voice in prayer reaches so very high. R. Naftali adds that the patriarch Jacob had two names: *Yaakov*, from the word *ekev*, 'heel', and Yisrael, composed of the word *lo rosh*, 'to him a head'. Thus Jacob in his own person suggests the path of spiritual ascent from the 'heel', the lowest part of the body, to the 'head, the highest part.

R. MOSHE TEITELBAUM OF UJHELY (1759–1841)

R. Moshe Teitelbaum's *Yismah Moshe* was published in Lemberg in 1861, has gone through a number of editions since the,[17] and is now one of the most important Hasidic works. R. Moshe's first comment on Jacob's dream is in the philosophical but anti-rational vein.[18] R. Moshe rejects the view of the philosophers that God is bound by the rules of logical thinking so that a logical impossibility – that two and two make five for instance – is impossible even to God. The Rabbis say[19] that the Ark in Solomon's Temple was situated there and yet occupied no space there, a logical impossibility if ever there was one. Maimonides[20] writes that God's foreknowledge is compatible with human freedom, even though the two are contradictory because God does not know things as outside Himself but He and His knowledge are one. R. Moshe understands this to mean not only that we can have no comprehension of God, but logical thought and all human wisdom and knowledge have no entrance into the mystery of God.

R. Moshe refers in this connection to the doctrine of the Sefirot. The higher Sefirot, appertaining to the divine thought processes, are the source of all human knowledge and hence human beings can have some faint apprehension of them. But the higher stages reaching to the En Sof are totally beyond all comprehension. Of God as He is in Himself only complete silence is permissible. It is not only that God is incomprehensible but that the whole notion of comprehension cannot apply at this stage. God invented logic and is not Himself bound by that which He has created. All this is hinted at in Jacob's dream. The ladder refers to the stage of the divine unfolding. The ladder is set up on earth, that is to say, creatures on earth can have some faint apperception of the divine wisdom. But the head of the ladder reaches to that which is higher than the highest of the Sefirot, to that which is beyond all rational thought because it is higher than rational thought.

R. Moshe provides, in all, ten different interpretations, of which the above is the first and the lengthiest. The other nine are here given in brief and in paraphrase. In all his expositions R. Moshe is less 'Hasidic' than the other masters considered above, perhaps because he became a disciple of the Seer of Lublin, under the influence of his son-in-law, only in his middle years and became a Hasidic Zaddik only after the death of the Seer. The numbers are R. Moshe's.

2. The ladder is the link between the upper worlds and those

beneath, the latter being a mirror image of the former. The angels of God are the Zaddikim whose thoughts are always on God.

3. The Zaddik is the ladder linking heaven and earth since even in his earthly activities he has God in mind.

4. The ladder represents God's judgments. The angels are the Zaddikim who ascend first to be judged since the greater the man the more severely he is judged.

5. Since the spiritual and the material are combined in man he is the link between heaven and earth and he is represented by the ladder.

6. The ladder is man, to whom God sends his angels (in the plural) since, as the Rabbis say, an angel can carry out only a single task. R. Moshe sees this as an expression of individual providence.

7. The ladder is man. The angels are his good deeds which ascend on high and other angels come down to protect him.

8. The ladder represents God's providential care. God cares for Israel whether they are worthy or unworthy but when they are unworthy, the angels can be said to descend to them and when worthy they ascend to the angels.

9. The ladder is the Temple. When the Temple stood there was an increase among the heavenly hosts and when the Temple was destroyed a decrease.

10. The ladder is the Community of Israel. Whether Israel is in a state of degradation or high in heaven God always cares for them.

R. SHOLOMO ZALMAN OF KOPUTS (1830–1900)

R. Sholomo Zalman's *Magen Avot*[21] is a late Hasidic work in the Habad line and can serve as a summary of Habad treatment of the ideas said to be implicit in Jacob's dream. R. Sholomo Zalman's exposition is, however, shot through with Kabbalistic terminology, all in the particular Habad understanding. It is consequently impossible to reproduce all the technicalities in English. Here is given no more than a brief paraphrase which, it is hoped, manages to capture at least the gist of the argument.

In the Habad understanding of the Lurianic Kabbalah the 'light' of En Sof pervades all to the extent that, from God's point of view, as it were, there is no universe and no creatures. But the Infinite light of En Sof had to be screened and partly removed, as it were, so as to leave room for the Sefirot and ultimately finite creatures on earth to emerge. There are four worlds, one higher than the other. These are the worlds of *Atzilut* ('Emanation'), the highest of the four, the stage of the Sefirotic realm; *Beriah* ('Creation'); *Yetzirah* ('Formation') and *Asiyah* ('Action', the source of this world and embracing this world). These four are abbreviated as ABYA. The Sefirot of each world are present in the world immediately beneath but in a fainter form, so to speak, since each lower world is more remote from En Sof. Thus the *Hokhmah* ('Wisdom') of *Beriah* descends from the *Malkhut* of *Atzilut* and so on down to the lowest of the Sefirot of *Asiyah*. This whole process is known as *hishtalshelot ha-olamot*, the evolution of the worlds, but there is a paradox here. If the En Sof is all, how can there be four worlds or, indeed, anything at all? The answer is that, from our point of view, the worlds are real enough, but it is God who keeps them in being, renewing them at every moment.

When the Jew recites the Shema and unifies God his mind should embrace the whole process of the evolution of the worlds. He should trace back all the different forces through world after world until he reaches the En Sof. He should then, when he prays, trace back the whole process and so bring down God's blessing, since cosmic energy is required to keep the universe in being at every moment.

This is the meaning of the ladder. The ladder represents the ascent of all worlds to En Sof, which the mystic contemplates when he recites the Shema and by so doing assists the process. This ascent of the righteous helps the angels to sing their songs of glory, as a result of which the divine grace flows freely throughout creation in glorious melody. But for the unification to be achieved the mystic has to sacrifice himself to God, that is to say, to become lost to himself as his mind dwells on the glorious scheme.

R. Sholomo Zalman adds that there are, in fact, two ladders, the holy one he has described and the unholy one in which the demonic powers also draw down their sustenance from the En Sof. The letters of the word *sulam*, when transposed, form the word *semel*, an image, since the unholy is a perverse image of the holy. This unholy ladder also reaches from earth to heaven and is influenced by human deeds, but in the opposite way to the holy ladder. The angels of God ascend the unholy ladder through man's evil deeds. The more the mystic's thought is on the holy ladder, the less the power of the unholy ladder. The more the angels descend the unholy ladder, the greater the ascent of the angels on the holy ladder and all through human deeds.

From this survey it appears that the interpretation of the ladder was widespread among all Hasidic groups, but each master tried to introduce his own original ideas. We simply do not have sufficient information to enable us to know how such ideas passed from master to master and Hasid to Hasid, although once the major Hasidic works had been published it was the book that was responsible for the spread of the ideas. Yet each master seems to have believed that he, too, could make his own individual contribution since the Torah has many facets. However, in later Hasidic works there is comparatively little on Jacob's ladder, perhaps because the later masters believed the subject to have been exhausted.

NOTES

1. Another version of this theme is found in my *Beyond Reasonable Doubt*, Littman Library, Portland, Oregon, 1999, pp. 197–202. A useful summary of Midrashic and medieval comments on Jacob's ladder is given by Nehama Leibowitz in her *Studies in the Book of Genesis*, Jerusalem, 1972, pp. 298–304.
2. On R. Jacob Joseph and his doctrine of the Zaddik see *The Zaddik* by Samuel H. Dresner.
3. Ed. Koretz, 1780, *va-yetze*, p. 22a.
4. *Shabbat* 119b. It is well-known that the Hasidim intentionally reinterpreted Talmudic passages which refer to the *talmid hakham* to refer to the Zaddik, see Joseph Perl's preface to his satire on Hasidism, *Megalleh Temirin*, Vienna, 1819, note 1: 'Even the name *talmid hakham*, which, at first glance, does refer to scholars ['*lomedim*'], as the *lomedim* say for our many sins, applies to the Zaddikim.'
5. *Toledot*, p. 23a.
6. Pietrikow, 1884, pp. 54a–d.
7. Cf. *Toledot*, p. 23b, where R. Jacob Joseph uses the illustration of a man who skilfully amasses great wealth for the accumulation of spiritual riches.
8. See R. Mahler, *A History of Modern Jewry 1780–1815*, London, 1971, Chapter 12, pp. 430ff. Cf. *Ben Porat Yosef*, where R. Jacob Joseph remarks that the *Sefer Ha-Kanah* observes that in all creation there is a struggle for sustenance from the animal kingdom to man and the interpretation of the *piyut* to mean that man gives his very soul for his bread.
9. Edition used, Jerusalem, 1963, pp. 40–1. I have discussed this passage in my *Hasidic Thought*, New York, 1976, pp. 44–7.
10. *Elimah Rabbati*, Brody, 1881, 1:10, p. 2b.
11. *Kedushat Levi Ha-Shalem*, Jerusalem, 1964, pp. 46–51.
12. Edition used ed. Gedalyah Nigal, Jerusalem, 1978; section on the dream, pp. 73–4.
13. This saying is not found in the Talmud but is often quoted as if it were.
14. Edition used with three columns to a side, Warsaw, 1901, pp. 76b–77d.
15. Edition used, Jerusalem, 1971, pp. 26d–28b.
16. Zohar I, 2b–3b.
17. Edition used, Jerusalem, 1976, pp. 71b–72b.

18. R. Moshe Teitelbaum studied the medieval philosophical works in his youth. For anti-rationalism in Jewish thought see my *Faith*, London, 1968, 'Jewish Parallels to the Tertullian Paradox', pp. 201–209
19. *Yoma* 21a
20. *Yad*, Teshuvah 8:5
21. Published in Berditchev, 1902 (photocopy, Brooklyn, New York, 1978) pp. 22a–23b.

7

The Doctrine of the Zaddik in Elimelech of Lizansk

R. Elimelech of Lizansk (1717–87), disciple of the Maggid of Mesirech, is famous in the history of Hasidism as the founding father of the Galician branch of the Hasidic movement and as the author of the Hasidic classical work, *Noam Elimelekh*, 'The Pleasantness of Elimelech', published posthumously (1788) by his son Eleazar.[1] Although Gershom Scholem[2] and others have demonstrated that it is a serious blunder to see the doctrine of the Zaddik – the Hasidic saint and miracle-worker – as a later aberration unknown to the founder and earliest teachers of Hasidism, it is generally acknowledged, with justice, that the doctrine receives its fullest treatment in the *Noam Elimelekh*, setting the pattern for future developments, particularly in Poland and Galicia. In view of Elimelech's importance in this matter, it is surprising that, so far as I am aware, there has hitherto been little detailed study of this master's doctrine of the Zaddik.[3] This chapter seeks to fill the gap.

In Hasidism, the Zaddik,[4] the holy man, has much closer affinities with the Hindu Guru or Sadhu than with the Christian saint. He is the master around whom disciples gather both for the spiritual guidance he can offer and for the blessings he can bestow as the intermediary between God and man. The *Noam Elimelekh* is in the form of brief homilies to the Pentateuch, arranged according to the weekly readings.[5] A major part of the work is devoted to the details of the Zaddik's training, his character, and function. The Baal Shem Tov, the founder of Hasidism, died in the year 1760. By the time the book was compiled there appear to have been circles of Hasidim, each with his own Zaddik. These Zaddikim were drawn from the disciples of the Baal Shem Tov and their disciples. Elimelech is thus dealing not with an innovation of his own but with an established institution which he seeks to justify and to further. Scriptural verses and Rabbinic comments on these are made to yield the thought that Zaddikism was, from the earliest times, an indispensable method of bringing down God's grace from above. The ancient sources are utilized for this purpose with as little sense of the anachronism and incongruity involved as the medieval Jewish authors had when they saw the very same sources teaching Aristotelian philosophy in its Arabic garb.

As found in the *Noam Elimelekh*, the doctrine runs as follows: God is the source of all goodness; His nature is such that He has to have recipients for His bounty, since it belongs to the nature of the good that it must give of itself to others. Hence, the world was created with man as its goal and culmination. By serving God man elevates himself and the whole of creation; he learns to respond to God as like to like and thus merits the reward of enjoying God forever.[6] But the paradox here is that God's love is too powerful for finite creatures to endure. Were that love to be revealed in its full splendour to creatures they could have no separate existence. Were the divine love in its fullness to have been submitted to their gaze individual souls would be swallowed up in longing by the infinite goodness and mercy of the Creator. Indeed, finite existence as such would have been impossible. Consequently, the Kabbalah speaks of a primordial 'breaking of the vessels';[7] that is to say, the creative powers containing the original divine light, as God emerged from concealment to become manifest in creation, were too weak to hold the light and they were shattered. As a result of this primordial catastrophe, which, for all that, was for the ultimate benefit of creatures, that they might endure in their finitude in the presence of the infinite light, the universe is able to enjoy an existence apart from God, as it were. Yet 'sparks' of the broken light now inhere in all things. It is these 'holy sparks' which nourish created things and allow them to exist. The task of man is to reclaim the 'sparks' by restoring them to their Source. This he can do by using worldly things in God's service and lifting them up in sanctity by means of his holy thoughts.[8] In this way the whole of human history is seen as an attempt to win the holy for itself, to rescue it from the denizens of the 'Other Side', the forces of evil and impurity. When the work of reclaiming the 'holy sparks' is complete, redemption comes to the Jewish people and through them to all mankind. God's Presence – the Shekhinah, personified as a female in the Kabbalah – in exile because of the sins of the children of Israel, is also redeemed and reunited with her Spouse.

When that happens the Messiah comes and the work of redemption is completed.

Originally, Adam had the task of reclaiming the 'sparks', but when Adam sinned the whole process became far more involved and difficult. The Torah was given to help the children of Israel in the mighty effort of restoration now required, this being their duty as the offspring of the righteous patriarchs. But Israel, too, sinned by worshipping the golden calf. Consequently, Israel's history now becomes a tremendous cosmic drama in which good men fight on the side of the holy to save the 'sparks' from the demonic powers. When, again as a result of Israel's sins, the Temple was destroyed, the Shekhinah, too, went into exile. For man's deeds have a cosmic effect. They influence the 'upper world' and cause grace or its opposite to come down from above. The very balance and harmony of the worlds on high, the correct relationship between the creative powers of the Godhead, 'the unification of the Holy One, blessed be He, and His Shekhinah', depend therefore on man's conduct. The sufferings of Israel, making it difficult for them to serve God, mirror the sufferings of God Himself, at least in His aspect of manifestation. (Of En Sof, the Limitless, God as He is in Himself, nothing can be said at all because this aspect is utterly beyond all comprehension.) Disharmony on earth is matched by disharmony on high. The Holy One, blessed be He, is parted from His Shekhinah. Through the rescue of the divine 'sparks' harmony is restored. The Holy One, blessed be He, and His Shekhinah are reunited and grace flows freely from on high.[9] When the tremendous task is complete the Messiah will come. All disharmony, above and below, will vanish and God will reign in all His glory over a perfected world.

Thus far we are on more or less conventional Kabbalistic ground. This, very briefly stated, is the highly charged mythological scheme as found in the Lurianic Kabbalah from the sixteenth century onwards. But, at this stage, Elimelech, like the other Hasidic spokesmen, introduces the notion of the Zaddik. The Zaddik's role in the process is that of the 'channel' through which the divine grace can flow.[10] It is impossible for all men to live in permanent 'attachment' (*devekut*) to God.[11] Great sins apart, there are the common sins of slander, malicious gossip, hatred, lust, pride, anger, sloth and envy, all of which set up a barrier to the flow of the divine grace. Even those who strive worthily to rid themselves, so far as it is humanly possible, of these evil character traits, rarely love God so much that they think of Him even when they engage in worldly and bodily pursuits. Only the contemplative Zaddik, with all his thoughts entirely God-centred, is able to reclaim the 'sparks' of holiness in *all* things.[12] Only such a spiritual superman can remove the barriers and it is only through their attachment to him that lesser folk can become attached to God.[13]

The Zaddik thus performs a double task: he brings man near to God and he brings down God's grace from heaven to earth. Through the Zaddik's close attachment to God he can influence others to fear God.[14] The Zaddik's prayers for 'life, children and sustenance' help other to attain these.[15] Through the Zaddik's prayers the sick are healed, and the people of Israel, saved from persecution and oppression, are able to earn their daily bread and are blessed with worthy sons and daughters. The Zaddik's followers support him with their worldly goods and in this way become attached to him through his dependence on them.[16] Their welfare thus becomes his welfare and his prayers on their behalf are more readily answered. It is meritorious to tell and retell the tales of the events that happened to the Zaddikim and such story-telling helps man to overcome the blandishments of his evil inclination.[17]

The occult aspect of Zaddikism has sometimes been overlooked by biased admirers of Hasidic spirituality ignorant of this side of Hasidism or refusing to admit that there is any such thing. It has not been sufficiently noted, for example, that the doctrine of the Zaddik's role is bound up with the belief in *gilgul*, the transmigration of souls.[18] There are three ways, says Elimelech, in which a man can become a Zaddik:[19] his ancestors may have been Zaddikim and he inherits his charismatic gifts from them; he may have been named after a famous Zaddik; or he may have been a Zaddik in a previous incarnation.[20] Although it is possible for one lacking any of these qualifications to become a Zaddik, through his own efforts in subduing his instincts and rising to God, this is both extremely difficult and exceedingly rare.[21] The semi-magical aid of either parental endowment or the force of the special name or the mysterious rebirth of the holy man are generally necessary.[22] Furthermore, the ability of the Zaddik to give adequate spiritual advice to his followers depends on his knowledge of their previous existences. He alone knows for which purpose they have been sent down again into this world, which matters to they to put right because of their failures in their other lives, so that he alone can guide them through their stormy path in this existence.[23] Elimelech refers repeatedly to belief in *gilgul*, a belief he never questions. The reason why, he observes, two men who had never before met in this life find themselves automatically attracted to one another as if they were old friends, is because they were neighbours in Paradise during the period or rest between their two existences on earth.[24] The soul of Moses often returns to earth to inhabit the body of a Zaddik, which is why Moses died outside the holy land. Had Moses entered the land and carried out there the special precepts that can only be carried out there, he would have had nothing further to rectify and there could have been no justification for his return to earth[25].The striking parallel of all this to Buddhist teachings is too obvious to require further elaboration.

The Zaddik is required to reflect in particular on two great themes – the way of love and the way of fear.[26] The way of fear involves contemplation of the Zaddik's own unworthiness. The smallest character defects should assume in his eyes the weight and burden of serious offences.[27] He should try ruthlessly to eradicate these defects by every means at his disposal, including confession to others.[28] The way of love involves contemplation on the sublime majesty of the Creator as revealed in His wondrous works. The Zaddik should accustom himself to see the acts of God in everything to the extent that he ceases to marvel at any particular miracle.[29] At first a strong dose of rigorous asceticism is useful to the Zaddik's spiritual development. He should mortify his flesh and deny himself all but life's bare necessities.[30] After he has engaged for a time in ascetic exercises he may eventually attain the more advanced stage in which he can enjoy the world in a spirit of utter consecration so that he is able to reclaim the holy 'sparks' inhering in food and drink and other worldly delights[31]. But the desire of the Zaddik for the things of the world is really foreign to his nature. So lost is he in heavenly thoughts that God has to put into his heart a desire for worldly pleasures, otherwise he would be incapable of reclaiming the 'sparks' and have no opportunity to take part in the worldly needs of those on whose behalf his prayers are offered.[32] God may even cause the Zaddik to sin, albeit a sin of a far from severe kind, in order for him to fall from his elevated stage. This fall is necessary both in order to provide him with some point of contact with the sinners for whom he prays and to help the sinners by raising therm together with himself as he rises from his sin.[33]

The Zaddik is enjoined particularly to avoid any sexual impurity or sexual imaginings of any kind. Seminal emissions during the night, even if involuntary, are treated as grave sins for the Zaddik. They are evidence of his lack of success in attaining the stage of complete attachment to the holy.[34] He should never gaze at women and if his wife is beautiful he should not be aware of it.[35] Although the Zaddik, as an observant Jew, is obliged to have marital relations, his mind, during the act, should be on the supernal mysteries.[36] It is clear that for all Elimelech's insistence on the Zaddik's duty to reclaim the 'sparks' in worldly things, he considers the sex act to be intrinsically unworthy. The true Zaddik would really be incapable of having congress with his wife were it not for the fact that God sends him a special desire on Friday night sufficient to enable him to carry out the divine command.[37] When Adam 'knew' his wife, Cain, the first murderer, was born (Genesis 4:1), Elimelech takes 'knew' in this context literally. The true Zaddik does not know that he is with his wife since his mind is absorbed at the time in meditation of the divine.[38] Abraham knew that his wife was beautiful (Genesis 12:11) only when he came near to Egypt. It was his proximity to the lewd Egyptians that brought him down from his stage of complete attachment.[39]

The Hasidic masters were wont to make strange gestures, particularly during their prayers.[40] Elimelech explains this on the grounds that every limb and organ of the Zaddik's body is under the control of his soul. As the soul journeys in the higher realms it influences the body to make gestures of an entirely uncontrived nature.[41] Because they are spontaneous, the gestures of the true Zaddik do not appear odd or grotesque. On the contrary, so attractive do they seem to observers that they are frequently copied. Naturally such aping of the Zaddik's gestures is inauthentic and invites ridicule.[42] The soul of the Zaddik is also capable of producing spontaneous song. Zaddikim with no ear for music have been known to burst forth in deliciously sweet melody during their prayers.[43]

The Zaddik is like a Seraph, burning in such enthusiasm for the divine[44] that he would be in danger of expiring in his longing for God were it not that God saves him by cooling his ardour.[45] The Zaddik's fiery worship creates around him an aura of sanctity so that it becomes easier for his associates to worship God.[46] The Zaddik's love for God finds its expression in study of the Torah and in prayer. But the Zaddik is, after all, human and can become bored with his routine. He experiences times of spiritual dryness when he desperately needs the kind of recreation good conversation provides. Yet the Zaddik never detaches himself from God. Even his worldly talk is full of spiritual guidance and elevated counsel.[46] Even when he discusses with the keenest interest the worldly concerns of his followers his true intention is on the heavenly matters on which his mind dwells constantly.[48] At times the Zaddik will curiously engage in fulsome self-praise, telling his followers of his great worth. But there is neither pride nor vanity in this. It is all no more than a clever ruse to justify his right to pray on behalf of others, necessary because of Satan's determined efforts to denigrate the Zaddikim and thus prevent them from achieving what is required in the upper worlds.[49]

The Zaddik has powers over life and death. Even when God has decreed that a certain person should die, the Zaddik's prayer can nullify the evil decree.[50] Again and again Elimelech returns to the theological difficulties in the idea of the Zaddik's intervention. God does not change His mind. How then can the Zaddik's prayer bring bring about a total change of fortune? Elimelech gives various answers to the question. The soul of the Zaddik soars so high that it reaches to those worlds where only mercy reigns so that there has never been there any decree of suffering or death.[51] Through his prayers for the sick and the unfortunate, the Zaddik attaches them to these worlds and the decree becomes automatically nullified. In another version, the Zaddik creates new heavenly worlds by the power of his prayer and deeds and in these worlds there has never been any evil decree.[52] Still another solution is that God's decree was in the first instance conditional; the evil decree would come into operation for a person only if the Zaddik did not pray on his behalf.[53] If it be asked why God should make the cure depend on the prayers of the Zaddik, the reply is that God so desires the prayer of the righteous[54] that He is ready, as it were, to provide any excuse to obtain these prayers.[55]

Elimelech is obviously embarrassed at the claims Hasidism makes for the Zaddik. He is fully aware of the Mitnaggedic taunts that even in the days of the prophets it was no easy thing to attain the holy spirit. Elimelech retorts that in earlier times, too, the objection was put forward by opponents of the holy men that there is a steady decline of the generations and yet now even the Mitnaggedim acknowledge the state of sanctity reached by these holy men.[56] Yes, it was harder to attain to the holy spirit in prophetic times, but now that the Shekhinah is in exile it is much easier.[57] Elimelech quotes the parable given in this connection by his master, the Maggid of Mesirech (described here as the Maggid of Rovno.[58]) When the king is in his palace he will leave it only to stay for a while in a splendid mansion where full regal honours can be paid to him. But when the king is on his travels he is prepared to enter the most humble dwelling if hospitality is there offered to him and it is sufficiently clean. In this way the Hasidic masters adopted a rationale for their insistence that miracle-working saints could exist in their day without abandoning what had become virtually dogma, that the generations suffer progressive deterioration. Nowadays, when the Shekhinah is in exile, God dwells in every soul free from sin. All that is required is a determined effort to cleanse oneself from sin as well as a degree of Talmudic learning.[59] This aspect of Zaddikism has also been ignored. The early Hasidim evidently believed that it was possible in their own day for men to be inspired and perform miracles. In a sense, Hasidism is a revival of prophetic ecstasy. The Hasidim not quite suggest that it is possible for the Zaddik to attain the higher states of prophecy. But they do contend that the Zaddik can be inspired by the holy spirit and that he can tap the source of miraculous powers to enable him, like the prophets of old, to perform supernatural acts.

In his zeal for Zaddikism, Elimelech borders at times on the blasphemous. Every word that proceeds from the mouth of the Zaddik causes an angel to be created, bringing about a flow of grace in both this world and the upper worlds and sweetening the divine judgments.[60] The Zaddik is called God's 'brother' and also His 'redeemer'.[61] By his holy living and separation from worldly matters the Zaddik redeems God from exile. The Zaddik also issues commands which God is obliged to obey.[62] By his self-sacrifice the Zaddik promotes harmony and creates unity and can thus be compared to God Himself, unique in the upper and lower worlds.[63] The Rabbinic saying[64] that there are three partners in man's creation, God, his father and his mother, is interpreted by Elimelech as referring to the Zaddik's function in turning God's judgments into mercy. The 'mother' referred to here is, accordingly, the Shekhinah, the source of the divine compassion, while the 'father' is none other than the Zaddik to whose intercession man owes his very life.[65] The true Zaddik is like the angels in his total separation from the material. His is the same love and fear of God which the celestial beings have and his stage is far more elevated than theirs.[66] Reminiscent of the Zen ideal of 'living like one already dead' is Elimelech's remark that the Zaddik who draws down the divine influence from above should have no thought of self but should conduct himself as if he were not in this world at all.[67] To insult a Zaddik or to speak evil of him is equivalent to speaking ill of God Himself.[68]

Not only does the Zaddik sin as a consequence of God's decree but, occasionally, he sins intentionally in order to establish some point of contact with sinners that he might help them in their ascent to holiness. The idea of a sin with good intention – *averah lishmah* – is found in the Talmud,[69] but it is notorious that in the Sabbatean heresy the notion was especially emphasised. From the Lurianic idea of the need for restoring the 'divine sparks' it was but a step to the suggestion that these are present in sin as well, so that the holy man is obliged to descend in order to rescue even those 'sparks' that have fallen into the evil side of existence.[70] On the whole, Hasidism is careful to avoid such anti-nomianism but the idea of the 'holy sin' is not completely lost sight of.[71]

In Elimelech's scheme not all Zaddikim occupy the same spiritual stage, though all are endowed with such rich intellectual gifts and holy power, that, like the Torah, they testify to God's glory and majesty. It is impossible to deny the existence of God when one considers the evidence of His wondrous wisdom as revealed in the Torah and in the character of the Zaddikim.[72] There are bound to be differences among the Zaddikim since the opportunities for serving God are as limitless as the Creator Himself. Even a Zaddik who has reached the loftiest rungs on the ladder of saintliness can see only the 'tops of the mountains'.[73] Thus not all Zaddikim live in complete separation from the world. Those who do, however, are superior to those actively engaged in commercial pursuits, exceedingly meritorious (*mitzvah gedolah*) though this is. The former, lost in complete attachment to God, need have no fear, for instance, of nocturnal pollution, but the latter must guard themselves against uttering any vain words, for these can cause pollution even where there are no impure thoughts.[74] Again, some Zaddikim are more mature than others. When the Zaddik is a mere tyro in the path of holiness, his newly discovered delight in God's service and the heightening of his spiritual powers are so novel and deliciously exciting that he can easily fall into the sin of pride. Mature Zaddikim, on the other hand, are never proud, knowing as they do from long experience in self-mastery how remote they still are from the goal and grieving as they do constantly over Israel's bitter lot.[75] Humility is the hallmark of the true Zaddik. He avoids every semblance of pride and treats worldly things as dreams rather than reality. He never thinks in terms of self-achievement but attributes it all to God.[76] No sooner does a Zaddik allow the thought to enter his mind that he is one than he immediately falls from whatever stage he has reached. The true Zaddik always sees himself as a fraudulent Zaddik.[77] The strange paradox in the life of holiness is that the person who imagines that he is near to God is really remote from Him while the true Zaddik, grieving over his remoteness from God, is, in the process, very near to Him.[78] Another distinction made by Elimelech is between the Zaddik in deeds and the Zaddik in thought. The latter is a contemplative, permanently attached to God in his mind, and he, not the other, can succeed in bringing down the flow of grace.[79]

In addition to these distinctions between Zaddikim, there are differences in their spiritual endowments from birth. A Zaddik who attains saintliness through his own efforts is less advanced on the way than one born in a state of sanctity because his father had holy thoughts at the moment of conception.[80] There are also differences among Zaddikim in their types of worship. There are in all three types: the Zaddik around whom people gather in order to learn from his saintly way of life (*Kehot*); the Zaddik who engages in bitter mortification of the flesh (*Merari*); and the Zaddik who is so humble that he sees himself as a stranger upon earth with no real right to existence (*Gershom*). All three types must exist if the world is to be perfected.[81] With regard to their capacity for assisting others not all Zaddikim are equal. There is the Zaddik who cannot afford to associate with lesser men because they will have a corrupting effect on him. But the true Zaddik by his close association with men of a vastly inferior rank can help them in their ascent without any risk of contamination.[82] Finally, Elimelech makes a distinction between the Zaddik who worships God in fear on weekdays and in love on the Sabbath and the Zaddik who worships God in love even on weekdays.[83]

Naturally Elimelech has much to say regarding the details of how the Zaddik should conduct himself. He must be 'sweet to God and to man'.[84] He must be humble in the extreme,[85] hiding his deeds from men and having all his thoughts on the upper worlds.[86] To be truly effective in his prayers he should not try to bring down the flow of grace by his own efforts, but should associate other Zaddikim with him.[87] Ordinary men require a greater degree of sanctity and freedom from distraction when they are praying. Not so the Zaddik, who can easily pray without too much distraction but requires special powers of concentration when eating and drinking and engaging in business, since his task is the elevation of the 'holy sparks'.[88]

Although the main theme of the *Noam Elimelekh* is the role of the Zaddik, many of the teachings in the book are aimed at the ordinary Hasid who may be no more than an aspirant for the higher reaches of saintliness or who may have no spiritual ambitions whatsoever of this kind. Indeed, although the term Zaddik in this work is generally employed in its technical sense of the holy master, it refers occasionally simply to the good Jew who wishes to lead a life of service and dedication.[89] It is on the whole possible to determine from the context in which sense Elimelech is using the term, but it would seem that much of his spiritual counsel is offered to anyone who wishes to have it, even though it is particularly relevant to the Zaddikim. The plain fact is that the book was used by the Hasidim as a devotional work and the people to whom the homilies were addressed in the first instance cannot have been considered to be Zaddikim either by the master or by themselves. It is illuminating to examine the kind of counsel Elimelech offers to his less exotic followers, those on the lower rungs of the ladder. The following ideas are found in the book addressed apparently to the mass of the Elimelech's followers and here there are no references to the special role of the Zaddik.

The duty of Torah study devolves on every Jew. Although the Talmud considers such study of value even when undertaken for ulterior motives,[90] the aim of Hasidism was to introduce only the purest motivation in this area of traditional Jewish piety. The early Hasidim were severely critical of scholars who studied the Torah for their own gain or to win fame. Elimelech does not abandon entirely the Talmudic principle but he points out that the Talmudic Rabbis permit study with unworthy motives only because, as they state, it will lead eventually to study for the only true motive, for the love of God. If, asserts Elimelech, a man spends all his days in study out of unworthy motives he will certainly go to hell.[91]

Together with his study of the Torah the good Jew must be careful to carry out all the precepts. The whole purpose of creation was for the good of God's creatures. This good consists of man coming nearer to God and the means for this are the practical precepts of the Torah. In addition to the general precepts binding at all times on every Jew, there is a special precept to be carried out in each age according to the precept's 'root' in heaven, namely its significance in the divine realm, its special place in the cosmic process. Elimelech cites as the example for his generation the precept of 'fringes' (Numbers 15:37–41).[92]

There are three hindrances to the good life. Man is addicted to worldly lusts, he possesses evil traits of character, such as anger and the like, implanted in him from birth, and he is prone to take pride in his genealogical tree. He must transcend all three if he is to tread the path of perfection. He can overcome worldly lusts by engaging in worldly things 'for the sake of heaven', as for his nature, he must struggle with himself incessantly. And he can rise above ancestral snobbery by reflecting on its utter vanity.[93] But it is not generally possible for a man to uproot entirely his evil traits. If, for example, a man is born with a propensity to anger he should not try to eradicate this completely but should rather use it for sacred purposes, the holy wrath directed against evil-doers, for example.[94] In addition to his avoidance of sin, man must satisfy his legitimate bodily needs 'for the sake of heaven'. In his eating and drinking he should have the intention of reclaiming the 'holy sparks'. In donning choice garments he should have the intention of adorning the divine image in man. The person who conducts himself in this way will always be satisfied with his lot. Not so the man who indulges himself for his own sake rather than for God's. He will never be satisfied and his life will never be his own.[95]

There are echoes of the conflict between the Hasidim and Mitnaggedim in Elimelech's work. The Mitnaggedim claim, Elimelech notes, that the controversy is 'for the sake of heaven' but if that were really so on their part why is it that they fail to agree even among themselves and are envious of one another? It can only be that they have come together filled with an itch of contention in their envy of the Zaddikim.[96] In a letter written by Eleazar, Elimelech's son,[97] the writer advises his correspondent to take no notice of those who speak ill of the Zaddikim. Eleazar quotes his father as saying that the marvellous deeds of the Zaddikim are no more than a drop in the sea compared with their inner life and spirituality. Among other things, so great is their degree of sanctity that they hardly ever set foot out of doors since the place where they walk may be unclean and it is quite impossible for them to be for any length of time without holy thoughts. Even when they converse with other men their thoughts are on God's glory. They sleep very little and rise from their beds to mourn the exile of the Shekhinah and the people of Israel. So great is the power of their holy prayers that no nation could ever succeed in oppressing Israel were it not for the fact that their opponents quarrel with the Zaddikim and denigrate them. It is true that the Zaddikim receive gifts from their followers, but they themselves give liberally to all good causes, especially for the purpose of marrying off Jewish girls, against which there are terrible governmental decrees.[98] These, too, would not have happened were it not for the opponents of the Zaddikim, who nullify the beneficial effects of the latter's prayers.

Both the doctrine of Zaddikism and Elimelech himself received a mixed reception in the Jewish world. The Hasidim venerated the man and his book, considering the latter to be so profound that few could hope to understand it. For the Hasidim Zaddikism is also so essential that a Hasid, by definition, is the adherent of a Rebbe. Even the so-called 'dead Hasidim' of Bratzlav, who have no living Rebbe, are no exception since R. Nahman continues to be their Rebbe even though he is no longer in the land of the living. On the other hand, the Mitnaggedim saw Zaddikism as a form of idolatry and they scorned belief in the miraculous powers of the Zaddik as sheer superstition. The Maskilim rejected many of the Hasidic ideas. Elimelech in particular was the target of their fierce attacks. Even an objective student of Hasidism like Dubnow[99] allows himself to describe Elimelech as teaching that the Zaddik is a kind of commission agent between God and man. The truth probably lies somewhere in between. For those who have eyes to see the Noam Elimelekh speaks of a wild piety coupled with a sincere and determined effort to promote holy living. That Elimelech was a child of his time, accepting as revealed truth ideas that moderns do not share, is not to be wondered at, since the greatest of thinkers have been time-bound in this sense. Let Hasidic legend have the last word. When the Rebbe Elimelech would proceed to the reading-desk to lead the congregation in prayer he would take out his watch and place it on the desk in front of him. When the Hasidim were asked why the Rebbe did this, they would reply: 'It is to remind him not to lose himself in eternity and return to the world of time.'

NOTES

1. The *Noam Elimelekh* (hereafter abbreviated as NE) has been published in a critical edition by G. Nigal, Jerusalem, 1978. The first edition was published in Lemberg. Friedberg's *Bet Eked* lists, in 1954, no fewer than thirty-five different editions.

2. G. Scholem, *Major Trends in Jewish Mysticism*, London, 1955. Samuel S. Dresner has given a comprehensive account of the doctrine of the Zaddik in the works of R. Jacob Joseph of Polonnoye, the first Hasidic author to be published, in *The Zaddik*, London, New York and Toronto, 1970. The doctrine as it appears in the work of the Seer of Lublin, Elimelech's disciple, has been studied by Rachel Elior, 'Between *Yesh* and *Ayin*: The Doctrine of the Zaddik in the Works of Jacob Isaac, the Seer of Lublin', in *Jewish History: Essays in Honour of Chimen Abramsky*, ed. Ada Rapoport-Albert and Steven J. Zipperstein, London, 1988, pp. 393–455.

3. On R. Elimelech see the full-scale but uncritical biography by B. Landau, *Ha-Rebbe R. Elimelekh Mi-Lizansk*, Jerusalem, 1963, D. Halahmi, *Hakhmey Yisrael*, Tel Aviv, 1957, pp. 165, 197; Martin Buber, *Tales of the Hasidim*, Vol. I, New York, 1957, pp. 253–64; Jiri Langer, *Nine Gates*, London, 1961, pp. 115f. A. Markus, *Hasidism*, Heb. trans., Tel Aviv, 1954, pp. 106–10; Louis I. Newman, *The Hasidic Anthology*, New York, 1944, Index 'Lizensker, The'; S. A. Horodetsky: *Ha-Hasidut Ve-Ha-Hasidim*, Tel-Aviv, 1951, Vol. III, pp. 147–53; E. Steinman, *Sefer Shaar Ha-Hasidut*, Tel Aviv, 1959, pp. 152–7 and 386; A. Walden, *Shem Ha-Gedolim He-Hadash*, Warsaw, 1879, Vol., p. 7a, Vol. II, p. 28a; M. Bodek, *Seder Ha-Dorot He-Hadash*, Lemberg, 1965, Chapter 5; H. S. B. Michelson, *Ohel Elimelekh*, Precemysl, 1910. For modern critical studies see the Introduction to Nigal's edition; S. Dubnow, *Toledot a-Hasidut*, Tel Aviv, 1960, Vol. II, Chapter 5, pp. 178–88; *The Encylopedia of Hasidism*, ed. Tzvi M. Rabinowicz, Northvale, New Jersey and London, 1966, pp. 111–12.

4. For the history of the term 'Zaddik' see my article 'Righteousness' in *Encyclopedia Judaica*, Vol. 14, pp. 180–4. Generally in Rabbinic literature the Zaddik is the ordinary 'good man' as opposed to the Hasid, the 'saint'. Since the term Hasid was used in Hasidism to describe the members of the group, a special term had to be found for the Master. This was the term Zaddik, thus reversing the older meaning of the two terms. The Hasid is now the follower, the Zaddik the holy saint. This enabled the Hasidic teachers to reinterpret Rabbinic sayings dealing with the 'just' or the 'righteous' so as to refer to the Hasidic Zaddik. Cf. my *Holy Living: Saints and Saintliness in Judaism*, Northvale, New Jersey and London,1990, pp. 9–20.

5. Eleazar, Elimelech's son, in his Introduction to the first edition of the NE, remarks that Elimelech's followers suggested that Eleazar approach his father to have his homilies recorded. Elimelech, however, refused to allow this during his lifetime but agreed for them to be published after his death. It was Eleazar who gave the book its title.

6. NE *Likkutey Shoshanah* to Isaiah 42:21, edn Nigal, p. 556.

7. Elimelech and the other Hasidic masters do not know the radical version of the Lurianic Kabbalah in which the 'breaking of the vessels' is a means of purging, as it were, the dross of evil from God, but they follow the more conventional interpretation of the doctrine; see I. Tishby, *Torat Ha-Ra Ve-Ha-Kelipah Be-Kabbalat Ha-Ari*, Jerusalem, 1968.

8. This theme occurs with the utmost frequency in NE; see e.g. *toledot* to Genesis 27:6 (ed. Nigal, p. 71) and *va-yiggash* to Genesis 44:18 (ed. Nigal, p. 135).

9. See NE *behukkotai* end (ed. Nigal, pp. 359–60) and *ki tisa* beg. (ed. Nigal, p. 274).

10. NE *hayye sarah* to Genesis 24:1 (ed. Nigal, p. 56). The idea that the Zaddik is the 'channel' through which the divine grace flows is found in very early Hasidic teachings, e.g. in Jacob Joseph of Polonyye's *Toledot Yaakov Yosef*; see Dresner, *The Zaddik*, p. 277, note 33 and p.378, note 34.

11. On *devekut* see Gershom Scholem, '*Devekut*, or Communion with God' in *The Messianic Idea in Judaism*, New York, 1971, pp. 203–27.

12. NE *mishpatim* end, to Exodus 23:19 (ed. Nigal, pp. 247–8).

13. NE *lekh lekha*, to Genesis 12:2–3 (edn Nigal, pp. 26–7).

14. NE *toledot*, to Genesis 26:15 (pp. 67–8).

15. This theme occurs very frequently in NE, e.g. *va-yerah* beg. (ed. Nigal, p. 43). The relevant Talmudic passage (*Moed Katan* 28a) reads: 'Life, children and sustenance depend not on merit but on *mazzal*.' *Mazzal* means, of course, 'luck', 'good fortune', 'fate', and the saying is astrological, but Elimelech and the other Hasidic masters take the term as

referring to the 'flow' (from the root *nazal*, 'to flow') of divine grace which can be influenced only by the Zaddik's prayers.

16. NE *pikkudey*, begin (ed. Nigal, p. 283); *korah*, to Numbers 18:8 (ed. Nigal, pp. 222–3). Cf. Dubnow, *Toledot a-Hasidut*, pp.182–3.
17. NE to Exodus 12:3 (ed. Nigal, p. 194). This became an important principle in later Hasidism, see the sources quoted in Joseph Perl's satire on Hasidism, *Megalle Temirin*, Vienna, 1819, Introduction, note 11.
18. See article 'Transmigration of Souls' in *Jewish Encyclopedia*, Vol. XII, pp. 231–4 and 'Gilgul' in Gershom Scholem, *Kabbalah*, Jerusalem, 1974, pp.344–50. On the occult features in Hasidism see Moshe Idel, *Hasidism: Between Ecstasy and Magic*, SUNY Press, Albany, 1995, and Gedaly ah Nigal, *Magic, Mysticism, and Hasidism: The Supernatural in Jewish Thought*, Northvale, New Jersey and London, 1994.
19. NE *bemidbar* to Numbers 1:2 (ed. Nigal, p. 368).
20. NE *ki tisa*, to Exodus 30:31 (ed. Nigal, p. 277).
21. NE *emor* beg. (ed. Nigal, p. 340). Cf. from a contemporary Hindu theologian: 'In the history of mysticism it is recognised everywhere that in exceptional cases illumination is possible and this takes place even when an external source is lacking. We know of the Pratyeka Buddha who neither received his wisdom from any previous Buddha nor communicated it to others,' quoted by Arthur Koestler, *The Lotus and the Robot*, London, 1960, p.72.
22. Cf. NE *emor*, to Leviticus 22:27 (ed. Nigal, p. 343).
23. NE *naso* beg. (ed. Nigal, p. 370).
24. NE *va-yehi*, beg. (ed. Nigal, p. 142).
25. NE *devarim*, to Deuteronomy 1:37 (ed. Nigal, p. 479).
26. NE *hukkat*, beg. (ed. Nigal, pp. 430–1).
27. NE *shemini*, beg. (ed. Nigal, p. 301). Hasidic legend has it that Elimelech did penance, when he grew to manhood, for having trampled on his mother's breasts when he was a babe in arms, Buber, *Tales*, pp. 254–5; Horodetsky, *Ha-Hasidut Ve-Ha-Hasidim*, p. 150.
28. *Tzettil Katan*, No. 13, printed at end of NE (ed. Nigal, pp. 616–17).
29. NE *va-yerah*, to Genesis 18:12 (ed. Nigal, p. 46).
30. NE *bo*, to Exodus 12:2 (ed. Nigal, p. 192). Cf. NE *hayye sarah* to Genesis 24:1 (ed. Nigal, pp. 56–7) that even true Zaddikim who attain saintliness without self-mortification do so only by the merit of those who are ascetics.
31. Ibid. Elimelech, as a former devotee of the Lurianic Kabbalah and asceticism, always tries hard to reconcile this with the new 'way' taught by the Baal Shem Tov in which asceticism is frowned upon. Cf. Dubnow, *Toledot qa-Hasidut*, p. 179.
32. *NE Likkutey Shoshanah*, to Psalm 145:19 (ed. Nigal, p. 554).
33. NE *va-yehi*, to Genesis 47:28.
34. NE *ki tetze*, to Deuteronomy 23:11 (ed. Nigal, p. 515)
35. NE *bereshit*, to Genesis 4:1 (ed. Nigal, pp. 10–11).
36. *Ibid*.
37. See the Letter of Zechariah Mendel at end of NE (ed. Nigal, pp. 603–8).
38. NE *bereshit* to Genesis 4: 1 (ed. Nigal, pp. 10–11).
39. NE *lekh lekha*, to Genesis 12:11 (ed. Nigal, p. 28) Cf. NE *va-yishlah* to Genesis 32:25 (ed. Nigal, p. 95) that the sex act can never be entirely pure, hence no benediction is recited over it, unlike eating, over which a benediction is recited. See Dubnow, *Toledot a-Hasidut*, p. 470, that in the writings of the Mitnaggedim the NE was criticized for its alleged obsession with sexual matters.
40. See my *Hasidic Prayer*, paperback edition, The Littman Library of Jewish Civilization, London and Washington, 1993, p. 54f.
41. NE *emor* end (ed. Nigal, p. 347). Cf. Elimelech's prayer before the Morning Service, freq. printed e.g. in *Siddur Harey Besamim*, Warsaw 1933–34, where the prayer is recited asking God to direct all man's 'movements', both conscious and unconscious, to Him alone.
42. NE *kedoshim*, to Leviticus 19:4 (ed. Nigal, pp. 330–1).
43. Letter of Eleazar at end of NE (ed. Nigal, pp. 593–602).
44. NE *noah* to Genesis 6:10 (ed. Nigal, p. 18; *beshallah*, to Exodus 14:16 (ed. Nigal, p. 208) in the name of the Maggid of Mesirech (Rovno).
45. NE *va-yishlah*, to Genesis 32:6 (ed. Nigal, p. 84).
46. NE *shemot*, to Exodus 3:11 (ed. Nigal, p. 173); *metzora* to Leviticus 14:2 (ed. Nigal, p. 317).

47. NE *tazria*, to Leviticus 12:2 (ed. Nigal, p. 305).
48. NE *reeh*, to Deuteronomy 12:19 (ed. Nigal, p. 501).
49. NE *kedoshim*, to Leviticus 19:10 (ed. Nigal, p. 335).
50. NE *Likkutey Shoshanah*, to Song of Songs 1:9 (ed. Nigal, p. 581). The idea of God fulfilling the degree of the righteous man (*tzaddik*) is found in the Talmud (*Taanit* 23a; *Sotah* 12a; *Ketubot* 103b) based on Job 22:28. This became a favourite theme in Hasidism when applied to the Zaddik.
51. NE *aharey mot*, beg. (ed. Nigal, p. 323).
52. NE *va-yetze*, to Genesis 30:36f. (ed. Nigal, p. 80).
53. NE *va-yehi*, beg. (edn Nigal p.142).
54. The saying that God desires the prayers of the righteous (*tzaddikim*) is Talmudic (*Yevamot* 64a; *Hullin* 60b). Again Elimelech interprets this as referring to the Zaddik in the Hasidic sense.
55. See NE *va-yishlah*, to Genesis 32:4 (ed. Nigal, pp. 93) where Elimelech gives a different solution. It is only the letters forming the words of the evil decree that are created on high and the Zaddik, by his prayers arranges these letters to form words not of curse but of blessing. These letters are those in which the Torah is written and the Torah was given in love. Consequently, only great love, beyond the capacity of ordinary human beings, can rearrange the letters in their right order so as to avert the evil decree. The Zaddik has such great love and it is for all men, Elimelech is careful to say, non-Jews as well as Jews, though, naturally, the Zaddik's love is reserved especially for Jews.
56. See Letter of Eleazar, referred to in note 43 above.
57. Eleazar's Letter. Cf. the lengthy defence of the Zaddikim in NE *mikketz*, to Genesis 41:1 (ed. Nigal, p. 123).
58. The Maggid lived in Rovno in his youth and returned there at the end of his life, after his stay in Mesirech, see A. Kahana, *Seder Ha-Hasidut*, Warsaw, 1922, pp. 143–4; Dubnow, *Toledot a-Hasidut*, p. 178 note 1.
59. NE *va-yeshev*, to Genesis 37:1 (ed. Nigal, pp. 109–10).
60. NE *shelah*, to Numbers 13:2 (ed. Nigal, p. 392).
61. NE *behar*, to Leviticus 25:25 (ed.n Nigal, pp. 354–5).
62. NE *hukkat*, to Numbers 19:2 (ed. Nigal, p. 434). Dubnow, *Toledt a-Hasidut*, p. 181, note 1, quotes NE *behar*, end (ed. Nigal, p. 356), where Elimelech states that God is like a 'slave' to do the bidding of his 'master', the Zaddik. But Dubnow omits Elimelech softening this, apparently blasphemous statement, with the conventional qualification *keveyakhol*, 'as it were'.
63. NE *hukkat*, to Numbers 19:2 (ed. Nigal, p. 434). One of the counts presented against the Hasidim, by the Mitnaggedim in their complaint to the Russian government, was that the Hasidim called their Masters 'God', see D. Z. Hillman, *Iggerot Baal Ha-Tanya U-Veney Doro*, Jerusalem, 1953, Documents 83, par. 6, p.142.
64. *Niddah* 31a.
65. NE *devarim*, beg. (ed. Nigal, p. 469).
66. NE *Likkutey Shoshanah*, to Psalms 119: 19 (ed. Nigal, p. 557).
67. NE *hayye sarah*, beg. (ed. Niga, p. 54).
68. NE *shelah* to Numbers 15:30 (ed. Nigal, p. 409).
69. NE *Nazir* 23a; *Horayot* 10b.
70. See Scholem, 'Redemption Through Sin' in *The Messianic Idea*, pp. 78–141; on the relationship between Sabbateanism and Hasidism see Scholem, *Major Trends*, pp. 330–4.
71. On the sin of the Zaddik see Dresner, *The Zaddik*, pp. 199f.
72. NE *bereshit*, to Genesis 1:1 (ed. Nigal, p. 7).
73. NE *noah*, to Genesis 8:5 (ed. Nigal, p. 21).
74. NE *hayye sarah* beg. to Genesis 24:1 (ed. Nigal, p. 61)
75. NE *shemot*, beg. (ed. Nigal, p. 159).
76. NE *va-yetze*, beg. (ed. Nigal, p. 74).
77. NE *noah*, to Genesis 6:9 (ed. Nigal, pp. 14–15).
78. NE *behukkotai*, end (ed. Nigal, p. 359). For this reason, remarks Elimelech, all benedictions begin in the second person, 'Blessed art Thou', but continue in the third person, 'Who hath sanctified us with His commandments'. See Dresner, *The Zaddik*, p. 282, note 10, that this thought is attributed to the Baal Shem Tov by Jacob Joseph of Polonnoye.
79. NE *terumah*, beg. (ed. Nigal, p. 250).

80. NE *mishpatim*, to Exodus 21:9 (ed. Nigal, p. 244).
81. NE *naso*, beg. (edn Nigal p. 370).
82. NE *shelah*, to Numbers 14: 24 (ed. Nigal, pp. 403–4) in name of the Maggid
83. NE *ki tavo*, beg. (edn Nigal p.518).
84. NE *devarim*, to Deuteronomy 1:1 (ed. Nigal, p. 475).
85. Ibid.
86. Ibid.
87. NE *mattot*, beg. (ed. Nigal, p. 457).
88. NE *korah*, end (ed. Nigal, p. 428).
89. *Cf.* the remarks of Dresner, *The Zaddik*, op. cit., pp. 275–6.
90. *Pesahim* 50b; *Sanhedrin* 105b.
91. NE *tzav*, beg. (ed. Nigal, p. 295).
92. NE *noah*, to Genesis 6:9 (ed. Nigal, p. 15). It is not clear why the precept of *tzitzit* in particular should have been significant in Elimelech's generation. Has it something to do with governmental decrees against Jewish garb? Cf. *nishmat* to *shelah* in NE (ed. Nigal, pp. 464–6).
93. NE *lekh lekha*, beg. (ed. Nigal, pp. 23–4).
94. NE *tzav*, to Leviticus 6:2 (ed. Nigal, pp. 298–9).
95. NE *hayye sarah*, beg. (ed. Nigal, p. 52).
96. NE *Likkutey Shoshanah*, end (ed. Nigal, pp. 587–8).
97. Letter I at end of NE (ed. Nigal, pp. 591–2).
98. The reference is to the decree of 1782 against marriage before the age of eighteen; see Dubnow, *Toledot a-Hasidut*, p. 185, note 2.
99. Dubnow, *Toledot a-Hasidut*, p. 183, quoting NE *Likkutey Shoshanah*, beg. (ed. Nigal, p. 530), where Elimelech does, in fact, speak of the Zaddik as a *sarsur*, a commission agent, but not as Dubnow allows his readers to assume, Elimelech here says that the Zaddik is the agent between God and the Torah, not between God and man.

8

Discipleship in Hasidism:
A Study of Two Masters

The relationship between the Hasidic teacher and his disciples, between the Zaddik and his Hasidim, still awaits full investigation by students of the movement. There are no full-scale scholarly treatments of this theme and even among Hasidic works the subject is treated only incidentally in the numerous works in which the doctrine of the Zaddik is developed. Problems still to be considered are: How did the early masters became disciples of their masters? What happened to convert an ordinary Hasid into a disciple? Why is it rare to find a disciple owing his allegiance to more than one master? In this brief study all that is attempted is to note two examples of the relationship between master and disciple in the life and work of two distinguished twentieth-century Hasidic masters; the term disciple being used here for both the general Hasidim of the master as well as for the disciple proper, totally committed to follow the master's path.

THE MUNKACER REBBE

R. Hayyim Eleazar Shapira (1872–1937), known as the Munkacer Rov as well as the Munkacer Rebbe, since he occupied both positions, discusses in his *Divrey Torah* (third edition, Jerusalem, 1974, Part 1, No. 5) the problem, which must have bothered many of the Hasidic Rebbes, of how a spiritual leader can remain humble without destroying his authority. The Hasidic master had to try to be at one with his followers and yet retain his aloofness. He had to be on the most familiar terms with his Hasidim without evoking the contempt on their part which familiarity breeds.

This problem has to be faced in every teacher–disciple relationship but is particularly acute in Hasidism since the Rebbe's calling demands that his inner life should control his external conduct, resulting, at times, in actions bound to appear strange, even unlawful, to the uninitiated. The tendency of the Hasidim was to emulate the Rebbe's behaviour patterns. Though they placed the Rebbe on a pedestal, the Hasidim still believed that his was the model life to which they could at least aspire. The dilemma the Rebbe faced is the inevitable one of the man in a position of extraordinary spiritual power over others, who is yet obliged to appear ordinary, rejecting any show of excessive saintliness. In other words, how can a Rebbe function as such while denying in his heart of hearts that he is a cut above his Hasidim.

The prophet declares: 'It hath been told thee, O man, what is good, and what the Lord doth require of thee; only to do justly, and to love mercy, and to walk humbly with thy God' (Micah 6:8). How is such an ideal to be realized, asks the Munkacer. If a man really practises justice and loves mercy, others are bound to know of it. How can one renowned for his righteousness and goodness walk humbly with his God? Surely the prophet does not mean to imply that good should be practised only in stealth with an outward appearance of profligacy and irresponsibility. (It is, in fact, widely rumoured that some of the Kotzker Hasidim used to turn conventional piety on its head, sinning in public and carrying out the *mitzvot* in secret.) Such conduct would amount to a *hillul ha-shem* (profanation of the divine name) by lowering the standards.

If, in order to avoid misunderstanding, the saintly man, while hiding his saintliness, informs his disciples that his strange outward conduct is only a mask, this defeats his purpose since the disciples then know that the saint's apparent irreligion is only make-believe. It must follow that a rabbi and spiritual leader (*rav u-manhig*) is obliged to practise his religion openly and as an example to others, conducting himself scrupulously in full adherence to all the laws of the Torah. But together with his external observance he should have a deeply spiritual inner life with hidden intentions in all that he does known only to his Maker.

Whitehead's definition of religion as what a man does with his solitariness is hardly acceptable to Judaism with its strong emphasis on community, but, for the Munkacer, it is sound, at least with regard to the inner life of religion. A very rich man may have a secret compartment in his safe where he keeps his most precious possessions, leaving some valuables in the outer compartment so that if he is forced by armed robbers to open the safe they will take only that which they find in the outer compartment. If the ruse is to work there must be a sufficient amount in the outer compartment to delude the robbers into thinking that there is no more hidden away. If the amount they find is far less than a man of his substance is likely to have, they will suspect that his real wealth is hidden away somewhere else and they will force him to reveal its whereabouts.

By the same token, says the Munkacer, a spiritual leader must parade his saintliness to the extent that his followers, witnesses of his rich spiritual conduct, will not imagine that, in addition, he has an even richer spiritual storehouse within. Paradoxically, the cultivation of secret piety is made possible only by a public exhibition of virtue sufficiently obvious to prevent the curious from probing more deeply into what really motivates the saint. It should be added that for the Munkacer this secret, inner life of which he speaks involves in the main the practice of *yihudim* ('unifications'), that is, profound reflections in all that the saint does on the various combinations of divine names relevant to each particular act.

The Munkacer's Boswell, Y. M. Gold, tells (*Darkhey Hayyim Ve-Shalom*, Jerusalem, 1974, p. 2), in illustration of this kind of reflection, that during the Omer period the Rebbe was observed gossiping at length to a select circle of his more learned Hasidim about a number of prominent contemporary Rabbis. It all seemed a mere pointless conversation until the Rebbe happened to let slip the observation that anyone who was aware of the particular Kabbalistic intentions attendant on that day of the Omer would understand the import of his remarks.

This stress on the need for the Rebbe to conform in his external conduct leads the Munkacer to reject blind hero-worship of the Rebbe on the part of his Hasidim. No Hasid, observing his Rebbe or any other famous Rebbe, carrying out acts that seem irregular or unlawful, should ever argue that the Rebbe knows what he is doing and he, too, will follow the Rebbe. In this connection the Munkacer quotes (*Nimmukey Orah Hayyim*, Jerusalem, 1968, No. 68) the early nineteenth-century Hasidic master, R. Zevi Hirsch Eichenstein of Zhydachov:

> Even if the rabbi is like an angel of the Lord of hosts, have no faith in anything he does to follow that practice until you have proven to your own satisfaction that it is proper ... To be sure you must find excuses for him. Heaven forfend that you view him with suspicion, but you must never follow him to do that which appears to be contrary to the Torah.

You must argue it out with him, asking him for his reasons. Only if he
can prove to you that what he does is in accordance with the Torah and
after he has explained it to you so convincingly that you are sure he is
right should you have faith in him. Otherwise have no faith in him
even if he tells you that he has received it from Elijah himself.

Gold (p. 13) states that it is for this reason that he is at pains, in his
account of the Munkacer's life, to find support for every one of the
Rebbe's practices in the standard Codes and other works recording
the established norm.

In addition to his role of Rebbe, the Munkacer headed a
Yeshivah in which young men studied the Torah. Gold (op. cit.,
No. 886, p. 325) describes an interesting pedagogical principle the
Munkacer adopted and with which he would preface his remarks
each year at opening session of the Yeshivah. The Talmudic Rabbis
make a distinction between the study of the Torah for its own sake
(*lishmah*) and the study of the Torah *shelo lishmah* ('not for its own
sake', i.e. with ulterior motives such as to win wealth or reputation
as a scholar). But the saying of the Babylonian teacher, Rav, is
quoted (Pesahim 50b): 'Let a man study the Torah even *shelo
lishmah*, for out of study *shelo lishmah* he will come to study *lishmah*.'
Rav's 'even' implies that study with ulterior motives is basically
unworthy but is tolerated because it will lead to study with worthy
motives. Hasidism generally tended to go much further, qualifying
Rav's statement so drastically that study of the Torah *shelo lishmah*
is seen to be positively sinful and to be avoided if at all possible.
This was, in fact, one of the chief bones of contention between the
early Hasidim and their opponents the Mitnaggedim, the latter
being much more lenient in the matter and refusing to denigrate
scholars simply because they studied in order to win fame. All the
more remarkable, then, is the Munkacer's advice to the young
students in his Yeshivah that they should, at first, study the Torah
with ambitious motives. It is sheer delusion, he maintains, for
young men to imagine that they are sufficiently God-intoxicated to
be able to study the Torah *lishmah*.

The truth is, says the Munkacer, that the driving force in the
beginning is bound to be one of self-interest. It is only when the
young student has become accustomed to the real delight in learning that he automatically comes to study *lishmah*. And this should
be the student's motivation. He should, indeed, study for ambitious reasons, otherwise he will never really come to enjoy learning, but at the back of his mind there should be the intention that

he studies in this way so that it will lead to study *lishmah*. A realistic insight into the mechanics of study!

Developing the principle of discipleship, the Munkacer (*Divrey
Torah*, Part 2, Nos 1 and 107–8) strongly supports the Hasidic practice of the Hasid visiting his Rebbe to sit at his table, especially on
Sabbaths and Festivals. He admits that, while the Talmudic Rabbis
speak often of a disciple staying with his teacher to learn from him,
there is no clear indication that he should partake of his meals. Yes,
states the Munkacer, the Hasidic practice of the 'tisch' ('table', the
sacred meal) is an innovation, but a very worthy one, and it finds
some support in earlier sources.

However, states the Munkacer (*Divrey Torah*, Part 1, No. 34), not
every man who claims to be a Rebbe is worthy of being one. There
are many who adopt the role because it is an easy way of earning a
living. Great discernment is required of the would-be disciple when
choosing which Rebbe to follow. The discerning have the capacity to
know whether a Rebbe is truly a holy man to be followed or a
phoney out for wealth and fame. 'I have heard,' says the Munkacer
in this connection,

> in the name of a holy man, may his merits protect us, in whose town
> many inferior and ignorant people supported and attached themselves
> to a man who made himself out to be a Rebbe and a Zaddik but he was
> really a hypocrite. This holy man said that Jews are 'believers, sons of
> believers' [i.e. they have an inborn faith but this can sometimes lead to
> sheer credulity] and it depends on their state of soul. For one who has
> been endowed with a good soul believes in a true Zaddik and has the
> merit of believing in that which is completely true. But one who has a
> lowly soul has faith in false beliefs and is a fool who will believe anything.

The Munkacer appears to have tolerated his disciples' doubts,
believing that they would eventually be stilled. He tells (*Divrey Torah*,
Part 1, No. 35) a story he claims to have heard from reliable people
about a disciple of Rabbi Baruch of Medziboz, grandson of the Baal
Shem Tov. R. Baruch had a disciple who was very well learned in philosophy. He did not tell his master of his interest in philosophical
thought but continued to reflect on problems of faith until he began
to question the very basis of his religion. R. Baruch saw by means of
the holy spirit the turmoil in the soul of his disciple and paid him a
visit in order to still his doubts. R. Baruch referred to the Rabbinic
statement that there are fifty gates of understanding. A philosopher,
when presented by a problem, seeks to find a solution and when he

succeeds in doing so he can be said to have entered one gate of understanding. But a further question presents itself to him and to this he also finds the solution and has entered the second gate. And so it continues until he has reached the fiftieth gate, at which stage there is no solution. For if a man were to enter the fiftieth gate the truth about God would be so unanswerable that freedom to act would be impossible. Were the truth to be so clear to a man he would have no choice but to obey God's will.

The Munkacer was known as a vehement fighter for the truth as he saw it, often attacking without restraint other Hasidic Rebbes with whom he disagreed. But in his relationship with his disciples he seems to have been extremely gentle and tolerant. He writes (*Divrey Torah*, Part 7, No. 47) that since a teacher learns from his disciples as well as teaching them, they are, in a sense, his teachers as well as his disciples. For this reason, the Munkacer approves of the advice given by the non-Hasidic Rabbi, Akiba Eger, that a teacher should avoid, whenever possible, referring to his disciple as 'my disciple' or signing a letter to him as 'Your teacher'. The Munkacer (*Divrey Torah*, Part 1, No. 114) tells a story, which he says came to him from the Hasidic tradition, of R. Zeev Wolf of Zbarazh who had intended for many years to journey to the court of the Seer of Lublin (both Hasidic masters in the late eighteenth century). When R. Zeev Wolf finally made the journey, the Seer came out to meet him. This shows, states the Munkacer, that, contrary to proto- col, in which the disciple goes to meet the master, where the disciple is worthy it is the right thing for the master to go to meet his disciple. The Munkacer (*Divrey Torah*, Part 3, No. 36) notes that when the Rebbe gives a general discourse to his disciples his eyes should be open so as to communicate the ideas face to face. But when he delivers his 'Torah' on the Sabbath or on the Festivals, the Rebbe's eyes should be closed so as draw on the inspiration he receives from on high when he is entirely closeted in his inner self. The Munkacer, in these observations, always speaks of a Rebbe in general but it is fairly obvious that he is referring to himself in his struggle to achieve the correct balance in the Rebbe–disciple relationship.

REB ARELE

Very different from the Munkacer, who belonged to an established Hasidic dynasty, succeeding as Rebbe his father and grandfather, was Rabbi Aaron Roth (1894–1944). Reb Arele, as he is called, came under the influence of Hasidism in his native Hungary. A group of youthful enthusiasts gathered around him and for these he acted as a spiritual guide. Eventually he was persuaded to don the mantle of a Hasidic Rebbe. He emigrated to Eretz Yisrael where his synagogue and Yeshivah, the *Toledot Aharon* in Meah Shearim, Jerusalem, was presided over, after Reb Arele's death, by his son-in-law and successor in the new dynasty. (Reb Arele also left a son who, claiming to be the real successor of his father, established a rival group, though, one gathers, the son and son-in-law and their Hasidim later made it up.) Reb Arele is thus one of the very few Hasidic masters since the early nineteenth century to found his own dynasty.

In the earlier period of Hasidism it was generally the disciple, not the son or son-in-law of the Rebbe, who became Rebbe in his stead. In this as well as in his attempt to recapture the simplicity of the early days of Hasidism, Reb Arele sought to revitalize the movement. Reb Arele was a prolific writer, his three major works are: *Shomer Emunim* (Jerusalem, 1964) on faith in God; *Shulhan Ha-Tahor* (Jerusalem, 1966) on eating as an act of divine worship; and *Taharat Ha-Kodesh* (Jerusalem, 1968) on sexual topics. In these works Reb Arele offers guidance to his followers based on the numerous Hasidic works he quotes throughout. The work *U-Vo Tidbak* by Mordecai Blum (Jerusalem, 1980) is an anthology of Reb Arele's teachings, culled from these works, on the high duty of attachment to the Hasidic masters, that is, on Hasidic discipleship. Blum states that Reb Arele himself wished to compile a detailed treatise on the subject but was unable to do so owing to pressure of work in other areas. Reb Arele's letters to his followers, published in his lifetime under the title *Iggerot Shomer Emunim* (Jerusalem, 1942) are an especially rich mine for students of the Rebbe–Hasid relationship. These letters are intensely personal, offering spiritual counsel to individuals who turned to their master in their need. The letters are in Hebrew but Reb Arele frequently breaks off in the middle to write in Yiddish, when he evidently feels that the formal Hebrew style is unsuitable to convey the warmth and intimacy of his involvement in the problems of his correspondents.

Little psychological acumen is required to realize that Reb Arele's followers were disturbed by their adherence to a Rebbe who did not have the backing of an established dynasty and whose strong sense of inferiority for this reason tempted them to make, in compensation, claims as to his holiness and miracle-working powers bordering on the grotesque. His son, for example, in his introduction to the *Shulhan Ha-Tahor*, states that when Reb Arele was a young Yeshivah student it often happened that his parents failed to send him the money for his expenses but so strong was the young man's trust in God that he persisted in his studies convinced that God would provide. And God did provide in that the money-box was miraculously replenished so that he was never in need. Reb Arele, in the letters, is extremely annoyed at the exaggerated claims his followers made on his behalf. He protests (letter 15) that he is, in fact, unworthy in his own eyes to be any kind of spiritual mentor, but since his friends do imagine that his spiritual counsel is effective he is obliged to offer it for what it is worth.

To give all the letters in translation would require a whole book. Here one of the most revealing (Letter 7) is rendered in English translation as conveying Reb Arele's attitudes and his method of approach. This letter is addressed to a disciple who had become a *shohet* in a small Hungarian village. It was written while Reb Arele lived in the town of Beregsas, after an earlier stay in Eretz Yisrael.

> Warmest greetings to my dear friend.
>
> I must inform you that I have received your delightful letter and it is more than two weeks that I made myself ready to reply but, for our sins, the many troubles in these times prevented me ...
>
> With regard to your query concerning my emigration to Eretz Yisrael ... Until now I go about thinking of emigrating to Eretz Yisrael if this is God's will, even though what is the significance of Eretz Yisrael since God can be worshipped anywhere and even in Eretz Yisrael it is possible to live like an animal and even worse than an animal. But what can I do? For from my youth my form of worship and my longing (when I witness the great decline in the Hasidic world, the point of truth being entirely lacking) is to strengthen breaches of the heart and to raise up a holy brotherhood to serve God in unison. Many sufferings have been visited upon me, wave upon wave, until I was compelled to go in exile from Eretz Yisrael because this was the will of the Creator, blessed be He. I left behind there young kids who have now grown to be goats [a Rabbinic idiom, respectively, for immature and mature scholars]. But in the course of time they have retreated from God's service and I am very concerned lest all my labours have been in vain. Our Rabbis, of blessed memory, say that a small group in Eretz Israel is more significant than seventy [members of the] Sanhedrin in the Diaspora. For this I entreat God to bring me to Zion with song, to serve Him in unison, to sanctify His name, if this be His will and His pity for me, the inferior one. But if God wishes it to be otherwise, I must nullify my will before His blessed

will, for this is the main thing. As our early teachers have said, worship consists in man doing that which God wants.

And so, too, for example, they have cast you into a little village and there you must find God's grace. For instance, in a large town there is much political manoeuvring, many lies are heard and witnessed, and one, especially a *shohet*, is exceedingly sold to immeasurable falsehood. Know my child, believe that which I have received from Zaddikim, that when one is sold, even to a single permanent falsehood, Heaven forfend, this causes the whole interpretation around and around stinks, such power is there in today's completely false style of worship. But now you live in a village, free from immeasurable falsehood, so you should be full of joy since the worship of God is in any event rare in today's world and there is no one with whom to converse. On the contrary, it seems comical to them.

But know, my dear child, the main thing is to keep count of every minute, not to make a habit of time-wasting gossip with your wife or childish talk with your children. You will see that whatever habits a man accustoms himself to, he is assisted by Heaven to continue in them one way or another. Recall the days of your youth when you spent all your strength in the assiduous study of the Torah and in the life of prayer with inwardness, which sanctifies and purifies inwardly and outwardly. I have spoken of this to you frequently how toiling in divine worship prevents one falling. And the main thing, at any rate, is never to despair. For even if one is among strangers, as the disciples of the Baal Shem Tov state, the rule is: Whatever one can grasp one must grasp and, if not, it is still forbidden to look at the way the world behaves and, if necessary, one must do the exact opposite of what the whole world does. One cannot grasp, and one is not permitted to grasp, the idea of prayer until one has immersed himself in this matter for many years. This is provided that one does not accustom himself to make strange gestures, as the stupid do, to sway violently backwards and forwards or to have glazed eyes or swing the head round and round and suchlike crazy gestures that are an abomination to God. The fact that the Zaddikim did, at times, these things was due to their powerful attachment to God which burned in their heart and they were unconscious and unaware of what they were doing. But one lacking in the effort to concentrate on the plain meaning of the words of the prayers or even the intentions of purification and the fear of God, does not belong in this category, as every intelligent person understands.

The root of the matter is that every son of Israel must seek all his days for 'lowliness of spirit and the point of truth' for this is the real form of worship for all one's days. As I have said, and am always in the habit of saying, the letters of the word *emet* ['truth'] are the initial letters of *emunah* ['faith'], *mesirat nefesh* ['self-sacrifice'] and *tekifut* ['stubbornness']. These are the root principles wherewith to attain truth. For the man of faith has no need to engage in flattery and has no need to resort to any kind of falsehood. As for self-sacrifice, this means a readiness to sacrifice oneself for the truth, and needs to be exceedingly

stubborn in order to stand firm, with the little truth one has appre-
hended, against any creature. As a result, in the course of time, God
helps man to attain lowliness of spirit since truth and a lowly spirit are
inseparable companions.

My dear son, it is now just before Pesah and a time which does not
allow writing a letter. Yet I have written out of my regard for you. I beg
you, keep this letter. Do not throw it away but take it out always to look
into it and, with God's help, it will do you good. Reflect and consider
at all times how much one can achieve in a spirit of self-sacrifice.
Consequently, my beloved son, do not cast away, God forbid, the point
you have received from me in your youth. For this is the meaning of a
true disciple, that he holds fast to the ways of his teacher and never
departs from them. For this is my entreaty, in all my functions as a
Rebbe, which I loathe and detest as is well-known to all who know me,
that God will help me to raise an intelligent disciple. All my disciples
are required to sanctify His blessed name wherever they go, for such is
the aim of aims. May it be God's will that I have merit of this for ever
and ever. Amen.

I want to ask you to rehearse by heart tractate *Berakhot* and see to it
that you complete it and do not be indolent in the matter for through it
much good will accrue to the soul. And repeat each day several pages
of the *Tikkuney Zohar* ...

Your friend ...

From both the Munkacer and Reb Arele there are strong indi-
cations of how these two late Hasidic masters, one the scion of a
notable dynasty, the other the Rebbe who founded a dynasty, tried
honestly to grapple with the problems of discipleship. Both
masters are at pains to reject any sense of superiority they have
over their disciples and yet, by allowing themselves to function as
Rebbes they must have accepted that they were sufficiently well
advanced to act as guides to those for whom the goal was more
distant. Hasidism had to face this problem from its inception,
particularly because it stressed to such a degree the elevated
nature of the Zaddik. Whether, in the final analysis, Hasidism succeeded in solving the problem adequately is another matter.
Perhaps R. Israel Salanter was right when he said, 'Both the
Hasidim and the Mitnaggedim are wrong. The Mitnaggedim are
wrong in thinking they do not need a Rebbe. The Hasidim
are wrong in thinking that they have a Rebbe.'

9

A *Pitka* from a Hasid to his Rebbe

The following is a translation of a *pitka* (a petition[1] a Hasid gives to his Rebbe) by a Hasid of the Gerer[2] Rebbe, R. Abraham Mordecai, author of *Imrey Emet*.[3] As the first *pitka* presented by this Hasid to the new Rebbe this amounts, in fact, to a declaration of loyalty to the new leader. This interesting document has been published recently in the work *Otzar Nehmad*, Machon Chasidei Polen, Tel-Aviv, Antwerp and New York, 1987, at the end of the book. The heading reads, 'A *pitka* written by one of the veterans among the Hasidim of Kotzk,[4] Ger,[5] Alexander[6] and the *Sefat Emet*,[7] may their merit be a shield to us, Amen, to his holiness, our master, Admur, the *Imrey Emet*, may the memory of the righteous be for a blessing, of Ger, at the beginning of his leadership in the year 665 [= 1905].'[8]

I belong to those born in Lipna[9] and was brought up among the first Kotzker Hasidim, outstanding Torah scholars, God fearers, seekers of truth, of whom it was said:[10] 'Who is a Hasid? He that conducts himself graciously towards his Maker [*ha-mithased im kono*].' My father, on whom be peace, was also a great scholar, an outstanding Hasid among the veterans of the Hasidim of Tomashov[11]/Kotzk and in the days of my youth I had a strong desire to take the next step[12] so that, after I had studied Gemara, Rashi and Tosafists in the Bet ha-Midrash,[13] I went to the Hasidic *stiebel* where I sought out Hasidic books in secret.[14] I had a great longing to flee to Kotzk but I was unsuccessful in this since the way there was so very great. But, at the age of seventeen, after my marriage, I journeyed to Kotzk. When I arrived there in his holy presence [of the Kotzker Rebbe] he asked me where I came from and what my name was. I was seized by a great dread and I lost my composure and all sense of individual existence. At that moment one thought only entered my mind. I imagined that Akavia ben Mahalaleel (*Avot* 3:1) was standing in front of me and was shouting: 'Consider ... know whence thou art come ...'. The impression this made on me has lasted until this very day. As I turned to depart from his presence I became a different person and my heart burned with clarity so that I applied to him the verse: 'And his sensitivity[15] [*e-hariho*] shall be in the fear of the Lord' [Isaiah 11:3] [i.e. the charismatic saint had an intuitive awareness of the Hasid's state of mind]. During this first journey I stayed there for eight Sabbaths so that when I went back home all worldly desires and pleasures had become abhorrent in mine eyes and my studies and prayers were mingled with joy and dread. If, occasionally, I fell [from my elevated state], I was easily capable of rising again as a result of his awakening [i.e. as a result of the saint's influence]. I was at Kotzk at five different periods[16] and at each of these journeys I sensed that it was not through my own strength and ability but was due solely to the fact that he, of blessed memory, had poured out to me from heaven the holy anointing oil.

And it came to pass when the ark of God was taken to heaven [i.e. when the Rebbe died], before there began to shine the light clear as the skies, the light that illumined the whole world, namely, his [the Gerer Rebbe's] great-grandfather,[17] our holy master, may the memory of the righteous be for a blessing, of Ger, his soul is in Eden, I fell fifteen degrees backwards until the spirit of the Lord was stirred within me and I journeyed to Ger for the first festival of Shavuot [i.e. the first after he had become a Rebbe]. When I entered his holy presence to hear his words proceeding from his holy, pure mouth, burning like coals of fire, I awoke like a man who wakes from his sleep. His words descended to the innermost parts of my stomach and entered into my bowels like the serpent's venom. Then I said to myself, this holy man has come into the world to teach the sons of Judah to use the bow[18] and how to wage the war against the evil inclination through knowledge of the innermost part of the Torah,[19] for this is the main thing. And we also find that only through the knowledge of the Torah can a man achieve the worship of God, blessed be He, and the more one is attached to knowledge the more will he find delight in worship. In the Torah [we find]: 'Unto thee it was shown, that thou mightest know' [Deuteronomy 4:37] and: 'Know this day' [Deuteronomy 4:39]. And in the Prophets [we find]: 'Know my son the God of thy father' [1 Chronicles 28:9]. And the prophet cries out: 'Because thou hast rejected knowledge' [Hosea 4: 6]. And in the *Ketuvim* [we find]: 'The Lord looks down…to see if there were any man of understanding that did seek …' [Psalms 14:2]. And our Sages, of blessed memory,[20] denigrate exceedingly even a scholar if he has no knowledge [i.e. good sense, profundity, here knowledge of religious sensitivity]. This [knowledge] it was that illumined the eyes of Israel to acknowledge the Creator by means of knowledge and the innermost parts of the Torah so as not to fall into the trap of the evil inclination concealed in the heart. When I heard words of Torah from him on the Sabbath my heart melted within me and all my limbs trembled. Many times I was prepared to take on oath that he knows the thoughts and intentions of my heart which I have even in my own home even when I am engaged in optional matters [i.e. non-religious concerns]. And his holy words would reach their target within a hair-breadth without missing. At times I would journey to Ger three or four times a year and each time I spent there at least four Sabbaths and yet when I came back home after each journey I became like one reborn. And with regard to all that I studied at home, whether Bible or Midrash, Halakhot and Aggadot or Gemara with Rashi and Tosafists, I discovered myself and my faults, but because I had heard and hearkened to his holy words on the holy Sabbath I was able to find counsel in order to refine and put right that which I had made crooked. When I heard a single word of Torah this then gave me the ability to interpret my way and to build great constructions like one of his holy disciples, men of renown. I neither rested nor sat quiet by day or by night. On numerous occasions *es hat fun bet arosgevorfen* ['it hurled me from my bed'] for my total vitality came from the words of Torah I heard from him whether in the innermost chambers in private [i.e. in private audience with the Rebbe] or in Sabbath in public [addresses of the Rebbe] just as a babe gains its nourishment from suckling at its mother's breast. I called these seven years the seven years of plenty.

After him there arose our holy master of Alexander,[21] his soul is in Eden. From him I learnt lowliness, patience and abasement for prayer by a soul inventory[22] at least twice each day, once in the morning before prayer and once at night before retiring to sleep. I served in holiness these three holy men.[23] All songs are holy[24] but the Song of Songs is holiest of the holy, namely, his father, our holy master,[25] of blessed memory, his soul is in Eden, may his merits shield us and all Israel, Amen. It is he who illumined the whole world from end to end with his Torah and his sanctity. Of him our Sages,[26] of blessed memory, say: 'There is one among us worthy that the Shekhinah should rest upon him like Moses our teacher, on whom be peace, but his generation is unworthy of it.'

It was he who sacrificed himself for the sake of the generality of Israel like Moses our teacher, on whom be peace, of whom it was said: 'And he looked on their burdens' [Exodus 2:11] on which Rashi, of blessed memory, comments: 'He set his eyes and his heart to be distressed by the troubles of Israel.' Of him our Sages, of blessed memory, say:[27] 'There is one pillar in the world reaching from the earth to the firmament and he is the Zaddik.' He is referred to as 'one' because he embraces and unifies all the stages from the earth to the firmament. From the end of the stages which are in earthly things, in the category of the *tav*, up to the firmament, which is the highest stage, in the category of *alef*,[28] it is well-known from books and from scribes that the Holy One, blessed be He, created the world, by means of the Torah, that is, by means of the twenty-two letters. For the Holy One, blessed be He, contracted Himself[29] in the letters and His first contraction was in the letter *alef* and then proceeding from letter to letter until the letter *tav*, at which stage there is free choice ,[30] either *tav, tiheyeh* ['live'] or *tav, tamut* ['die'].[31] The true Zaddik is obliged to bind himself to the lowest stages, the place of free choice, the category of *tav*, and draw them stage after stage until they reach the letter *alef*, representing the *aluf*[32] ('Lord') of the world. This is why the *talmid hakham* [the sage] is also called ALL[33] for 'all is in heaven and earth" [1 Chronicles 29:11] and the *talmid hakham* who unites heaven and earth embraces all stages and unites Heaven and earth. This is why our Sages, of blessed memory, say:[34] 'The world endures because of one Zaddik', as it is aid: 'The Zaddik is the foundation of the world' [Proverbs 10:25]. For were it not for the Zaddik the world could not endure as a result of the deeds of the wicked who cause the world to descend and divide it from the Lord of the world, as the verse says: 'And a complainer separateth *aluf*' [Proverbs 16:28]; they separate the category of the *alef* from the category of the *tav*. But, as a result of the Zaddik's attachment to all the stages, the world ascends after it has fallen, which is why Sages are referred to as 'builders', as the Rabbis say:[35] 'Read not "sons" but "builders"', for they erect the whole construction of the world. And this is why the world endures even because of a single Zaddik for he binds together all the lower stages from the letter *tav* to the letter *alef*, just as the YESOD,[36] when it rises, elevates the whole construction [of the Sefirot]. I heard this from the holy mouth of his great-grandfather, our holy master of Ger, of blessed memory, on the verse: 'in the eleventh month, on the first day of the month, took Moses upon him to expound this Torah' [Deuteronomy 1:5], which Rashi, of blessed memory, explains that it means in seventy tongues. Now he, of blessed memory, asked: Why was it necessary for Moses to explain the Torah in seventy tongues, since the nations of the world did not want to receive the Torah,[37] as it is written: 'and rose from Seir unto them; He shined forth from mount Paran' [Deuteronomy 33:2]. He, of blessed memory, replied in these words: Rashi means [the following in Yiddish] that Moses, on whom be peace, digged deep into the recesses of the Torah. Even if a Jew would fall into all the evil lusts of all seventy nations the Zaddik of the generation should know how to release him from the nethermost rungs of hell through the power of the Torah. And this is, as above, from the letter tav, representing death, to the *aluf* of the world.

Now no proof is required for that which everyone knows to be so: that his holy great-grandfather, of blessed memory, was a great Gaon in keen dialectics, the whole world [of learning] being,in comparison to him, like a skin of garlic,[38] and that he was among the elite in the dialectics of the Halakhah and that all kinds of novellae of Torah and the secrets of the Torah which proceeded from his holy mouth in Hasidic topics were also in the style of great sharpness. For I have never seen such sharpness in all the holy Hasidic works as is found in his studies. For all that, a very little I understood and of that which I did not understand I kept: 'If you walk in My statutes' [Leviticus 26:2], which Rashi explains to mean toiling in the study of the Torah. I worked hard and thank God I found good sense and knowledge. But as for the Torah of his grandson, that is to say, his father, our holy master, may his memory be for a blessing, what can I say, what can I speak! I have been in Ger more than a hundred times during the past thirty-five years. I have heard much Torah from him. Generally speaking, that which I understood I understood very easily, but as for that which I did not understand, it is not enough that I failed to grasp his full thoughts but I did not manage to grasp even the beginning of his thoughts. For everyone with eyes to see and a heart to under-stand was able to see in his mind's eye that the Shekhinah uttered from the throat[39] of that Zaddik profound words, mysteries of mysteries, secret and concealed. And whosoever claims to have had some grasp of the meaning of his holy words is mistaken, except for a very few of the elite. I laboured and toiled and poured out my prayers and many times my hair stood on end that God should give me the grace to understand his words, but my prayers were unanswered. I suffered greatly on this score for two reasons. The first is that the Torah states: 'But if you will not hearken unto Me', [Leviticus 26:14], explained by Rashi, of blessed memory, to mean: To labour in the study of the Torah and to know the exposition of the Sages, from which it follows that a man must sacrifice himself in order to understand the exposition of the Sages. Secondly, the Torah states: 'But the Lord hath not given you a heart to know, and eyes to see, and ears to hear, unto this day' [Deuteronomy 29:3], which Rashi, of blessed memory, explains to mean: To recognise the kindnesses of God and to cleave to Him. The *Baal ha-Turim*[40] notes that in the adjacent verse it says: 'And I have led you forty years in the wilderness' [verse 4], hinting that no man grasps the full mind of his teacher until forty years have elapsed. But I have spent more than fifty years studying the topic and am unable to grasp even the beginning of my teacher's thoughts. But this is my comfort in my distress: that even though I have said that I have learnt nothing from him I did learn from him nevertheless one thing for which he can fittingly be called my revered teacher. For this I did learn from him, that all that I have learnt from our holy masters, their souls are in Eden, in the days of my youth, and I thought that I had learnt from them much wisdom and knowledge, in his day it became obvious to me that, in fact, I had not learnt from them as much as a drop in the ocean. Moreover, whatever I managed to grasp when I was with his father, our holy master, of blessed memory, in my first journey to him, during my second journey I realized that in my first journey I had grasped nothing, and so during my third journey and so on, whenever I returned home it became known to me that I had understood nothing. For God's holiness is infinite and the final end of knowledge is to know that one does not know. Concerning this our Sages,[41] of blessed memory, say: 'If you have acquired knowledge what do you lack?' For the main aim of knowledge is to know what is lacking. 'If you lack knowledge what have you acquired?' If your knowledge has failed to uncover what you lack it is evidence that you have not learnt anything at all. With regard to this King Solomon, on whom be peace, said: 'I said: "I will get wisdom" but it was far from me' [Ecclesiastes 7:23]. He should have said: 'I said I would get wisdom but I am not a wise man', and then it would be a positive statement and its converse. So why did he say that it was remote from him? But, as above, the holiness of God, blessed be He, infinite so that the more one's stage of comprehension the more one grasps that he has understood nothing. For only he can be called wise who recognizes what he lacks and from this there stems a sense of humility. For the wiser a man the greater is his degree of humility.

To return to the first matter, to what I said above that I am greatly aggrieved that I have failed to understand many of the sayings of our holy teachers, of blessed memory. I said that it depends on no other but on myself so I scrutinized my deeds and I rehearsed a saying I had heard in the name of the holy master of Kotzk, of blessed memory. Right at the beginning of Kotzk[42] he said that anyone who studies the Zohar without first stripping himself from corporeality[43] does not understand a single word and whoever thinks he does understand is mistaken. Thus far his holy words. And the Kotzker Hasidim during the lifetime of the holy master of Kotzk, of blessed memory, did not study the Zohar, except for a few of the elite, and the Torah novellae of his father, our holy master, of blessed memory, are most elevated, standing in the highest places of world, hence I failed to understand them.

I have heard from true Hasidim who heard the following statement from the holy master of Kotzk, of blessed memory, which was uttered as early as the time when his sun began to shine in Tomashov. This is what he said [in Yiddish]: 'The heart must be broken; both shoulders must be crushed and heaven and earth totter and yet one must not depart from one's own.' Thus far his holy words. The Hasidim who heard this from the holy master did not know what he meant by thi. He replied as follows. 'It is stated in the writings of the holy *Ari*,[44] of blessed memory, that the majority of souls have been created only to put right one or two character traits which they had corrupted in this world and if they fail in this they will be obliged to undergo a further transmigration [45] in this world,' and he, of blessed memory, said: 'How can a man know which character trait he has been created to put right and elevate in this world? It is that which his inclination entices him constantly to transgress.' And he said [in Yiddish] as follows: 'That which causes him trouble to carry out provides him with clear evidence that it is this for which he was created to put right and to elevate and for this self-sacrifice is required.'

Now it is well-known that the Holy One, blessed be He, created the world by means of the Seven Holy Qualities[46]. These are ten including KETER but in the main they are seven, and for average folk[47] only five are main ones in order to know how to serve the Creator, blessed be He, in love and fear, TIFERET, NETZAH, HOD. YESOD is combined with MALKHUT, which embraces the 248 positive precepts and the 365 negative precepts, and this is called a complete configuration. It is also well-known that after Adam's sin, as a result of the filth of the serpent,[48] there fell from him many souls into the depths of the KELIPOT[49] and all creatures became corrupt and we are obliged to put them right. In the generation of the Flood they were completely wicked to the extent that they separated the world from its cause, namely, from the Torah which comes from the Creator, blessed be He, hence the world was destroyed by the Flood. The Torah hurled them into the KELIPAH of Egypt and Canaan, for these Princes on high are higher than all the other seventy Princes. For they [the people at the time of the Flood] converted the seven Qualities to serve their own bodies, to love external objects of love and external fear etc. They (the Princes of Egypt and Canaan) contaminated all the nations and their main aim was to contaminate the people of Israel. Therefore, KNOWLEDGE was exiled[50] and the Torah is in the category of KNOWLEDGE. Therefore, Israel had to go down to Egypt in order to elevate the Torah from the KELIPAH of Egypt, as it is stated in the *Tikkuney ha-Zohar*:[51] '*And the Egyptians made the children of Israel ... with hard service, in mortar, and in brick, and in all manner of service in the field ... with rigour* [Exodus 1:13-14]. *With mortar* [homer] this refers[52] to the *kal va-homer; with bricks* [lev-enim] this refers to the clarification [bbun] *of the laws; in all manner of service in the field* this refers to the Torah; *with rigour* [farekh] this refers to refutation [pirkha]'[53] until they brought up the letters of the Torah from the depths of the KELIPOT and they despoiled the Egyptians, bringing forth from there the holy sparks, and then, when they went out, they were able to receive the Torah in three months' time. After the Torah had been received the Qualities emerged from their exile. Had Israel not sinned by worshipping the golden calf, once the Torah had been given, the world of rectification would have come into being, and if Israel had carried out 'do not let any soul live' [Deuteronomy 20:16] the work of rectification would have been further completed. And if Saul[54] had not had pity on the best of the flock the work of rectification would have been further completed. Therefore, God, blessed be He, commanded: 'After the doings of the land of Egypt, wherein ye dwelt, and after the doings of the land of Canaan, whither I bring you, shall ye not do; neither shall ye walk in their statutes' (Leviticus 18:3). For they contaminated the land by their evil traits and their whole aim was to cause Israel to stumble through these evil traits. Now in Egypt KNOWLEDGE was in exile and when KNOWLEDGE came out of exile the Holy One, blessed be He, commanded that the SEVEN QUALITIES be brought out as well, as it is written: 'And ye shall count seven sabbaths of years' [Leviticus 25:8],[55] representing the seven clean days,[56] in order to elevate the SEVEN QUALITIES to the domain of the sacred. And after this Israel became worthy to receive the Torah. At the time of the giving of the Torah the filth of the serpent departed from them and two crowns[57] were attached to them. But when they sinned these were stripped away from them and to this day the QUALITIES are in exile. So that this is the main aim of our worship to elevate the QUALITIES to their SOURCE. The Midrash Rabbah[58] explains that the 'flaming sword' (Genesis 3:24) as referring to Gehinna and 'to keep the way of the tree of life' as referring to *derekh eretz*.[59] This teaches us that *derekh eretz* precedes the Torah, which is the Tree of Life. I have found in the holy books that *derekh eretz* means the[60] SEVEN QUALITIES.[60] These , indeed, precede the Torah, for if a man has not put these right it is said that if, heaven forbid, a man is unworthy[61] the Torah becomes for him a deadly poison and this in itself constitutes his Gehinna since he does not understand the Torah correctly. I have seen in one of the works of the disciples of the Baal Shem Tov, his soul is in Eden, a comment on the saying of our Sages, of blessed memory, that a scholar who has no knowledge[62] etc. of the KELIPAH is called a 'carcase', and whoever studies the Torah without knowledge the KELIPAH benefits[63] greatly from his studies for then his studies give energy to the KELIPAH and the KELIPAH has nourishment from the sacred.

I, too, humble and poor, even though unworthy to write Torah, yet since the following idea came to mind as I was writing the above, I am bold enough to offer my own proof that *derekh eretz* precedes the Torah and that *derekh eretz* refers to the Qualities. It is written: 'In the beginning God created the heaven and the earth. But the earth was desolate and void ... And God said: Let there be light' [Genesis 1:1.3]. Rashi, of blessed memory, comments:

'R. Isaac said: The Torah should have begun with "This month shall be unto you" [Exodus 12:1]. Why does it begin with "In the beginning?" Because of: "He declared unto His people ..." [Psalms 111:6 .' At first glance this is unintelligible. Rashi, of blessed memory, generally explains verses of Scripture in their plain meaning and what simple meaning is there here? But it comes to teach us the stage of the holy Torah. For as long as a man has not torn out of himself completely every evil trait and still retains even a faint trace of them, his studies will be an abomination in the eyes of the Lord and he will never attain to the light of the Torah. And this is what R. Isaac means when he says: 'What is the reason?' and 'Because He declared'. That is to say, just as the Holy One, blessed be He, Himself created the world out of darkness and converts the darkness into light, as it is written: 'And he said ... and there was light', so did He teach His people Israel that they cannot have the merit of understanding the Torah unless they have torn out of themselves every evil trait, called 'darkness'. Hence the Torah first records the deeds of the wicked whose works are darkness, as it written: 'And their works are in the dark' [Isaiah 29:15] and they say: Who knows of it and who can see us? The Torah therefore also records their severe and bitter punishments: the pain over the overthrow of Sodom; the narratives of Lot, Pharaoh and Abimelech; of Esau and Laban; of Egypt's putting Israel in bondage; all of them were smitten with extraordinary plagues because they did not conduct themselves in the proper manner [*be-derekh eretz*]. Afterwards, the Holy One, blessed be He, commanded the destruction of the seven nations, as it is written: 'thou shalt save nothing alive that breatheth' [Deuteronomy 20:16]. Their punishment, too,was brought on them because they caused the whole world to fall into their evil traits and they did not conduct themselves in the proper manner. If the nations say to Israel:[64] You are robbers in conquering the lands of the seven nations, they will reply: It is all from the Holy One, blessed be He. He has created them for His glory with the seven holy traits, to serve Him, laud Him and praise Him and to declare His splendour, as the prophet declares: 'Everything that is called by My name, it is for my glory I have created it, I have formed it, yea, I have made it' [Isaiah 43:7], that is to say, all the worlds of Creation, Formation and Action, were created only for His glory, and you have destroyed all the worlds through your evil traits. Therefore, He took it from you and gave it to those He saw fit in order that they

may put right that which you have corrupted. They cause the
world to endure because of their good traits as it was at the time of
Creation. But if you had not made it all corrupt, the Holy One,
blessed be He, would not have been obliged to wait for twenty-six
generations[65] before giving the Torah and to you as well the Torah
would have been given. But now not alone has He not given you
the Torah but Egypt has been punished with plagues and Canaan
has had to suffer the decree of no soul shall be left alive. Israel, on
the other hand, even though they were humbled and in bondage
to the Egyptians 'whose issue is the issue of horses' [Ezekiel 23:20],
yet they conducted themselves properly and kept themselves
always from all the evil traits, from theft, from unchastity and from
all ugly things, as the Torah testifies when it refers to them as the
Reubenites, the Simeonites.[66] To them not alone was the Torah
given with goodwill, so that it should not appear to them to be like
a stale declaration[67] and the precepts like rules learned by rote, of
which a man becomes sick and tired, but the good tidings were
given to them of: 'this month[68] shall be for you', namely, that they
will have the merit of expounding on every single title[69] heaps and
heaps of laws and they have the ability to to introduce new ideas
everywhere, new things and secrets of the Torah. And even that
which a diligent student[70] will find as new, all has been given to
Moses at Sinai. As it is written: 'which I command thee this day'
[Deuteronomy 19:9] that it should be in your eyes as if they had
been given this very day at Sinai and each day to become newly
created to acquire fresh vitality in understanding the Torah. Just
as the righteous, who study the Torah for its own sake, introduce
new ideas and secrets of the Torah daily so, too, the Holy One,
blessed be He, in His goodness, renews daily the work of Creation.
Were it not for their discovery of new ideas in the Torah[71] the
world could not endure for a single moment. Consequently,
R. Isaac tells us a great thing right at the beginning of the Torah,
teaching us that no man can merit the light of the Torah unless he
first uproots from himself all the evil traits that are under the
dominion of the seventy Princes on high, as I have said above in
the name of the holy master of Ger, of blessed memory, that when
Moses expounded the Torah he taught in all the seventy tongues,
as Rashi explains, and He will then humble them and are them
under the power of the sacred. And leading from one thing to
another, we can explain the saying in the Gemara; Samuel[72] said:
There is no difference between this world and the days of the

Messiah except for servitude to the government. His words seem very strange. Is it for such a small matter that we offer our prayers thrice daily: 'and to Jerusalem thy city return in mercy' and 'the shoot of David' apart from sabbaths and festivals? It is certain that what he really means is that in the days of the Messiah the government, namely, the evil traits and evil lusts of the seventy nations, will be utterly annihilated and they become subservient to the sacred and they will be under the control of Israel. Then all the external KELIPOT will be no more and the earth shall be full of the knowledge of the Lord as the waters cover the sea and the Lord's name will be whole and His throne whole.

I have heard in the name of the Kotzker Rebbe, may his merits shield us, his soul is in Eden, that he gave the following interpretation to the verse: 'Take heed unto yourselves, lest ye forget the covenant of the Lord your God ... and make you a graven image which the Lord thy God hath commanded thee' [Deuteronomy 4:23]. The point made is well-known. The verse should have said: 'which the Lord hates'. And he, of blessed memory, said that when the Torah warns us not to make any image it is to teach us that if our worship of God is without proper intention and without thought of God alone it is as abominable and repulsive in God's eyes as a real idolatrous image.[73] Thus far his holy words. And from the holy Rebbe of Ger, his merits shield us, his soul is in Eden, I heard as follows: (the Talmud says)[74] Habakkuk came and based them on one principle: 'The righteous shall live by his faith' [Habakkuk 2:4]. He said (in Yiddish) as follows: Faith [*emunah*] means to nurture, as in the verse: 'And he brought up [*omen*] Hadassah' [Esther 2:7]. We must be so nurtured in holiness that there is not even a hair-breadth of hatred or of envy or of lust or pursuit of fame. Thus far his holy words. And I have heard from the holy mouth of the Alexander Rebbe, his soul is in Eden, may his merits shield us, the following exposition of a passage in the holy Zohar.[75] The verse says: 'Wherefore criest thou unto Me? speak unto the children of Israel, that they go forward' [Exodus 14:15]. The Zohar asks where could they have gone forward since they were at the sea? But the meaning is that they should go on since it does not depend on prayer but it depends on *atika*[76] ['the old']. This passage in the Zohar is unintelligible. What is the meaning of it depending on *atika*? He explained it thus. Of what use is prayer and crying out, first uproot your evil traits by the roots. This is the meaning of *atika*, meaning to move away from your evil traits. And this is the main and perfect repentance and then your prayers will be automatically successful. Then He will answer even before you call, but of what use is prayer and crying out for help without uprooting the evil traits.

It follows from all that has been said above, even if a man keeps all the precepts of the Torah it is not considered to be true worship as long as he has not succeeded in uprooting his evil traits. For this is the main thing in worship by every Jewish soul for all his days on earth. Now it is well known that all depends on KNOW-LEDGE. When knowledge prevails the evil traits are humbled and the converse is also true, when the one rises the other falls. Hence I come on this first journey to arrange my speech before him and the defects in my conscience. There are times when my mind is broad and the words proceeding from my mouth in my studies are with great delight and my prayers are also uttered with great delight and with a broken heart. [In Yiddish] it learns of its own accord, it prays of its own accord, out of the innermost parts of the heart. I know only too well that it is not through my own strength that my prayers are so fluent in my mouth from heaven; generally this happens on sabbaths and festivals. There are other times when I need much preparation and a good deal of deliberation until I get myself into the right frame of mind. On the other hand, there are times when my heart lies like a stone and I have to labour hard with every kind of toil and every kind of self-encouragement for knowledge has been removed from me – not entirely, heaven forbid, only it is present in a very small way. Then my world becomes dark for I sense a great partition between the right ventricle of the heart and the left ventricle with all that is left to me only free choice and then I am obliged to wage the war of the Lord with prayer and supplication, as it is written: 'Their heart cried out unto the Lord' [Lamentations 2:18]. Occasionally the Lord sends me His help from His holy place and has pity on me from heaven. But at other times I am obliged to pray as it comes and over this I am always anxious and my heart sick for it would seem that I have still not escaped death. For who can declare I have refined my heart, I have been purified of my sins? And the prophet cries out: 'Behold I will enter into judgment with thee, because thou sayest "I have not sinned"' [Jeremiah 2:35]. Every man is always in great danger and suffers numerous temptations. There is no moment without its obstacle. A man rises early in the morning. He prepares himself with powerful concentration to take upon himself the yoke

of the Kingdom of Heaven and he recites the Shema with great unification. A great king, called Nimrod, then comes to confuse him, as
it is written: 'Like Nimrod a mighty hunter before the Lord'
[Genesis 10:9], meaning, even when he actually stands before the
Lord, going to the synagogue to pray, he confuses his thoughts and
overcomes him in the presence of the One before whom he stands.
As Ravnai[77] said: 'I am grateful to my head in that when I reach "We
give thanks to Thee" it bows of its own accord.' Even though in this
saying of our Sages, of blessed memory, there are many mysteries
yet the plain meaning is also true. He goes to the Bet ha-Midrash to
study the Torah and Esau comes with his hunting in his mouth and
he studies with him. For I have found in the holy books that Esau
is the Prince who governs any study of the Torah that is not for its
own sake. He goes out to to the market and he is in great danger, as
it is stated in the Midrash:[78] You imagine that the evil inclination
stands in the sideways, he actually stands in the market place. And
when he sees a man feeling[79] with his eyes and dressing his hair he
says: This one is mine. I would imagine that when the Midrash
speaks of adjusting the hair it refers to the fact that the market is
always the place where, if he forgets for a single moment that the
Holy One, blessed be He, knows all, thoughts, he can easily fall into
the deep pit of destruction. This is the meaning of: The difference
between the upper waters and the lower waters is as little as a hair-
breadth.[80] And so, too, the reference to feeling with his eyes, for a
man is wont to feel his pockets,[81] namely his innermost being, all
the time. Even though our Sages,[82] of blessed memory, say: 'I have
created the evil inclination and I have created the Torah as the anti-
dote', they obviously refer to those who study the Torah for its own
sake. As our Sages, of blessed memory, say:[83] 'It is a life-giving balm
to those on the right', which Rashi explains as those who engage in
the study of the Torah with all their might and trouble themselves
to know its secrets. And even though our Sages, of blessed memory, have given us the advice:[84] 'If this ugly wretch meets with you
draw him into the Bet ha-Midrash', meaning, remind him that you
have studied in the Bet ha-Midrash that you are forbidden to pay
heed to him to do as he wishes you to do, but his hope is vain since
this ugly wretch also studies with him and engages in dialectics
with him and says to him: Let the law pierce the mountain. In the
process he causes him to forget what he has studied and causes him
to stumble in the thoughts of his heart. For there is an angel
appointed over forgetfulness and he causes him to forget to engage

in soul assessment afterwards. The name of that angel is Sihon king of Heshbon.[85] So have I heard it from my father, of blessed memory.

To sum up, a man is faced all day with numerous tests, whether spiritual or material such as the difficulty of earning a living and the pain of rearing children. And it is impossible to overcome the evil inclination with its many eyes. So how much more must a man have many eyes to look to it that he does not fall into the trap, heaven forbid. These [eyes] are those of the men who have girded their loins with the light of the Torah and who engage in the study of the innermost Torah for its own sake. As I have heard it with my own ears from his great-grandfather, of blessed memory, of Ger his soul is in Eden, on the night of the holy sabbat section Shemot in the year 626 [= 1866], after the Sabbath has been welcomed, a few months before he departed this life. This is what he said: The Midrash states[86] that the tribes were called by names suggesting redemption; Reuben after: 'Because the Lord hath looked upon my affliction' [Genesis 29:32]; Simeon after: 'Because the Lord hath heard that I am hated' [Genesis 29:33]. And he commented [in Yiddish]: *Redemption means: when it is very restrictive, extremely dark, but not, heaven forbid, because of coarseness, and then from this in itself light is produced, namely, that we are in no way disturbed by it. And this is the meaning of: 'The excellence of the light is from the darkness'* [Ecclesiastes 2:13]. At this he stopped speaking. After a minute or two his holy words proceeded with burning fire and it seemed as if the prophet Isaiah was standing there prophesying. He said as follows [in Yiddish]: *The very same tests that existed at the time when Israel conquered the land, of which it is said: 'Now these are the nations which the Lord left, to prove Israel by them' [Judges 3:1] will apply nowadays as well. And we should not fool ourselves into thinking that we shall be able to cope. No! Anyone who will not be strongly involved with the innermost parts of the Torah will stand from afar. There will come a time when Jews will stand in the field and will have nothing to eat any longer except grass. And the nations of the world will roast their food in the field and the Jews will have to swallow greedily the smell in the roasting. And we should not fool ourselves that we shall then be able to cope. It will be restricted and ever more restricted for Jews, dark and ever darker.* And he ended with (in Yiddish): *It is certain that at that time will be fulfilled: 'In sitting still and rest shall ye be saved'* [Isaiah 30:15]. It seems to me that this prophecy applies to our time.

And now that I have become aware of the great power of the innermost parts of the Torah to save men from the snares of death, what is past is past but when the sun has set the sun shines, before the sun of Moses had set[87] etc. And it is stated in the Midrash Rabbah[88]: The names of Abraham, Isaac, Jacob, Samuel, Moses are doubled in the Torah for there is no generation without its Abraham etc. And the Zohar[89] states that the soul of Moses extends to six hundred thousand in every generation until the six thousandth generation. I am this day like a newborn infant for I know that his holiness is the foundation of true knowledge. Teach me, our holy master, long may he live, the way in which we should go in the worship of the Lord and teach us knowledge that we may understand the inner Torah. And let the verse be fulfilled for me: 'The ear that hearkeneth to the reproof of life abideth among the wise' [Proverbs 15:31]. And let him pray for me to remove from me the thorns and thistles which surround the Supernal Rose[90] that my worship should be clear and pure only for the Lord alone. And let my name be engraved upon his holy and pure heart that my old age should not put to shame my youth and my spiritual sense in wisdom and knowledge for this was my capacity in the days of my youth and with me and let them not leave me in my old age. And I hereby bind myself with a strong and powerful tie, in both body and spirit, as I was bound to his father, the holy Zaddik and to the holy Zaddikim who preceded him, their souls are in Eden. I cast my burden upon his holiness and to him I lift my breath, spirit and soul to put right my soul where appropriate that my worship, my Torah and my prayer be bound to the service of God by the Zaddik of this generation.

From me, his servant who bows before him, dust am I under the soles of his feet, Yaakov Yitzhak known as Zelig son of Hayyah Rachel[91] descendant of our master author of the *Bet Yosef*[92] Karo, of blessed memory, of Vallachovek.

Further information about this remarkable document is now available. In the recently published biography of R. Abraham Mordecai, to whom the letter was addressed, *Rosh Galut Yisrael* by A.M. Segal, Jerusalem, 1990, the document is printed in full as a Supplement (pp. 477–87). Here it is stated that the document was first published in the journal *Talpiot*, which came out in Shanghai in the year 1946. The editors of this journal state that in the year 1939 the Rebbe, before the festival of Shavuot, showed the document to his son R. Israel, later to become his successor (see pp. 187–8 for fur-

ther details). In note 70, page 186, it is told that the Hasidim of Ger
studied this document as an example of how the old Hasidim venerated their Rebbe.

This interesting document sheds light on how Hasidism was
actually lived in the second half of the nineteenth century and
beginning of the twentieth century. The Hasid's loyalty to his particular Rebbe and the latter's dynasty is evident throughout the
missive. The writer clearly belonged in his 'soul root', as the
Hasidim put it, to the Gerer dynasty, the successor of Kotzk.
R. Hanoch Henoch of Alexander, like the Kotzer, belonged to the
then newly formed Psychsa school. Once the *Rim* had assumed
leadership of the Gerer school it seemed entirely natural that, after
the passing of the *Rim*, the writer should express his loyalty to the
Rim's successor, the *Sefat Emet*, and afterwards to the latter's son,
the Gerer Rebbe, even though the writer was so much older than
the Rebbe. It is not only humility that prevented the writer from
even entertaining the thought of becoming a Rebbe himself.

To be noted especially is why the Hasid needs his Rebbe.
Although the Gerer Rebbes were very learned in Talmudic studies,
as the writer remarks, it was not to learn Talmud that the Hasid
repaired to the Rebbe. The story has often been told of the disciple
of the Maggid of Mezirech, R. Laib Sarahs, who declared that he
did not journey to the Maggid to learn Torah but to see how he tied
his shoelaces. In the language of our hero, the Hasid goes to the
Rebbe for instruction in the 'inner Torah', meaning presumably
guidance for the conduct of one's inner life. The writer never fails
to study the 'revealed Torah', especially Talmud and the
Commentaries of Rashi and Tosafists, but he is haunted by the fear
that this is not enough to 'put right' that for which his soul had
been sent down to earth. To be noted especially is how the writer
utilizes the Zoharic passage about the *kal va-homer* not to denigrate
Talmudic learning. Even in Egypt Talmudic dialectics were the
means to redemption but only a means for all that. This was
basically the bone of contention in the matter of Torah study
between the Hasidim and the Mitnaggedim. The basic thrust of R.
Haim of Volozhyn's *Nefesh ha-Hayyim* was to demonstrate that the
study of the Torah was not a means to an end, as the Hasidim held,
but the sublime end in itself. It is well-known that some of the early
Hasidic masters totally subordinated traditional Talmudic learning
to the ideal of *devekut*, attachment to God in the mind. For them
the study of the Talmud was itself an exercise in *devekut*, with God

in the mind even during study. R. Hayyim retorted that such study is not really study at all since in studying difficult passages of the Talmud it is neither possible nor desirable to have in mind anything other than the particular passage studied. The Gerer Hasidim seem to have coped with the problem by keeping Talmud study and *devekut* in two separate compartments. The Hasid would acquire much learning in Talmud in the conventional sense but for *devekut* he would go to the Rebbe for guidance.

Also to be noted is the idea that the true Rebbe succeeds in showing the Hasid the ineffability of the divine. The aim of the gnosis is to appreciate that there is no gnosis in divine matters; the Infinite recedes as knowledge increases and this in itself is a most important form of knowledge.

The universalistic note is also present in the writer's attempt at describing the fate of the nations of the world. Israel was only 'chosen' as a last resort because the 'nations' had failed to live up to what God demands of them in terms of righteous conduct, *derekh eretz*.

The document also provides some insight into religious psychology. In the presence of the charismatic leader the Hasid loses all sense of individuality and, when he recovers it, he imagines that the saint's words were directly attuned to the particular problems of his soul life. He tries hard to pray in a proper spirit of devotion and, at times, this comes so easily to him that it is as if the prayers proceed out of his mouth effortlessly and with great joy. At other times he suffers from the mystical 'dark night of the soul' (the actual term is not, of course, found in Hasidic literature) but he still perseveres, with the Rebbe's guidance, to reach higher devotional stages. It is noteworthy that he makes no mention of his material situation. As a veteran Hasid he had long outgrown 'the vanities of the world' and evidently finds it objectionable even to mention his material needs to the Rebbe.

We are not given much information about the life and career of this Hasid. He does not seem to have been well-known in Gerer circles since he has to tell the Rebbe who he is. Perhaps this why he signs the letter by referring to his illustrious ancestor, R. Joseph Karo. At all events, we have here one of the most revealing and moving documents in the history of Hasidism, one which historians of the movement would do well not to ignore.

NOTES

1. On the Hasidic practice of giving the Rebbe a *pitka* or *kvitel* see A. Wertheim, *Halakhot ve-Halikhot be-Hasidut*, Jerusalem, 1960, pp. 161–4.
2. The Hasidim refer to the Polish town Gora Kalwaria, nineteen miles south of Warsaw, as Ger, hence the Gerer Rebbe, i.e. the Zaddik of Ger.
3. Published posthumously, Tel Aviv, n.d.
4. Menahem Mendel (1787–1859), Hasidic Zaddik first in Tomsshov and later in Kotzk. See A. J. Heschel, *A Passion for Truth: Reflections on the Founder of Hasidism, the Kotzker and Kierkegaard*, London, 1973, and the same author's Yiddish work, *Kotzk*, Tel Aviv, 1973.
5. Isaac Meir (1789–1866), the great-grandfather of the Gerer Rebbe, known as the *Rim*, after initial letters of his name.
6. Hanoch Henoch of Alexander (1798–1870).
7. Judah Aryeh Laib Alter (1847–1905), author of *Sefat Emet*, grandson of the *Rim* and father of the Gerer Rebbe.
8. Thus the Rebbe was thirty-nine years of age when he succeeded to the leadership of Ger. The title *Admur* (initial letters of *Adonenu, Morenu ve-Rabbenu*, 'Our Lord, Teacher and Rebbe') is given to the Hasidic masters by their followers.
9. Lipno is a town in central Poland.
10. This saying is found in Zohar, II, 114b; III, 222b and *Tikkuney ha-Zohar*, I, ed. Reuben Margaliot, 1b.
11. Where R. Menahem Mendel first served as a Rebbe.
12. Lit. 'to pass over to the over side'.
13. The usual course of studies for boys and young men.
14. In secret because young men were discouraged from studying Hasidic works at too early an age.
15. See *Sanhedrin* 93b where this verse is understood as referring to the Messiah (punning on *reah*, 'smell') who can smell out sinners.
16. Since the writer was seventeen when he first journeyed to Kotzk and since he was there five separate times after that he must have been at least twenty-two years of age (probably older) in 1859 when the Kotzker died, which makes him at least sixty-eight when he stated his loyalty to the new Rebbe of Ger in 1905, when the Rebbe was thirty-nine.
17. R. Isaac Meir, the *Rim*.
18. 2 Samuel 1:15 in David's lament over Saul and Jonathan; for the Hasidim the warfare of the Bible is applied to the inner struggle with the evil inclination.
19. The mystical, as opposed to the plain meaning. 'Knowldge of the Torah' means here knowledge of this inner meaning, which, for the Hasidim, is the ultimate meaning, though they do not reject study of the plain meaning.
20. Midrash Leviticus Rabbah 1:15.
21. R. Hanoch Henoch, whom the Kotzker and Gerer Hasidim acknowledged as a Rebbe belonging to the same school.
22. The Talmud (*Bava Batra* 78b) interprets 'Come to Heshbon' in Numbers 21:27 as referring to the *heshbono shel olam*, 'inventory of the world', i.e. self-scrutiny with a view to self-improvement.
23. The three holy men are the Kotzker, the *Rim* and the Rebbe of Alexander.
24. Based on Mishnah *Yadaim* 3:5 and referring to the biblical Song of Songs, but here applied to the Rebbes – all Rebbes are holy but this one is holiest of holies.
25. The *Sefat Emet*, grandson of the *Rim*.
26. *Sanhedrin* 11a.
27. *Hagigah* 12b, 'The world rests on one pillar and its name is Zaddik ("Righteous") for it is said: "But Zaadik is the foundation of the world" (Proverbs 10:25).' Here this is interpreted as referring to the Hasidic master, called the Zaddik.
28. The letter *alef*, the first letter of the aphabet, to the letter *tav*, the final letter of the alphabet.
29. In the Kabbalistic doctrine the *En Sof*, the Infinite, withdraws 'from Himself into Himself' to leave 'room' for creatures to come into existence. The letters of the Hebrew alphabet are the form taken on earth by the various spiritual entities by means of which the world was created.

30. In the creative process the stage is eventually reached at which the universe is sufficiently at a distance from the Infinite for human freedom of choice to be possible; otherwise all would have been determined by the nearness of God.
31. See *Shabbat* 55a; *tav* is the first letter of both *tiheye* and *tamut*.
32. Pun on *alef* to denote *aluf*, 'Lord of the universe'.
33. In the Kabbalah YESOD, 'Foundation', the sixth of the seven Lower Sefirot, is called the Zaddik and if referred to in the verse quoted as ALL, hence the parallel drawn with the Hasidic Zaddik, and see *Yoma* 38b. The term *talmid hakham*, used in the Talmud for a scholar, is applied by the Hasidim to the Zaddik.
34. *Yoma* 38b.
35. *Berakhot* 64a.
36. YESOD is represented, as above, by the Zaddik on earth.
37. *Sifre* 343 to the verse quoted.
38. A saying of Ben Azzai in *Bekhorot* 58a.
39. This saying is not found in the earlier sources but is used frequently in the later literature, see M. Sabor, *Mikhlol ha-Maamarim ve-ha-Pitgamim*, Jerusalem, 1967, Vol. III, p. 1771. For the Hasidic belief that the Shekhinah takes over when the Zaddik speaks see Rivka Schatz Uffenheimer, *Quietistic Elements in Eighteenth Century Hasidic Thought* (Heb.), Jerusalem, 1968, pp. 117–19.
40. By Jacob b. Asher (d. 1340).
41. A saying in *Nedarim* 41a meaning: 'If you have knowledge what do you lack? If you lack knowledge what do you have?', but interpreted here as: 'If you really know, then you must know what you lack in knowledge', i.e. the more one knows of the divine the more one knows that one does not know.
42. When the Rebbe first moved to Kotzk.
43. The Hasidic term for transcending corporeal awareness, a near to a trancelike state.
44. The *Ari* is the famous Safed Kabbalist, R. Isaac Luria (1534–72).
45. Like the Kabbalists the Hasidim believe in the transmigration of souls (*gilgul*). A soul that has not 'put right' some defect is obliged to return to earth in another incarnation to rectify the fault.
46. The Seven Qualities are the Seven Sefirot, the powers or potencies in the divine. These are ten in number, the highest of which is KETER ('Crown') but those with the closest link to earth are the Lower Seven listed here.
47. The average folk should be primarily concerned with representing the five Sefirot mentioned, i.e. unlike the Zaddik who represents the union of YESOD and MALKHUT.
48. See *Shabbat* 146a for the idea that when the serpent cohabited with Eve he infected her and her descendants with his filth but when Israel received the Torah at Sinai they became immune from the serpent's filth.
49. The KELIPOT ('Shells') are the demonic forces which feed on the holy.
50. KNOWLEDGE is Daat, an intermediary between the Sefirot of HOKHMAH ('Wisdom')) and BINAH ('Understanding').
51. Tikkun 21, ed. Reuben Margaliot, 44a and see Zohar I, 27a. In the context there are echoes here of the tension between the mystical approach of the Kabbalists and that of the Talmudic and Halakhic studies; see I. Tishby, *Mishnat ha-Zohar*, Vol. I, Jerusalem, 1957, p. 384. But here the passage is explained to mean that, on the contrary, Talmudic style argumentation was essential in order to put everything right.
52. The argument from the minor to the major.
53. 'Refutation', the term used for the refutation of an argument in the Talmud. There is a pun on *homer* ('severe' i.e. the 'major') and *homer* ('mortar') and on *pirkha* ('refutation') and *perekh* ('rigour').
54. 1 Samuel 15:8.
55. The writer, no doubt quoting from memory, seems to be referring to Leviticus 25:8 but, since he uses the singular, he is probably thinking of Leviticus 23:15, which refers to 'counting the omer' and is interpreted in the Kabbalah on the analogy of a menstruant counting her days until she can be united with her husband.
56. *Shabbat* 88a that at Sinai each Israelite received two crowns, which were taken away when the golden calf was worshipped.
57. The seven days during a woman's purification during which she has no show.
58. Genesis Rabbah 21:9.

59. That *derekh eretz* precedes the Torah is not found in the Midrash Rabbah but in the Midrash *Tana de-Vey Eliyahu* I.
60. The meaning is probably that the Sefirah MALKHUT, the last of the Sefirot, is known as ERETZ ('The Land') hence 'the way of the land' is the way to the Sefirot by righteous conduct.
61. *Yoma* 72b.
62. Midrah Leviticus Rabbah I:15: 'A scholar who lacks knowledge, a carcase is better than he'
63. The writer takes 'better than he' ('*tovah hayemenu*') to mean that the 'carcase' , the KELI-PAH, is all the better for it through him, i.e. the demonic forces are nourished by the sacred when they are brought into the study of the Torah by the scholar who studies with a selfish motive.
64. This is in the saying of R. Isaac quoted by Rashi. The nations say to Israel: You are rob-bers because you have taken our land away from us.
65. *Pesahim* 118a.
66. They preserved their family purity and hence knew who their fathers were.
67. *Sifre*, Deuteronomy 33.
68. The word for month, *hodesh*, means 'renewal'.
69. *Eruvin* 21b.
70. Jerusalem Talmud *Peah* 2:4 (17a).
71. By discovering new ideas in the Torah the righteous release the creative energy latent in the Torah and hence keep the world in being.
72. *Berakhot* 34b.
73. The Kotzker's interpretation is do not make a graven image out of that which the Lord has commanded you.
74. *Makkot* 24a that Habakkuk based all the precepts of the Torah on the one great princi-ple of faith (*emunah*).
75. Zohar II, 48a.
76. Taking *atika* as connected with *yaatek*, 'he removed', not as 'old'.
77. The reference is to Jerusalem Talmud *Berakhot* 2:4 (5a) but there the reading is not Ravnai but R. Matnah or R. Mani. This saying was well known in the middle ages and is quoted, for example, by the Tosafists to *Bava Batra* 164b.
78. Genesis Rabbah 22:6.
79. In the context the meaning seems to be arranging the eyebrows to make a man attrac-tive to women.
80. Tikkuney ha-Zohar 19, ed. Reuben Margaliot, p. 38a.
81. A man feels his pockets all the time, *Bava Metzia* 21b. Pocket or money bag is *kis*, mean-ing 'that which is usually covered', hence the intrepretation that it refers to the inner Torah.
82. *Kiddushin* 30b.
83. *Shabbat* 63a on Proverbs 3:16.
84. *Kiddushin* 39b.
85. See *Bava Batra* 78b, as above, for the connection between Heshbon and *heshbon* in the sense of soul inventory, Sihon is the king of *heshbon*, i.e. he has dominion over it and seeks to frustrate it.
86. See Exodus Rabbah 1:15, but the verse quoted there for Reuben is Exodus 3:7 and for Simeon Exodus 2:24.
87. Midrash Ecclesiastes Rabbah 1:5 on Ecclesiastes 1:5.
88. Exodus Rabbah 2:6.
89. Zohar III, 273a.
90. The Supernal Rose is the Sefirah MALKHUT, the Shekhinah, attacked by the KELIPOT, the 'thorns'; see Zohar I, 1a.
91. When a Hasid presents a *kvittel* he signs it with his mother's name not his father's, hence 'son of Hayyah Rachel'.
92. The great work by Joseph Karo (1488–1575).

10

The Book *Rahamey Ha-Av*

The little book *Rahamey Ha-Av*, one of the most popular Hasidic works from its first appearance in Lemberg in 1868 down to the present day, was compiled by Jacob Katina (= Klein), Dayan in the Hungarian town of Huszt for forty years until his death in 1890.[1] During the major part of Klein's career as a Dayan, he served under Rabbi Moses Schick, the *Maharam Shik*, who was appointed Rabbi in Huszt in 1861. Huszt was largely a Hasidic town, adopting, for instance, the Hasidic liturgy. Schick tried to change to the Ashkenazi liturgy, whether or not successfully we are not told.[2] This fact, as we shall see, probably has implications for the nature and form taken by the book. The work first appeared without the author's name, but his identity was disclosed once the book had gone into further editions in which Klein is given as the author.[3]

> In the frontispiece the author states his aim as follows: This book was compiled by a person on behalf of his sons in order to train them in the right way. But when he saw that the light was good [Genesis 1:4] he resolved to apportion it to Jacob and spread it abroad in Israel [based on Genesis 49:7 and probably hinting at his name, Jacob]. For, he said, although these words are small in both quantity and quality, perchance someone will find in the book some good quality that will be of credit to his soul. The honour of the Lord demands secrecy [based on Proverbs 25:2] so the authorship remains undisclosed. But the Sages have said:[4] Accept the truth from whichever source it comes and it is written: From all my teachers have I gotten wisdom [based on Proverbs 119:99 as interpreted in tractate *Avot* 4:1].

The author appended to the fifth edition a little prayer of thanks, the opening letters of the four stanzas of which form his name *Yaakov*. He continues:

For what am I and what is my life that God should have given me the merit of compiling this anthology and that, thanks to His name, these words have become popular. Before this time the book has been printed four times: once in Chernowitz, twice in Lemberg, and for the fourth time in Warsaw. And now it appears in a fifth edition with many further additions. May it be His will that I utter an acceptable word and that these words should find favour and make an impression in the hearts of the children of Israel so that perchance I might be rebuilt from it to restore my lost ones so that I do not enter the Presence of the Holy King in a state of embarrassment.[5]

The book is arranged in 58 paragraphs and according to the letters of the Hebrew alphabet from *alef* to *tav*. 58 in Hebrew is *nun* and *het*, forming the word *hen*, 'grace' or 'favour' and the book has been divided into 58 paragraphs with this in mind. (The word *hen* is also an abbreviation of *hokhmah nistarah*, 'the hidden science', i.e. the Kabbalah). As the author modestly acknowledges, the book is more of an anthology than an original work but a competent arrangement of material in an anthology constitutes a strong degree of originality. The author's sources are, naturally, the Bible and the Rabbinic literature, but there is also a good deal of material from the Hasidic classics as well as anecdotes about the Hasidic masters. The author was, evidently, a Hasid but not a Rebbe. There is no indication of whether he belonged to any particular Hasidic group or was simply an admirer of Hasidism in a general way.

In the Preface the author addresses his sons:

Gather ye and hear O ye sons of Jacob [Genesis 49:2], may God increase you a thousandfold [Deuteronomy 1:11] and may you grow immeasurably in Torah and good deeds so that the Creator obtains from you great satisfaction. For this is my prayer at all times that your deeds and your Torah should be to afford satisfaction to His great name and that, God forfend, I should never suffer shame and embarrassment through you in the world on high, that, may God save us from it, they should not say: Just look at the shoots you have raised [*Ketubot* 45a]. My sons, more pleasant than fine gold and bound on the tablets of my heart, you should know that numerous troubles and worries have been my lot in the matter of raising children. Many tears have I shed, on numerous occasions have I bothered the Zaddikim of the generation to awaken mercy until I had the merit of having you. And now I am old, advanced in days, and who knows what the next day will bring, whether I shall have the merit of training you in the way of the Lord as it is in my heart, and as there is an obligation on every father to do, as it is said: *As a man disciplines his son* [Deuteronomy 8:5] and as it is written in connection with our father Abraham, on whom be peace, *That he may instruct his children and his posterity to keep the way of the Lord by doing what is just and right* [Genesis 18:19], I therefore decided to write down for your benefit some good qualities which seemed in my poor mind suitable for a man to follow for as long as he sojourns in this lowly world. And if you will hearken unto me you will fulfil two precepts, that of honouring God and that of honouring a father, for these words will be as if I were addressing you personally. I record all this for you in accordance with my limited perception of how to serve God as I have understood it from authors and from books and as I have personally tried to implement it. As for you, if you will have the merit of possessing greater powers of perception, as I hope you will, the verse will be fulfilled: *And he that hath clean hands waxeth stronger and stronger* [Job 17:9]. However, you should not be too hasty' to refute my words since destruction by the aged is really constructive [*Megillah* 31b]. I have called this tract: *Rahamey Ha-Av* ['A Father's Mercies'] for it is true mercy when a man disciplines his son to train him in God's ways for this is the whole duty of man. And so should you do, my children, for your own children to the end of all generations: to watch carefully over your offspring, young and old, that every step they take and every move they make should all be for the sake of affording satisfaction to His blessed name. I have based my words on the twenty-two letters of the Torah, the letters of the alphabet, and thus I begin with the help of the Rock of my salvation.[6]

It would seem that the author did intend the work in the first instance for his own children, but by publishing the little book, albeit anonymously, he obviously looked forward to a much wider readership. We shall examine later on whether the omission of his name was due to modesty or whether there was another reason for it.

Short of translating the book in full, its flavour and particular stance can best be appreciated by noting its main thrust. For instance, here is the first paragraph on *emet*, 'truth':

Truth is the all-embracing balm.[7] There is no finer quality and it is the seal of the Holy One, blessed be He.[8] Take the utmost care to speak the truth in your heart as in connection with the story of Rav Safra related at the end of tractate *Makkot*.[9] At the very least, take care not to utter any falsehood for the mouth is the entrance to all the limbs of the body and their sovereign. Consequently, it must never be contaminated by false utterances and those who do so will not receive the countenance of the Shekhinah,[10] as it is said: *He that speaketh falsehood shall not be established before mine eyes* [Psalms 101:7]. Even though it can happen that a man is compelled to tell lies, where, for example, it is to save life or in those instances stated in the Gemara[11] where Rabbis avoid the truth, yet even here every effort should be made to utter whatever is said in such a way that it is not an explicit falsehood, as stated in the *Sefer Hasidim*.[12] If you will have the merit of speaking only the truth in your mouths you will unite through this the quality of Truth with that of the Mouth, namely *Tiferet* and *Malkhut*,[13] the Holy One, blessed be He, and His Shekhinah, and this is the whole purpose of our worship in this world. This embraces the idea that all your deeds and all your study of the Torah should be entirely sincere and not out of ulterior motives, God forbid, for such is a deadly poison in the service of our Creator and even the smallest amount disqualifies. Very few people escape. There are many who engage in self-torture, who study the Torah and perform good deeds, and yet their worship is disqualified by this trait and they are not held in esteem in God's eyes, as it is said in the Gemara regarding the two men who roasted their Paschal lambs.[14] It is necessary to pray long for this that the few good deeds a man performs should be solely for God's sake without any ulterior motivation so as not to inherit two hells.[15] May the All-Merciful grant us the merit to worship Him in truth.'

In this short paragraph all the ingredients of the Hasidic approach are contained. From its inception Hasidism fought against the Rabbinic scholars who, the Hasidim maintained, did not really worship God but studied and carried out good deeds solely in order to acquire a reputation as great scholars and righteous men. On this view, ulterior motivation, to win fame and fortune and the like, disqualifies Jewish worship. Study and practice with such motivation were not worship of God but only a means to the realization of selfish ambition. The Mitnaggedim, the opponents of Hasidism, retorted that, as they saw it, according to the Talmud[16] a man should still study the Torah and perform good deeds even if his motive is less than pure, for out of impure motivation he will eventually attain pure motivation. R. Hayyim of Volozhyn (1749–1821), foremost disciple of the great opponent of Hasidism, the Gaon of Vilna, in his *Nefesh Ha-Hayyim*,[17] uses the Talmudic text about the two men and their Paschal lambs to yield the exact opposite conclusion from that of our author. The Talmudic passage states that the man who eats the lamb solely in obedience to the divine command is righteous whereas the man who eats it because he enjoys roast meat is a sinner. Our author understands this to mean that the whole worship of the 'sinner' is totally unacceptable because of his impure motivation. On the contrary, R. Hayyim argues, even the 'sinner' has the credit of carrying out a divine command and will be rewarded for it, whereas one who has the most elevated thoughts about the significance of Passover and the Exodus but does not actually participate in the offering is, in the Biblical expression, 'cut off from his people'. Our author was undoubtedly aware of R. Hayyimys critique but, as a follower of Hasidism, against which R. Hayyim offers his critique, stresses purity of motive in such a way as to rule out impure motivation entirely, though he is fully aware of how difficult it is to have completely pure motivation when studying the Torah and carrying out the precepts. It is possible that this is one of the reasons, perhaps the main reason, why the author published his work anonymously. As a Dayyan of the Court of a non-Hasidic Rabbi, the author no doubt felt himself to be inhibited from expressing openly what, from the non-Hasidic view, is, after all, a heretical opinion.[18]

The author's Hasidic stance can be seen throughout the book. He advises the study of the Kabbalah but believes that such study should not be undertaken before the student has acquired a thorough knowledge of Talmud and Codes. Moreover the study of Kabbalah should be in private and accompanied with subservience to 'the Zaddik of the generation' (No. 3). This latter remark probably means that the Hasidic Rabbi should first be consulted since there is to be observed in some Hasidic circles a degree of opposition to young men studying Kabbalah.[19] The author advises his sons (No. 5) to associate with older people and to avoid as much as possible the company of youths. 'It is very good to associate with the old, good men and not with the youths called *junge leit*, for counsel is not with children',[20] obviously a reference to the young rebels and trouble-makers, which were not lacking in Hasidic circles. Interestingly enough, however, in the section on clothes (No. 9), while he urges his sons not to wear Western clothes (*malbush deutsch*, lit. 'German garments') and not to be ostentatious in their dress, he makes no mention of the specific Hasidic garb, the *streimel* for example. He urges his sons to avoid wearing, if at all possible, any garments of wool. These may contain linen threads and the garments would then constitute a forbidden mixture of wool and linen – *shaatnez* – 'a very serious offence which contaminates the soul'. There are echoes here of the debate in the first half of the nineteenth century between R. Moshe Sofer of Pressburg, the *Hatam Sofer*, and the Hasidic master, R. Moshe Teitelbaum, the latter upholding the Hasidic custom of his time not to wear woollen garments during the prayers.

Very interesting are the author's remarks on tobacco (No. 11).

He frowns on young men especially becoming addicted to the weed, among other reasons because of vanity. Many Hasidic masters believed it to be exceedingly meritorious to smoke a pipe because of the subtle 'holy sparks' imprisoned in tobacco which the saint, when smoking in mystic meditation, rescues for the sacred.[21] But for young men to smoke is nothing but pride and vanity, especially if they smoke cigars. He continues:

> Although it is said in the holy books, in the name of the disciples of the Baal Shem Tov, that for the Zaddikim this is considered to be as if incense had been offered and that there are subtle sparks that cannot be elevated through eating and drinking but only through smoking ... yet all this applies only to the great ones of the generation, all of whose deeds are for the sake of heaven. But for young men this is no more than pride and an unnecessary waste of money. I have heard it told of our Master, Rabbi Shalom of Belz, that, in his youth, he was wont to smoke. It once happened that while he was studying in the Bet Ha-Midrash he saw a young man cleaning his pipe and filling it with tobacco. During the time all this was going on, Rabbi Shalom managed to study a whole page of Gemara, whereupon he said: If this instrument can waste time that could be spent in study it will not be allowed in my mouth from now onwards, and he never smoked again, even though he was a world-renowned Zaddik. And so, too, the holy Gaon, our Master Rabbi Moshe Teitelbaum of Ohelje, never used this instrument.

It is not without significance that the author seeks support for his opposition to smoking in the conduct of two Hasidic masters. He is aware of the importance some masters attached to smoking but seeks to limit this to the greatest of Zaddikim and is ready to show that even among two renowned masters there was opposition to the habit.

Naturally the author pays attention (No. 16) to the Hasidic ideal of *devekut*, 'attachment' to God in the mind.[22] At all times one should be aware of God's presence, even, from time to time at least, during the study of the Torah. No heed should be paid to those who say that the study of the Torah itself constitutes *devekut*. In fact, this is precisely what the Mitnaggedim did say,[23] the author obviously having in mind and taking sides against them. For the Mitnaggedim to engage in *devekut* during study was not to study at all. During the study of the Torah the mind must not be diverted from the particular subject studied, not even by thoughts on God. For the Mitnaggedim the study of the Torah is a sublime end in the religious life. For the Hasidim, important and highly significant though Torah study is, it is a means to an end, never an end in itself. The true end, for the Hasid, is that of *devekut*. Here, too, the author, whether or not a totally committed Hasid, prefers the Hasidic view to that of the Mitnaggedim.

The author's Hasidic stance can also be seen in the great emphasis he places on sexual purity. In the section on *hirhur*, sexual arousal (No. 18), he praises the Polish custom that unmarried youths are discouraged, until just before their marriage, from studying the sections of the Talmud and the Codes that deal with sexual matters. In the section on *kedushah*, 'holiness' (No. 49) he is even more emphatic. A youth should keep away from women in every way. He must never soil his mouth with obscenities. When a marriage has been arranged, the young man is allowed to meet his prospective bride but, apart from this, all familiarity between the young couple before their wedding is strictly forbidden. For the young couple to engage in courting before the wedding is as dangerous as 'fire burning in the nethermost regions of hell'. The author continues: 'And even after marriage let him not imagine that, God forbid, the rope has been unwound so that the wife is treated as if she were a piece of meat. Of this the Rabbis say.[24] "Sanctify yourself in that which is permitted to you." And he should depict to himself that God sees all his deeds so how can he avoid being ashamed. And everyone can depict to himself how many obstacles result from familiarity on occasions other than the time of the marital act so one who watches over his soul will keep away.'[25]

In addition to his general acceptance of the Hasidic way, the author considers specifically, in a number of sections, the pursuit of this way. In the section on *hasidut* (No. 25) he states that the title *hasid* is superior to that of *tzaddik* and he strongly disapproves of the proliferation of Zaddikim. It is better to have the superior title of *hasid* (a follower of a Zaddik) than to have the title of Zaddik, unless one is really such. As he writes:

> For our many sins, nowadays, the generation seems to imagine that there has been an improvement and most people go to be received by a Zaddik but only God knows who really goes [with sincerity]. There is a sect known as the *hevra* ['gang']. They are notorious, among them great scholars and men of good deeds.[26] My sons, for God's sake keep far away from them and do not go along with them for there is great risk in this. Even if they quote proofs from the Torah and from the tales about the Zaddikim, pay no heed to them and refuse to listen to them. God forbid that one should say that only his Rebbe is the true Zaddik

and none other. I have heard it told of our Master, the holy Gaon
Hayyim of Zanz, that on one occasion he declared in the Sukkah: 'If I
ever hear one of my followers declare that only his Rebbe is the Zaddik
and none other, I shall remove him from his roots.' For the Glorious
King has many servants. If only there was peace among the Zaddikim
and the Hasidim the son of David would come so why should one
denigrate the mode of worship of others?

Consequently, the author advises his sons to follow the Hasidic way
but to be circumspect and reject those Hasidic practices that seem
odd. He seems to accept without qualification the doctrine of
Zaddikism but is extremely reluctant to confine it to any one Zaddik,
and he evidently disapproves of the more bizarre Hasidic customs:

You, my sons, follow the way of the Hasidim but take that which is good
and cast away the strange practices. It is not exactly the will of God that
one should dance on tables ... nor is there any obligation to be among
the 'snatchers'[27] ... Also to make strange motions during prayer is not
obligatory but each person should conduct himself in accordance with
the root of his soul[28] ... And God forbid that you should depart even
slightly from application to the study of the Talmud and the Codes.[29]
And if there are some Zaddikim of our time who, so far as we can see,
spend little time in study, their way is beyond our comprehension and
no proof can be adduced from the conduct of angels.

In the section on the Rabbinic role, *rabbanut* (No. 51), the author
urges his sons to avoid at all costs taking on the role of a Hasidic
master. Nowadays, he remarks, anyone descended from a famous
Zaddik sets himself up as a Rebbe and seeks to earn his living in
this way:

Satan strives mightily to attract people to any God-fearing person who
then sets up as a miracle-worker. May God deliver you from such
falsehood except in dire need when a Torah scholar is compelled to sell
himself for a loaf of bread, as the situation nowadays is, for our sins,
when business opportunities are few and when expenses and taxes are
so heavy. But one who is compelled to come to this, to become a Rebbe
... should exercise the greatest care not to imagine that he is a 'some-
body' ... And the main thing is that he bend his head as a reed to the
Zaddik of the generation and he will then realize that he is a
'nothing'.

The author is saying here that if, through force of circumstances, a
person has to become a Rebbe, he should, at the same time,
become a Hasid of a 'real' Rebbe. Many Hasidic masters did, in

their humility, consider themselves to be mere Hasidim in relation to more saintly masters.

In the section on *tefillah*, 'prayer' (No. 56) the author attacks the Hasidic fondness for reciting prayers in small conventicles (*stieblech*). The Jewish ideal, according to the Talmud, is for Jews to worship in large synagogues, not in small prayer halls.

> Now in the time of the heels of the Messiah chutzpah is abroad.[30] Many are to be found who break away from the community to build a private high place for themselves, each to be the head of his own *minyan* and to ascend as the sixth to the reading of the Torah.[31] Woe to them for they do evil to themselves in that not only do they receive no reward for it but it is possible that they will be punished since they destroy the building of the Omnipresent. I do not speak of a place where there are brazen folk who stir up strife and mischief in the synagogue; or where there are ascetic scholars who make many preparations for prayer[32] and are unable to pray early in the morning with ordinary folk who pray without preparations in their concern to get away in order to earn a living; or where some use the Ashkenazi liturgy and others the Sephardi. In all such instances it is certainly permissible to separate oneself ... But as for those who separate themselves from the community out of pride or because they live too far away from the synagogue they will be called to account for they have severed that which should be joined.

It seems probable that our author, appointed originally as a Dayyan in a largely Hasidic community, eventually had to face difficulties, possibly aggravated when Rabbi Schick was appointed Rabbi of Huszt. Thus he tries to be as 'establishment'-minded as possible, rejecting the more rebellious aspects of Hasidism and seeking to discourage any proliferation of Hasidic Rebbes and conventicles, while, at the same time, advocating that the spiritual values inherent in Hasidism be accepted wholeheartedly. He may still have been uneasy about his stance so that, choosing discretion as the better part of valour, he published his book anonymously. Yet precisely because the book was not partisan, favouring no particular Hasidic group over others, it became popular among all Hasidim, to take its place in the library of Hasidic classics.

NOTES

1. From the tombstone, a photograph of which appears in the Jerusalem ed., 1979, of *Rahamey Ha-Av*, we learn that the author was a Dayyan in Huszt 'for about forty years' and that he died in the month of Shevat, 5650 (=1890). He is also described there as hav-

ing lived to a ripe old age. In the later editions of the book his name is given as Jacob Katina. Katina means small in Aramaic, hence the name Klein, a very popular name among Hungarian Jews. Freidberg, *Bet Eked, s.v. Rahamey Ha-Av*, gives the family name as 'Gottlieb'. J. J. Greenwald, *Peer Hakhmey Medinatenu*, Maramosziget, 1910, letter *yod*, No. 156 (p. 90) describes the author as 'a great Rabbi and Zaddik, author of *Korban He-Ani* and *Hen Tov*', but this latter work is our *Rahamey Ha-Av*, subtitled *Hen Tov* because it contains fifty-eight sections. Greenwald also states that he had been told of 'a marvellous event' that took place between the author and the *Maharam Shik* but fails to give any details. In the Index to his book Greenwald also gives the author's family name as 'Gottlieb'. It is something of a puzzle where this name in Freidberg and Greenwald comes from.

2. See B. Fuchs, *Yeshivot Hungaria*, Jerusalem, 1977, Chapter 31. pp. 478–99, that when the *Maharam Shik* was appointed Rabbi of Huszt in 1853 he endeavoured to get the towns-folk to change over from the Sephardi to the Ashkenazi version of the liturgy.
3. I have used the latest edition of *Rahamey Ha-Av*, Jerusalem, 1979, published by the author's grandson, E. Katina. Freidberg, *Bet Eked*, lists the following editions: Lemberg, 1868; Lemberg, 1870; Warsaw, 1874; Lemberg, 1875; Munkacs, 1894; Munkacs, 1898; Lublin, 1923; Cracow, 1937; Devo, 1934 (with notes by S. Z. Ehrenreich); Jerusalem, 1950 (with *Toledot Yitzhak* by I. Weiss) and a translation in Arabic (*sic*) by Hayyim Hori, Djerba, 1939.
4. Maimonides, Introduction to *Avot*, ed. Kapah, Jerusalem, 1965, *Nezikin*, p. 247.
5. This Introduction is stated in the Jerusalem edition to be the Introduction to the fifth edition but no date is given. The author lists the four previous editions as: once in Chernowitz, twice in Lemberg and once in Warsaw. There is, consequently, some confusion in Freidberg, who makes no mention of the Chernowitz edition. The author's reference to 'my lost ones' may mean if his sons stray from the true path but, more probably, it may mean the 'holy sparks' lost through his sins which the publication of the book will help restore to the sacred realm.
6. A list of good customs (*hanhagot*) taken from the author's *Korban He-Ani* (published in 1872) is appended to later editions of *Rahamey Ha-Av*.
7. Balm is *sama* and this is probably a pun on the Ashkenazi/Yiddish pronunciation of *emet*, 'truth', as *emes*.
8. *Shabbat* 55a.
9. *Makkot* 24a.
10. *Sotah* 42b.
11. *Bava Metzia* 23b.
12. *Sefer Hasidim*, ed. R. Margaliot, Jerusalem, 1973, No. 47, p. 107.
13. In the Kabbalistic scheme of the Sefirot, the male principle is *Tiferet*. This, as the harmonizing principle, symbolizes truth. The Sefirah *Malkhut*, the female principle, is symbolised by the mouth and represents the divine creative processes. According to the Kabbalah the purpose of human worship is to assist the unification of the Holy One, blessed be He, *Tiferet* with His Shekhinah, *Malkhut*.
14. See *Nazir* 23a: 'Two men roast their Paschal lambs. One eats it with the intention of carrying out the divine precept and the other eats it with the intention of enjoying a gross meal. To the first the verse applies: *And the just do walk in them* [Hosea 14:10]; to the other the verse applies: *but transgressors do stumble therein* [Hosea ibid.].'
15. That is, the 'hell' of living the hard life of study in this world and hell in the hereafter, based on *yoma* 72b: 'Rava said to the scholars: I beg you, do not inherit a double Gehinnom'.
16. *Pesahim* 50b.
17. See *Nefesh Ha-Hayyim, Shaar* III, Chapter 5, ed. Y. D. Rubin, Bene Berak, 1988, p. 197.
18. On the debate on this issue between the Hasidim and the Mitnaggedim see Norman Lamm, *Torah Lishmah*, Jerusalem, 1972.
19. Many of the Hasidic masters tended to place the emphasis on the ideal of *devekut* and while they believed in the Kabbalah as revealed truth they tended to favour the study of Hasidic works, especially for young men.
20. See my *Hasidic Prayer*, new ed, Littman Library of Jewish Civilization, London and Washington, 1993, pp. 154–9. I have noted some passages from *Rahamey Ha-Av* in the new introduction to this edition.

21. See my *Hasidic Prayer*, Chapter 4, pp. 46f. In point of fact the idea that in smoking the 'holy sparks' are raised and that smoking resembles the offering of incense in the Temple is found only in very late Hasidic works. The early Hasidic masters did smoke a pipe but only as an aid to contemplation; see my article, 'Tobacco and the Hasidim' in POLIN, vol. 11, London and Portland, Oregon, 1998, pp. 25–30.
22. See G. Scholem, '*Devekut*, or Communion with God', in his *The Messianic Idea in Judaism*, New York, 1971, pp.203–26.
23. See Norman Lamm, *Torah Lishmah*, which deals comprehensively with the whole debate.
24. *Yevamot* 20a.
25. On the strong Hasidic reservations regarding sex see J. A. Kamelhaar, *Dor Deah Tzaddikey Ha-Dor*, II, Jerusalem, 1970, pp. 203–5.
26. The identity of the *hevra* is not clear; probably either the Kotzker or the Bratzlaver Hasidim, both of whom were considered to be rebels by other Hasidic groups.
27. The reference is to *shirayyim*, the practice of the Hasidim to snatch food from a dish the Rebbe had previously tasted a little. See I. Tishby, 'Zevi Hermann Schapiro', *Ke-Sofer Haskalah, Molad*, February 1972, p. 568, note 66, that the practice of snatching *shirayyim* is never referred to in the Hasidic–Mitnaggedic polemics. The practice seems to be late.
28. According to his individual temperament.
29. The reference here is to a tendency among some Hasidim to dethrone the traditional study of the Talmud and the Codes in favour of greater concentration on *devekut* and the study of devotional works; see Norman Lamm, *Torah Lishmah*.
30. *Sotah* 49b.
31. The Hasidic Zaddik was usually called up to the reading of the sixth portion of the Torah because the sixth of the lower Sefirot, *Tiferet*, is called the Zaddik.
32. On Hasidic preparations for prayer see Chapter 4 in *Hasidic Prayer*.

11

A Hasidic Boswell on his Rebbe

It is more than a little surprising that for all the vast proliferation of Hasidic hagiographical literature we have hardly any information, until photographs were taken, of what the various Hasidic masters looked like; whether they were tall or short, thin or fat, dark-skinned or fair and so forth. It would seem that the followers of the masters thought it too disrespectful even to attempt such portrayals which might thereby imply that their heroes possessed all too human characteristics and that the physical form of the saints has any bearing on their spiritual stage. This kind of reservation is to be observed in non-Hasidic circles as well. We are not told, for instance, of what Maimonides looked like for all the rich biographical material on the famous sage or, for that matter, how Isaiah or Micah appeared to their contemporaries. The well-known legend of the king who instructed his artist to depict Moses and to whose consternation the great lawgiver's face gave evidence of severe signs of character degeneration was decried by a host of staid Polish and Russian Rabbis in the last century.[1]

An exception to all this is found in the work *Zikkaron Tov* by Isaac Landau, a disciple of the Hasidic master R. Isaac of Neshkhiz (1788–1869), youngest son of R. Mordecai of Neshkhiz (1752–1800).[2] Landau makes it clear, in the section of his work entitled *Inyan Or Panav*, 'On the Topic: The Light of His Countenance',[3] that in describing the actual appearance of his master he is being extremely innovative. While Landau's biography of his master in the *Zikkaron Tov* is in no way different from the run of such works, miracles, tales and all,[4] this section of the work, based on his personal experience, is factual, very unusual and strikingly 'modern'. (The letters in the book also seem to be authentic, though this requires further investigation.) This document is here given in English translation with a few notes to help clarify the meaning.

ON THE TOPIC: THE LIGHT OF HIS COUNTENANCE

1. I am about to record in writing a certain novel topic. This is as a result of that which I have heard twice from his holy mouth. One of these occasions was when he paid a visit to the town of Kolk in the year 618 [=1858]. He usually came to the town at nightfall and all the people came to look through the windows of the house where he was staying so as to look at his honour, Admur [*adonenu morenu ve-rabbenu*, 'our master, teacher and rabbi'], his memory is for a blessing for the life of the World to Come, so as to gaze at him. Some men wanted to close the shutters, called lodens, so as prevent the people looking at him. But he, of blessed memory, ordered that the shutters should not be closed and he had the windows opened entirely and stood leaning on the window-ledges with his face outside, saying: 'If the children of Israel want to look, let them do so.' He continued that his honoured father, our Master R. Mordecai, his memory is for a blessing for the life of the World to Come, of Neshkhiz said: 'Just as now it is considered to be of great merit for anyone to have known the Baal Shem Tov, the day will come when it will be considered to be of great merit to anyone who had known me. The [Hasidic] world will then ask if there is anyone who knew the Rabbi of Neshkhiz,' namely, the father of Admur. I also heard this tale from Admur when he was staying in Ratner. Then also, before he went to sleep, he ordered that they should not shut the windows when he arrived there. He again related this tale [about his father]. Consequently, I determined to relate, as a reminder, something about the appearance of the glorious visage of our Master, his memory is for a blessing for the life of the World to Come. Even though I have never seen anyone write this kind of thing of any Zaddik in the world, I beg my readers to forgive me and they should not complain since as a result of these accounts the topics become most valuable to us by allowing them to be retained in the memory as much as possible. And of those who judge others favourably may it be the divine Will that they be judged favourably.

The reader should consider as well the following. For woe to us that, for our many sins, we no longer have the merit of having bequeathed to us a remembrance of the light of the world, our Master, his memory is for a blessing for the life of the World to Come, except for his work: *Toledot Yitzhak*. Who was like unto him to spread abroad in the world the sanctity of God's name, blessed be He, to the very ends of the earth, so that the earth trembled at the mighty wonders He wrought through his holy merit which showed forth the power of divine providence to the ends of the earth. The old and venerable men have related that they cannot recall in all their days such renown as there existed in the days of our Master, his memory is for a blessing for the life of the World to Come. And now, for our sins, days will come when it will all be forgotten since he did not leave offspring in the world, except for the blessed memory of his holy deeds. Therefore, dear reader, do not be astonished if we have departed from custom to record as a memorial in a book all these matters concerning our Master, his memory is for a blessing for the life of the World to Come, even though our predecessors never followed such a practice when they compiled books about our holy Masters, their souls are in the Garden of Eden. I do not think it to be impossible that readers of this book when they recall, as a result, that which they had had the merit of seeing with their own eyes, they will find healing for their souls and will bestir themselves for good.

2. I want to record that which we know of the genealogy of our Holy Master, Our Rabbi, R. Isaac, son of the Gaon, Our Master, R. Mordecai, son of the Holy Rabbi Dov Baer, who was known as The Scribe of the Four Lands, son of the Holy Rabbi Leibush who was a Rabbi in Neshkhiz, son of the Holy Rabbi Isaiah, head of the Court of the holy community of Kovla, who was a descendant of Rabbi Heschel of Cracow and of Rabbi Nathan Shapira, author of the work *Megalleh Amukot*. And I have heard from our Master that he is of the seed of the Davidic dynasty. Our Master's mother was the Rabbanit Reiza, daughter of Rabbi Joseph of the city of Leshnov in the realm of His Excellency [the Czar of Russia]. The wife of this Rabbi Joseph was the sister of Rabbi Shlomo Zalman of Biala and their father was Rabbi Jacob, head of the Court of the holy community of Ludimir, son of Rabbi Ephraim Fischel, who was known as The

Trustee of the Four Lands, son of the Great Rabbi Laib, son of Rabbi Zechariah Mendel. The sister of the aforementioned Rabbanit Reiza was the wife of the Rabbi, the Gaon, Rabbi Tzvi of Lokotsch, author of the work *Mendel Tzvi*, he, too, was a son of the aforementioned Rabbi Shlomo Zalman of Biala since Rabbi Tzvi married his sister's daughter.

And I have also heard that the descent of our Master, his memory is for a blessing for the life of the World to Come, can be traced to the Holy Rabbi Abravanel, may the memory of them all be for a blessing for the life of the World to Come.

3. Let the memory of our honoured Admur, our Master, R. Isaac, his memory is for the blessing for the life of the World to Come, son of Our Master, R. Mordecai, his memory is for a blessing for the life of the World to Come, be for an everlasting memorial. May it be the Will from before Our Father in Heaven that we have the merit to recall his shining countenance and the appearance of his form all the days of our life, as we find in the holy books the advantage of this topic.

4. His facial appearance was most attractive. His hair was as white as pure wool from many years back, as the members of his family who knew him in his youth recalled. His holy skull was full all around as mentioned in the books regarding brainy people. He used to shave the hair [of his head] so as not to let it grow even a little, for it was hard for him to bear the hair. He was wont to remark that it is necessary the remove the judgments [the hair of the head represents sternness and judgment in the Kabbalah]. He had a kind of groove on his head, like a thread dividing his holy skull. The world calls this, having two heads. His forehead was wide on top and was full-featured. His holy eyes were fitly set [Song of Songs 5:12], evenly set, as mentioned in the Holy Zohar.[5] The pupils of his eyes were lightly tinged. His eyebrows were rather bushy. His holy ears were long and thin, reaching towards the neck. They were adjacent to the skull and did not protrude. All his hair was bright and sparkling. His ear locks were somewhere in between curly and straight but the hair of his holy beard was curly and was very bright and sparkling and each strand of hair could be seen separately. It was his habit occasionally to to grasp the left side of his beard[6] for a division could be seen between the two parts

of his beard, forming two sections from where the hairs began to where they ended.

His holy nose was of normal size but at its end towards the lips it became a little fuller than the norm. It was not round but rather square. The holy lips were of average size, neither thick nor thin.

His height was a little less than average and he was slightly bent in his old age. The palms of his hands were very shiny and clear. His fingers were thin and his fingernails somewhere in between long and round.

5. His whole body was clear and shining. In his old age he once showed his valet in the bath house a mark on one of his legs, remarking that this came upon him from the decree of conflagration that was issued against the town of Ratner, Heaven spare us.[7] For, as is well-known, there were frequent outbreaks of fire, Heaven spare us, in the town of Ratner. Our Master ordered that money for a *pidyon*[8] be collected in that town on the eve of the New Moon which they would bring to him and, as a result, they were spared from the conflagrations. Also towards the end when he was weak just before he passed away a *pidyon* was collected as was their wont in Ratner and bought to him. When the valet brought the *pidyon* to him our Master offered many supplications on their behalf for the purpose of bringing more blessings than usual to them. At this time miracles of miracles, far more than anything that could have resulted from natural means, were wrought and when the conflagration advanced only two Jewish houses were burned down etc., as is well known to the inhabitants of that town. Our Master said many times that he bore great sufferings in his body but he did not tell of them.[9]

6. His facial cheeks in his earlier days were not as lean as his body, which was thin and emaciated, especially in his old age and especially just before he passed away, when he became very weak. He used to say that he no longer had any flesh on which to sit or lie. When the purification[10] took place it was observed that he was nothing more than skin spread over his holy bones.

7. His honour, our Master, his memory is for a blessing for the life of the World to Come, would often see without spectacles and his eye was not dimmed. Even after he had passed away his

appearance suffered no change, heaven forbid. During his final months in this world he would on occasion cast dread by his piercing gaze, especially among the members of his family. His gaze used to penetrate outwardly and inwardly into the very innards and kidneys.

8. In his last days just before he passed away he was very prone to become weak as a result of the evil eye when anyone looked at him. They used to utter incantations over him to ward off the evil eye, especially during the last weeks before he passed away.

9. Generally his holy form was not the same all the time, especially on the Sabbath and Festivals. When they greeted him with 'Good Sabbath' after the evening prayers the burning enthusi asm of his prayers had so changed his face that he looked like a different person. Without exaggeration, those who did not know him could not tell from one time to another if it was the same person. This kind of change took place many times.

10. All who saw him said: 'What a beautiful Etrog.'[11] His form testified to what he was and the light of his countenance to his holiness.

Note on the picture of R. Isaac of Neshkhiz.

On page 95 in Yitzhak Alfasi's *Ha-Hasidut*, Tel-Aviv, 1974, there is a picture of R. Isaac of Neshkhiz in which are portrayed the special features mentioned in Landau's account, such as the divided beard. Alfasi does not tell us the origin of this picture. It is extremely unlikely that in the very early days of photography a photograph was taken of R. Isaac, and if the saint had sat for a portrait, extremely unlikely in itself, it is hardly likely that Landau would not have known of it and referred to it. It is virtually certain that the picture in Alfasi is, in fact, a painting or drawing based on the details provided by Landau.

NOTES

1. For the legend of Moses and the king's artist see Israel Lipshitz, *Tiferet Yisrael* to the Mishnah, *Kiddushin* end, note 77; Ginzberg's *Legends of the Jews*, Vol. V, p. 403, note 68; and my *Principles of the Jewish Faith*, ed. Northvale, New Jersey and London, 1988, p. 215.

2. The very brief article on Isaac of Neshkhiz in *The Encyclopedia of Hasidism* by Tzvi H. Rabinowicz, Northvale, New Jersey and London, 1996, pp. 343–4, relies on the fuller account by A.I. Bromberg, *Admorey Neshkhiz* etc., Jerusalem, 1963, pp. 40–50. (Vol. 20 in the series *Mi-Gedoley Ha-Torah Ve-Ha-Hasidut*). Bromberg, in turn, relies almost entirely on Landau's account in *Zikkaron Tov*. For Mordecai of Neshkhiz see EJ, Vol. 12, p. 315, and for Isaac of Neshkhiz see the brief reference in Levi Grossman, *Shem Sheerit*, Jerusalem, 1989, p. 65. Dubnow, *Toledot Ha-Hasidut*, Tel Aviv, 1967, p.385 refers to the *Zikkaron Tov* in his list of Hasidic legendary sources. Y. Raphael, *Sefer Ha-Hasidut*, Tel-Aviv, 1955, pp. 386–90 gives some of the teachings of Isaac of Neshkhiz from the other work of Landau, *Toledot Yitzhak*, Pietrikow, 1869. The *Zikkaron Tov* was published in Pietrikow in 1892. Both works have been republished in the series *Sefarim Kedoshim Mi-Talmidey Ha-Baal Shem Tov Ha-Kadosh*, Vol. 3, Brooklyn, New York, 1981.
3. *Zikkaron Tov*, Part 2, pp. 62–4 (Arabic numerals).
4. See, however, the interesting comment on p. 18 (No. 26) that Isaac of Neshkhiz reported that his father, Mordecai of Neshkhiz, attached no significance to the numerous tales of the Hasidic Masters since many of them are made up and contain many mistakes, except for the tales told of the Baal Shem Tov, which do have significance since even if the events related did not really happen such was the power of the Baal Shem Tov that he could perform miracles. Yet see Landau's remark on the same page (No. 26) that according to Isaac his father, Mordecai, revived the dead and Landau adds that he personally belonged to the families who were revived from the dead. On miracle tales in Hasidism see the Introduction to Sippurey Hasidim by S. Sevin, Tel Aviv, 1957, pp. 3–6; and Gedalyah Nigal, *Magic, Mysticism, and Hasidism: The Supernatural in Jewish Thought*, Northvale, New Jersey and London, 1994.
5. See Zohar II, 72b, on the character of a person derived from his face, 'A man whose eyes are evenly set is straightforward and free from guile.' But most of the other terms used by Landau (such as hair white as wool and the holy beard and nose) are taken from the 'facial' characteristics of 'The Holy Ancient One' in the *Sifra De-Tzeniuta* (Zohar II, 176b–179a); the *Idra Rabba* (Zohar III, 127b–145a); and the *Idra Zuta* (Zohar III, 287b–296b). Landau hints here that the Image of God is reflected in the form of the saint.
6. The meaning is probably that the saint stroked the left side of his beard as a symbol of his control over the sinister side so as to bestir the forces of mercy on high over the powers of judgment.
7. The meaning seems to be that the saint so tormented himself in order to pray that the conflagrations cease that this produced a miraculous sign of burning on his leg, unless it simply means that his leg was actually burnt during a fire.
8. The *pidyon* ('redemption') is the money given by the Hasidim to their Master that he should pray on their behalf.
9. Here the meaning may be that the saint actually burned himself in sympathy with those who suffered through the outbreak of fires.
10. When the ritual washing of the body took place.
11. The Etrog, taken on the festival of Sukkot, is described as 'the fruit of a beautiful tree' (Leviticus 23:40), hence the idiom.

12

Honour thy Father:
A Study in Hasidic Psychology

Avigdor ben Hayyim, Rabbi of Pinsk, the fiery opponent of Hasidism, drew up a list containing nineteen counts against the, to him, heretical sect for the consideration of the Russian authorities. (It is a sad fact that both sides in the eighteenth-century controversy between the Hasidim and Mitnaggedim brought their cause to the Russian government. As a matter of fact, the first to do this were the Hasidim.) Avigdor, involved in the struggle and under heavy attack by the Hasidim, sought to justify his stance to the Russian authorities by demonstrating that the Hasidim formed a subversive sect, a threat to ordered society.[1] Count 12 reads: 'They [the Hasidim] have no regard whatsoever for their parents. For, they argue, a father only brings his child into the world to satisfy his lust and there is consequently no obligation for a child to honour his father. The same applies to the mother except that some measure of respect is due to the mother by the child she suckled.'

Allowing for the bias of a highly prejudiced observer, it would be a mistake to dismiss out of hand the contention that the Hasidim treated parental authority lightly. Indeed, this was one of the charges the Hasidim hardly bothered to reject. Thus R. Shneur Zalman of Liady (1745–1813), the founder of the Habad version of Hasidism and Avigdor's protagonist, in a letter to a non-Hasidic Rabbi,[2] defends the right of his youthful followers to disobey their parents, who objected to the young men offering their prayers in the newly established Hasidic conventicles in which numerous changes had been introduced into the liturgy. Quoting earlier authorities in Jewish law,[3] R. Shneur Zalman declares that the duty of honouring parents, stated in the fifth commandment, does not include an obligation to obey their dictates. In point of fact, the authorities are somewhat divided on this question of obedience,[4]

and even those to which R. Shneur Zalman refers deal with the
more limited question of whether a son has to give up the woman
he wants to be his wife because his father objects to the match. But
it is significant that the Hasidim favoured that interpretation of the
law according to which the duty of honouring parents does not
include obedience to their wishes where this interferes with a son's
desire to follow his own religious path.

In this connection the story told of the Hasidic master R. Israel
of Ruzhyn (d. *c.* 1853) is very revealing.[5] It is said that many heads
of families in Berditchev tried to convice the Ruzyhner that it was
his clear duty to persuade the young men, who had left their wives
and families in order to become his disciples, to return home. The
Ruzhyner told them of a man in the days of the Ruzhyner's great-
grandfather, the Maggid of Mesirech (d. 1772), who had been compelled to divorce his young wife, at the instigation of the Rabbi of
the town and the wife's father, because the young disciple spent
too much time at the Maggid's court. Soon after, the heartbroken
young man died. When the Messiah comes, declared the
Ruzhyner, the young man, his father-in-law and the Rabbi of the
town will be called to judgment. The Messiah will present his decision. To the father-in-law he will say: 'You followed the ruling of
the Rabbi of the town and so you are justified.' But the Messiah
will then add: 'But I have come for those who are not justified.' It
is clear, in other words, that the Hasidic attitude involves a departure from normative Jewish law. But a revolutionary movement
cannot afford to abide by a rigid interpretation of the law when
this is invoked to read the movement out of existence.

At its inception, or at least from the time the movement grew
under the leadership of the Maggid of Mesirech, Hasidism was a
movement of insurrection. On the theological level, Hasidic
panentheism – the doctrine that all is in God – was highly unconventional. On the educational and social level, it challenged the
supremacy of the Talmudic scholars and the vested interests of the
powerful Kahal, the body of communal leaders. In such a movement the normal tensions between parents and children are cast in
relief, prominence being given to those features of the conflict that
remain dormant when both parents and children are bent on pre-
serving the status quo. Young men, inspired by the new and exciting ideas, would leave their parental homes for lengthy periods to
stay with their Hasidic master, and the journey itself was often
very expensive and time-consuming. The liturgy they adopted,

following the Kabbalah, was different from the established one, itself a potent source of contention in a milieu in which prayer and ritual contributed to the shaping of social as well as religious life. The young men would contribute generously to the Zaddik of their worldly goods set aside for the upkeep of their families by their parents and parents-in-law. In another of his counts against the Hasidim, Avigdor ben Hayyim says: 'They steal money from their fathers and mothers to give to their masters with the approval of the latter.' They would often be found advancing in public ideas, such as that the divine is found in all things, considered to be rank heresy by their staid elders. It even happened in the early days of the movement and, occasionally, even later, that parents of children who had gone over to Hasidism would observe the mourning rites over them as if they had died. The frequent comparison, in the anathema pronounced against the Hasidim, of the Hasid to one who beguiles others to idolatry,[6] was hardly conducive to an attitude of benevolent tolerance or avuncular condescension on the part of the older generation to the youthful enthusiasts, and the feelings of strong dislike must have been reciprocated. Scripture-reading Jews must have known that of the beguiler to idolatry it is said: 'Neither shall thine eye pity him, neither shalt thou spare him, neither shalt thou conceal him' even if he is 'thy brother, the son of thy mother, or thy son' (Deuteronomy 12:7–12).

It would not be difficult, of course, to adduce parallels to this type of conflict among other religious movements of reform and rebellion. One thinks of the 'Great Retirement' of the Buddha abandoning his wife Gopa as she slept and renouncing the delights of his father's palace; of Jesus: 'For I am come to set a man at variance with his father, and the daughter against her mother, and the daughter-in-law against her mother-in-law' (Matthew 10:35) and his 'Who is my mother and who are my brethren?' (Matthew 12:48); of Mohammed as a posthumous child who lost his mother when he was six years of age. On the Jewish scene there were the great upheavals caused by the sectarian groups in general and especially when the Shabbateans broke with traditional Judaism, whether or not, as the Mitnaggedim maintained, Hasidism sprang out of Shabbateanism. No man can succeed in the spiritual path, taught the Hasidic master R. Elimelech of Lizansk (1717–85), until he has rid himself of pride in his ancestry; hence Abraham was told to leave his father's house.[7]

The seeds of conflict between the generations are sown deeply in Hasidism. The legendary biography of the Baal Shem Tov, *Shivhey Ha-Besht*, depicts him as a child bereft of his parents at an early age.[8] Moreover, once the note of rebellion had been sounded, its effects were not confined to a revolt against the old order. A Hasidic tale[9] tells how the Maggid of Mesirech came, after his death, in a dream to his son, Abraham the 'Angel', to rebuke him for leading an ascetic life contrary to Hasidic teachings regarding worship through corporeality, on hearing which the 'Angel' disowned his father. 'I have only one father,' declared the 'Angel', 'my Father in Heaven.' The legend continues that, as a symbol of his severance with his earthly father, the coat of the 'Angel' he had inherited from the Maggid caught fire and was burned to a cinder. Of R. Baruch, father of R. Shneur Zalman, it is said that, unable to bear the honour paid to him by his distinguished son, he left his home town and wandered to Hungary, where he died without mentioning the names of his children.[10] Many of the early Hasidic masters who gave shape to the movement were late-comers to Hasidism, after it had been established; few were born into it. R. Jacob Joseph of Polonnoye (d. *c.* 1784), author of *Toledot Yaakov Yosef*, the first Hasidic book to be published, was, at first, a determined opponents of the Baal Shem Tov.[11]

In view of what has been said, it is not at all surprising that many traces of the conflict between the generations should be found in Hasidic literature. A phenomenon that has not received sufficient attention, for example, is the marked preference in this literature for the biblical father–son symbol, to describe the relationship between God and man,[12] rather than the erotic symbolism in earlier Jewish mysticism.[13] It is possible to account for the substitution on the grounds of the more prudish society in which the Hasidim moved as well as a reaction to the Frankist excesses, in the name of supposed mystical teaching, in the sphere of sexual morality.[14] There is no doubt truth in this connection, but it is not the whole truth. A careful examination of early Hasidic literature shows that the preference for the father–son symbol was due, in part at least, to a deeply felt need to atone for filial lapses and for Hasidic teachers to make their peace with the parents and teachers against whom they had rebelled. There is an almost obsessive preoccupation with the theme of God as the Father seeking His lost children, or, when the simile is varied, of God as Teacher correcting the immature comprehension of His disciples.

Examples abound in early Hasidic literature but, for the purpose, it suffices to refer to illustrations in the work of the Maggid of Mesirech, the great organizer of the Hasidic movement and its most influential mentor.[15]

The doctrine of *Tzimtzum* ('withdrawal' or 'concentration'), taught in the Lurianic Kabbalah, is adopted by the Maggid as a major theme in his philosophy, especially as the doctrine applies to man's inner life. The doctrine runs that the En Sof, the Ground of Being, 'withdrew from Himself into Himself' in order to leave an 'empty space' into which the universe and space and time as we know these could emerge. *Tzimtzum* is illustrated by the Maggid[16] on the analogy of a father who indulges in 'baby-talk' in his desire to find a point of contact and communication with his infant son. The father forces himself to love childish things that he might associate with his little boy as an equal. From the aspect of eternity, past, present and future are all one for God. God is beyond time. Consequently, when God 'saw' that the righteous in Israel were to be born, He withdrew into Himself and so controlled the divine love which, otherwise, would have gathered into itself all creatures, and they could not then have enjoyed an independent existence. As a father, contrary to his adult nature, voluntarily became childish in order to play with his little son, God, contrary to His infinite nature, brings the finite world into being by imposing limitations on Himself in order to take delight in the righteous.

The Maggid[17] offers a novel interpretation of 'Let us make man in our image' (Genesis 1:26). This means, according to the Maggid, that God had before Him, as it were, a picture of man as he would be when created. The biblical 'image of God' refers to the 'image' which God had of man before He created him. Now a human father whose son has left him will retain in his memory a picture of the child he loves. But a childless person can have no such picture in his memory. Since for God past, present and future are all one, it can be said of Him that He had a mental picture of how man would be even *before* He created man, in exactly the same way in which a human father retains in his memory the picture of a son who once lived with him.

The human deeds have cosmic significance is a basic idea in the Kabbalah. When man is virtuous he beings down from on high the flow of divine grace for the benefit of all creatures. When man sins he sends baneful impulses on high to produce an imbalance in the upper worlds and the flow of divine grace is impeded. In the

Maggid's view, it is only by divine pretence that man has the power to exert an influence on the cosmos. God, out of His love for him, endows his life with significance by giving him the illusion that he can exert cosmic influence. The Maggid[18] gives the illustration of a little boy who wishes to ride on a stick in make-believe that he is riding on a horse. The father cannot give his child a real horse who would not be entirely subject to the child's whim. On the other hand, the father has no wish to destroy the child's illusions because he wants the child to enjoy himself. The father acquiesces in the child's game by providing him with a stick which he can pretend is a real horse.

The Psalmist's injunction: 'Exalt ye the Lord' (Psalms 99:5) is explained as follows by the Maggid.[19] In order for a father to find some point of contact with his infant child who has not yet learned to talk, he is himself obliged to behave like a baby who cannot talk, performing actions and making undignified gestures totally ridiculous for a normal grown-up. Once the infant is able to talk the father can communicate with him in some measure through speech, but only at a level suitable for a child. He can talk to him, but only of childish things which in themselves have no appeal to the father. Once the son has grown to full manhood the father is able to converse with him as adults do, and he has no need to lower his dignity through his love for his child. God, in His great love, converses with man, no matter how lowly man's spiritual state. God imposes limits on himself, so to speak, in order to converse with man at the state at which he finds him. But the greater man's advance in spirituality, the nearer he is to God, and there is less need for God's self-limitation. Thus man's spiritual advance enables God to be Himself, as it were, and there is no longer such need for God to 'lower' Himself, hence the Psalmist's call for man to exalt God.

The verse 'And I, I taught Ephraim to walk, taking them by their arms' (Hosea 11:3) is given a bold anthropomorphic interpretation by the Maggid.[20] When a father lifts up his infant son in his arms the child is able to play with the father's beard. Similarly, God endows man with the love and fear of Him that are the arms which enable man to reach Godwards. Once man is near to God, when he is near to God's arms, he is able to draw down God's mercies and compassion into the words. Since God needs these not for Himself but for the world, they are symbolized by the beard extraneous to the person.

The Maggid[21] offers an explanation of why, according to one Rabbinic opinion, the penitent sinner is greater than one who has never sinned. The Maggid's illustration, resembling that of the Prodigal Son, is of a son who lost his way but found it again. The father rejoices over him far more than he does over the son who has never lost his way. For the latter has never known the thrill of being rescued from danger, whereas the son whose life was at risk rejoices all the more when he is rescued, and the father's joy, too, is increased by the greater joy of his rescued son. God rejoices over the sinner who returns to Him, for His joy is increased by the joy the sinner experiences at being saved from sin.

The Maggi teaches[22] that man can offer his praises of God whenever he is so moved, whereas the angels can praise him only at allotted times. A king's courtiers have specific times allotted to them when they are allowed to enter the king's presence. When the courtiers sense during their audience that the king is in a state of displeasure they will cut short their visit and remain in his presence for as little time as possible. Not so when the king's beloved son appears before the royal throne. Since the king loves his son, the son can stay for as long as he wishes even when the king is in a state of displeasure.

The great error of the ancient idolaters, remarks the Maggid,[23] was to imagine that God is so far beyond this world of error and evil that it is an affront to His dignity to pay homage to Him, rather than to lesser beings, for having created such a world. Yet Scripture commands that parents be honoured, even though, it might have been argued, all the indignities of human existence are the result of character defects and lack of ability that humans inherit from their parents. The command to 'honour' parents is to see dignity even where there is no dignity. Indeed, this is man's dignity that he has to struggle with the obstacles put in his way by his heredity and rise above them. In the same way, God's glory is to be seen in the created world for those who have eyes to see.

In the works of the Maggid there are references time and again to parables drawn from the relationship, often a tortured one, between father and son,[24] and it is by no means difficult to find such illustrations in the works of the Maggid's disciples and in early Hasidic literature in general. R. Shneur Zalman, for instance, comments[25] on the verse: 'Ye are the children of the Lord your God' (Deuteronomy 14:1) that the 'Jewish' soul[26] derives ultimately from God's wisdom. The semen of a human father, he observes, is drawn through his brain (according to the medical knowledge of R. Shneur Zalman's day). Although the semen undergoes many changes until it is formed as an embryo in the mother's womb, it still derives from the father's brain, and this applies even to the nails of the child. On this analogy it can be said that even the soul of the lowliest Jew is derived ultimately from the Supernal Wisdom.

Discussing the role of melancholy in the religious life, R. Schneur Zalman remarks[27] that a distinction has to be made between 'sadness', which is religiously harmful, and 'bitterness', which is beneficial. Sadness is evidence of a lack of spiritual vitality. It questions whether the life of religion is at all worthwhile. But bitterness at the soul's remoteness from God provides spiritual energy, since a Jew cannot truly rejoice in the Lord unless he appreciates that his 'divine soul' is imprisoned in the body and thus distant from her source in God. Through the grief that results from this awareness the soul reaches out to her source in God. The illustration given is of a prince who is freed, after long incarceration in a loathsome dungeon, to be brought into the presence of his father, the king.

The pervasiveness in early Hasidic literature of the father–son illustration is best explained on the grounds that the early Hasidic masters were moved, consciously or unconsciously, by strong guilt feelings regarding filial piety, inseparable from a movement of rebellion. Such feelings wedded to a mystical type of thinking gave a powerful thrust to the generation of thoughts in which the theme of reconciliation between father and son is elevated into a cosmic principle.

The fruits of this attitude are to be found in not a few manifestations of later Hasidic life. Among these mention should be made of the exaggerated deference to parents and teachers which made Hasidism, with few exceptions, a reactionary movement in many areas of Jewish life. The reaction against an earlier orthodoxy that was Hasidism became, in turn, an orthodoxy of its own. (Hasidic literature and life abound in such expressions as: 'My saintly father, of blessed memory, said'; 'My holy grandfather said'; 'It is the Hasidic custom'.) And although we are on highly speculative ground here, might it not be that the cult of the Zaddik, the Hasidic saint, whatever other factors may have been at work in its formation, owes something, in its later development, to the need for a well-nigh infallible father-figure of authority to compensate for the rejection of the older authority? Certainly, it is far from improbable that the idea of Hasidic dynasties, in which authority is automatically inherited by the son of the Zaddik and in which every grandsom (*einikel*) of a Zaddik enjoys the esteem of the masses, owes much to the oft-repeated idea that the father–son relationship mirrors forth ultimate reality. One thinks in this connection of the exquisitely tender prayers of R. Levi Yitzhak of Berditchev (1740–1809), who spoke to God as a child speaks to the father who loves him tenderly. To this day, it is not unusual for Hasidim to cry out in their prayers: '*Tatter Sisser'* ('Sweet Father').

It has been said that if Darwin had not been a problem child we would not have had *The Origin of Species*. Applying this saying, we might observe with justice that if the parent–child conflict had not touched the very heart of Hasidism in its formative period, the whole course of the movement might have been, for better or for worse, very different.

NOTES

1. The Avigdor affair is treated in well-documented detail in Mordecai Wilensky, *Hasidism U-Mitnaggedim*, Jerusalem, 1970, Vol. 1, pp. 230–95. For the list of Avigdor's counts against the Hasidim see S. Dubnow, *Toledot Ha-Hasidut*, Tel Aviv, 1967, pp. 270-3; M. Teitelbaum, *Ha-Rav Mi-Ladi*, Warsaw, 1910, pp. 106–11; D. Z. Hillman, *Iggerot Baal-Ha-Tanya U-Veney Doro*, Jerusalem, 1953, pp. 142–5; and Wilensky, *Hassidim U-Mitnageddim*, pp. 273–7. Avigdor wrote his attack in Hebrew, from which it was translated into Russian for the benefit of the Russian authorities.
2. Hillman, *Iggerot*, pp. 48–9.
3. R. Joseph Colon, Responsa *Maharik, shoresh* 167 and Isseries, *Yoreh Deah*, 240:25.
4. See Gerald Blidstein. *Honour Thy Father and Mother: Filial Responsibility in Jewish Law and Ethics*, New York, 1975, Chapter IV, 'Responsibility and Conflict', pp. 75–136.
5. M. Buber, *Tales of the Hasidim*, Vols 1 and 2, New York, 1947–8, in Vol. 2, *The Later Masters*, p. 57. Buber does not give his source for this tale and it is not in the collection: *Ner Yisreal*, ed. Dov Stern, Bene Berak, 1987, on the Ruzhyner. But see Stern Vol. 2, p. 150, in the name of Duber of Leboi, son of the Ruzhyner, who for a time, left Hasidism and the traditions of his father, that Gentiles honour their parents more than do Jews their parents, the reason being that Jewish life involves a desperate struggle against temptation. Jews cannot be entirely grateful to their parents for bringing them into this world of struggle. As the Rabbis say (Eruvin 13b), it were better for man not to have been created than to have been created.
6. See e.g. the proclamation in Vilna in the year 1781, Wilensky, *Hasidim U-Mitnaggedim*, pp. 106–9, in which the Hasidim are said to belong to a sect of 'beguilers and enticers' and frequently in the anathema published in Wilensky.
7. Commentary to Genesis 12:1, *Noam Elimelekh, lekh lekha*, ed. G. Nigal, Jerusalem, pp. 23–4, and see *Noam Elimelekh, to va-yeshev*, ed. Nigal, p. 73 for the idea that Gentiles honour their parents more than Jews do theirs. Cf. the story told of the Maggid of Mesirech in A. Kahana, *Sefer Ha-Hasidut*, Warsaw, 1922, p. 143. When the Maggid was still a child his parents' home was burned to the ground. His mother wept bitterly not so much at the loss of her home but over the loss of the family tree in which their descent was traced back to King David. The child consoled his mother saying: 'I shall start a new lineage.'

8. *Shivhey Ha-Besht*, ed. S. A. Horodetsky, Tel Aviv, 1960, English translation: 'In Praise of the Baal Shem Tov', ed. Dan Ben-Amos and Jerome R. Mintz, Bloomington, Indiana and London, 1960.
9. Buber, *Tales*, Vol. 1, p. 115.
10. Hillman, *Iggerot*, p. 1, note 1.
11. See A. Kahana, *Sefer Ha-Hasidut*, p. 103 and Samuel H. Dresner, *The Zaddik*, London, New York and Toronto, 1970, pp. 37–44. Among other early masters who came later to Hasidism are the Maggid of Mesirech, R. Pinhas of Koretz, R. Yehiel Michal of Zlotchov, R. Shneur Zalman of Liady, R. Elimelech of Lizensk and R. Levi Yitzhak of Berditchev, all of them becoming leading figures in the movement.
12. For the father symbol in the Bible see Deuteronomy 14:1: 'Ye are the children of the Lord your God' (although there is no direct reference to God as Father in the Pentateuch); Malachi 1:6; Isaiah 63:16; 64:7; Psalms 103:13 and see 27:10. For this symbolism in the Mishnah see *Rosh Ha-Shanah* 3:8; *Sotah* 9:15; *Avot* 3:14.
13. Although Gershom Scholem, *Major Trends in Jewish Mysticism*, London, 1955, pp. 226–7 observes that erotic symbolism is used generally in the Zohar only for the relationships between the Sefirot, except with regard to Moses, who 'had intercourse with the Shekhinah', 1. Tishby, *Mishnat Ha-Zohar*, Jerusalem, 1957, Vol. 2, pp. 280–301 has shown that there are passages in the Zohar in which erotic symbolism is used for the relationship between God and other human beings apart from Moses. The later Kabbalists, such as Cordovero, interpret the Song of Songs as a Cordovero God and the individual soul. Cf. Elihah de Vidas, *Reshit Hokhmah Ha-Shalem*, ed. J. Waldman, Jerusalem, 1980; *Shaar Ha-Ahavah*, Chapter 4, pp. 408–26, especially the story, p. 426, told by Isaac of Acre about the lover of the princess who became a hermit. Cf. my *Hasidic Prayer*, paperback edn, Littman Library of Jewish Civilization, London and Washington, 1993, pp. 60–1, where this question of erotic symbolism in Hasidism is discussed. See p. 60 for the passage from *Tzavaat Ha-Ribash*, Jerusalem, 1948; p. 7b in which it is stated that the Baal Shem Tov compared swaying in prayer in the presence of the Shekhinah to the motions of physical union between man and wife. But this does not contradict the thesis of substitution since such passages are extremely rare in Hasidism. In his anthology of Hasidic texts entitled *Derekh Hasidism* (Jerusalem, 1962, no. 42, p. 411), Hahman of Tcherin gives only a bowdlerized version of this saying. Joseph Perl's satire of Hasidism, *Megalle Temirin*, Vienna, 1819, gives (no. 75, p. 29b, note 7) a list of obscene passages he claims to have discovered between God and man. Such few references are scanty compared with the parent–child relationship.
14. See Scholem, *Major Trends*, pp. 217f.
15. The works of the Maggid quoted here are: *Maggid Devarav Le-Yaakov*, ed. Rivka Schatz-Uffenheimer, Jerusalem, 1976 (abbreviated MDL) and *Or Torah*, ed. Brooklyn, New York, 1980 (abbreviated OT).
16. MDL, no. 1, pp. 9–13.
17. OT, pp. 2b–3a.
18. To Psalms 103:3, MDL, no. 7, p. 21; OT, section on Psalms, pp. 71b–72a.
19. OT, section on Psalms, p. 72a.
20. MDL, no. 37, p. 56. This saying of the Maggid is based on the Zohar III, 131a, regarding the Sefirot and the 'Beard' of the 'Holy Ancient One'.
21. MDL, no. 119, pp. 193–5, section on Amos, 9:11, pp. 90b–91a.
22. OT, first comment in Psalms section, pp. 65a–67a.
23. MDL, no. 87, pp. 150–3; OT, *Yitro*, pp. 34a–b.
24. Rivka Schatz-Uffenheimer in her edition of MDL (Index *s.v. mishlev av*) gives a complete list of all the Maggid's parables based on the father–son relationship.
25. *Tanya*, Chapter 2, ed. Vilna, 1930, pp. 61–7a.
26. R. Shneur Zalman deals here with the 'divine soul', the divine spark in the soul, which, he holds, is possessed only by Jews. See my article 'The Doctrine of the "Divine Spark" in Man in Jewish Sources', in *Studies in Rationalism, Judaism and Universalism in Memory of Leon Roth*, ed. Raphael Loewe, London and New York, 1966, pp. 87–114.
27. *Tanya*, Chapter 3, pp. 39b–41a and see Chapter 45, pp. 64a–b.

13

Eating as an Act of Worship in Hasidism

Three differing attitudes have obtained among religious people towards the gratification of the physical appetites where their indulgence involves no breach of the religious law. These may be called the ascetic, the puritanical, and that of thankful acceptance. The first considers abstinence to be a virtue. On this showing body and soul are in permanent conflict, so that to indulge one is to frustrate the growth of the other. The ideal is for humans to reduce their physical needs to the bare minimum required for existence. The state of holiness is attained by means of fasting and a general mortification of the flesh. The puritan attitude, on the other hand, is not necessarily ascetic. It can be fully aware of the physical and spiritual perils that may easily result from ascetic exercises – ill-health, morbidity, rebellion, masochism, pride and lack of charity. But it is as uncompromising as asceticism in rejecting any enjoyment of the physical as an end in itself. Macaulay was unfair to the Puritans when he accused them of objecting to bear-baiting not because it gave pain to the bear but because it gave pleasure to the spectators. After all, pleasure at the spectacle of animal suffering is an ugly emotion. But it seems to be true that the puritan mind considers pleasure to be somehow unworthy. The physical appetites, it seems to hold, were implanted by the Creator in order to guarantee the survival of the human species, but they are more in the nature of a necessary evil than a positive good or, in any event, are good only because they can serve higher things. The third attitude sees the physical appetites as a gift of the Creator. In this view physical pleasure is not the highest pursuit of humans but neither is it shameful or sinful or of value only as a means to an end.

Each of these attitudes has had its Jewish adherents. While there are undoubtedly to be found ascetic views among the

Talmudic Rabbis,[1] the prevailing view in the Rabbinic literature, if one can speak of such a thing as a prevailing view, is that of thankful acceptance.[2] The enjoyment of the Sabbaths and Festivals, involving as it does eating as a religious obligation,[3] and the numerous benedictions in which thanks are given to God for food and drink,[4] all indicate a frank, at times joyous acceptance of physical pleasure as a divine gift to man. The ascetic attitude is to be found among some of the medieval Jewish philosophers (notably Saadiah[5] and Maimonides[6] with regard to sex), the Hasidey Ashkenaz,[7] and the Lurianic Kabbalah.[8] Puritanism is the attitude of many of the medieval Jewish moralists.[9]

Which is the attitude adopted by Hasidism? With few exceptions it is not ascetic. Indeed, the movement arose partly in opposition to Lurianic asceticism.[10] Nor, as Buber would evidently have it,[11] is the attitude of Hasidism that of thankful acceptance. As we shall try to demonstrate, Hasidism is puritanical in essence but with certain subtle ideas of its own. We are concerned, however, not with the more general question of how Hasidism views physical pleasure but with the Hasidic idea of eating as an act of worship. That the Hasidic masters themselves thought this worthy of treatment as a separate and most important theme[12] is justification enough for us to do so.

Basically, the Hasidic view is a development of the Lurianic doctrine of the 'holy sparks'. As En Sof (the Limitless), the Infinite Source of all being, emerges from concealment to become manifest in the finite universe, its infinite light has to become progressively coarsened so that the abyss between the infinite and the finite may be crossed. In the process the original light is slit up into 'lights' (*orot*) and 'vessels' (*kelim*) in which the 'lights' are to be contained. But at one stage of the process the 'lights' become too powerful for the 'vessels' to contain them, with the result that there takes place 'the shattering of the vessels' (*shevirat ha-kelimj*). These 'vessels' are later reconstituted in a form that enables them to contain the 'lights'. Yet the 'shattering of the vessels' causes some of the light to be spilled over so as to provide cosmic energy. The overspill from each world provides the divine force required to sustain the world immediately beneath it, until, eventually, this finite world emerges. Even here there is an overspill, and this provides the energy to sustain the existence of the *kelipot* (the 'shells'), the demonic aspect of being. Thus in all things there are 'holy sparks' of the divine light; the task of humans being to elevate these by using the things of the world in a spirit of purity and as a means of serving God. In the Lurianic system all this is spelled out in intricate detail.[13] While the Hasidic masters undoubtedly believed in the Lurianic Kabbalah as revealed truth, their main interest was far less in its theoretical aspects than in the motivation it provided for inwardness in their religious life.

Another Lurianic idea, used by the Hasidic masters, is that the letters of the Hebrew alphabet are not mere symbols, but the manifestation on earth of the various spiritual realities involved in the divine creative processes. According to this 'Neo-Platonic' idea, God actually 'said', for example, 'let there be light', in the sense that He combined the letters *alef, vav, resh* in their spiritual form on high, to produce the word *or*, 'light'. Light continues to enjoy existence; these potencies continue to be combined by the divine fiat. Every kind of food, to give another illustration, exists as it does because of this kind of divine combination of letters, those of that particular food, and when a man eats that food, he assimilates the energy it provides. Ideally, then, his mind should be directed to this divine force rather than be on the physical pleasure that he receives from the food itself.

Long before the rise of Hasidism the Kabbalists had described the eating of food in a spirit of purity as an act of divine worship. Isaiah Horowitz (d. 1630), in his gigantic compendium of religious thought and practices, *Sheney luhot ha-berit* (the *Shelah*), writes:[14]

> Eating involves both the general and the particular. By this I mean that although it is carried out with the aid of particular organs of the body, namely, the mouth and the gullet, yet in general it sustains the whole body. Similarly, with regard to the act of copulation, although it depends on that particular organ at the body's extremity, yet, since it is the cause of the birth of the child, it is a general cause. In my youth I studied the Torah at the feet of the great Rabbi, the illustrious and distinguished saint, our master Rabbi Solomon [Leibush of Cracow] of blessed memory. When I took leave of him to get married I said to him: 'Rabbi, give me your blessing and advise me how to conduct myself.' He replied in these words: 'Sanctify yourself in these two matters, in food and in copulation, and be exceedingly careful to keep at a distance of a thousand cubits from having to do with the illicit and be exceedingly strict in sanctifying them. For all the other precepts of the Torah make no physical impression. But with regard to these two, food sustains the body and copulation brings the body into existence so that there is a lasting impression.' Thus spake the holy mouth, may his memory be for a blessing for the world to come.

A verse quoted frequently in Hasidic literature to convey this idea of eating as an act of worship is: 'and they saw God and they ate and drank' (Exodus 24:12). This application of the verse goes back in the first instance to Elijah of Smyrna (d. 1729) in his *Midrash Talpiyyot*,[15] who quotes it from the thirteenth-century teacher Bahya Ibn Asher.[16]

> When a man needs to eat he should free his mind from other thoughts so that it can soar aloft to think of God while each mouthful is being swallowed. As Scripture says: 'And they saw God and they ate and drank' – this resembles the exposition of the rabbis[17] of blessed memory on the verse 'Let everything that hath breath praise the Lord' [Psalms 150:6] – 'For every breath give praise to Him'. In this way man's eating is counted as true eating, like one of the acts of divine service in the Temple or like the performance of one of the religious precepts. This is the main intention of a meal at table, the body being nourished, obtaining its bodily share from the physical act of eating, while the soul is sated, fattened and satisfied by means of this intention. The positive act of eating in this fashion is like fatness in the ways of the Lord and their pleasantness. It is in this connection that Scripture says: 'And that which is set on thy table is full of fatness' [Job 16:16].

In the same passage this author continues: 'Man's thoughts when he eats should be attached to God more than at any other time. The source of this idea is to be found in the verse: "And they saw God and they ate and they drank", which means, they had the intention of seeing the Glory in their hearts while they were eating and drinking.'

In the writings of the early Hasidic masters this idea of having holy thoughts while eating is repeatedly stressed. R. Jacob Joseph of Polonnoye observes[18] that for this reason it is preferable to eat in private rather than with a company at table, because only then can there be achieved adequate concentration on the divine without distractions. The same author speaks of two kinds of *tzaddikim*, those who eat frugally and those who enjoy good food and drink. The task of the latter is much more difficult since the more enjoyable the meal the greater the effort required in order to concentrate on God without succumbing to the blandishments of the physical appetite that has been aroused.[19] R. Jacob Joseph[20] remarks that there are two kinds of intention while eating. The simple intention is to eat in order to have strength for God's service. But the higher and more difficult intention is to elevate the 'holy sparks' and raise in thought all the spiritual forces residing in the food, all in accordance with the Kabbalistic mysteries. That is why God makes man experience hunger and thirst. The desire for food and drink is an inducement to man to eat and drink so that he may elevate the 'holy sparks' in that which he imbibes and digests. The spiritual aspect is concealed by the physical pleasure just as an honest woman whose face is veiled may be mistaken for a harlot; but the Zaddik knows how to see the reality and his thoughts are exclusively on the 'holy sparks' to be elevated.[21]

This theme is taken up by the grandson of the Baal Shem Tov, R. Moses Hayyim Ephraim of Sudlikov, in his *Degel Mahaney Efrayim:*[22] 'When the Zaddik eats, his sole intention is to sate his soul with the spiritual aspect of the food so that he may attach himself to the service of God. So it is with regard to all the material things in which he is engaged. He does not attach himself to the material side of that thing, but to its inward nature, the secret of God's portion within it. That is why there are to be found *tzaddikim* whose very body is pure.'

A number of Hasidic authors develop the thought that this spiritual aspect of food is to be detected in its taste.[23] The tastiness of food is a very pale reflection, in this material world, of those spiritual forces that are responsible for the existence of the food. Man should allow his mind to move on from his awareness of the physical pleasure of taste to the source of taste in the divine realm.

A comprehensive account of the whole theory is to be found in R. Nahum of Chernobyl's *Meor Enayim.*[24] The world was created by God's word and it is this that keeps it in being. In every thing there is a 'holy spark' that sustains it. It is these 'sparks' that become united with man's essential being when he eats, to provide him with energy and vitality. This 'spark' is spiritual food because the divine nature is therein contained but covered as though by a garment. When he eats, man should have this thought in mind and he should use in God's service the fresh energy and vitality imparted to him by the 'holy spark' once it has been assimilated. By so doing he unites the 'spark' to its source in God and releases it from its exile. The whole task of man is to rescue the 'holy sparks' from their captivity among the *kelipot*. All this is effected by the benediction recited over the food and the use of the fresh energy in God's service. Fasting is sinful,[25] because it is a refusal by man to engage in the task allotted to him. The Nazirite who denies himself wine sins against the soul[26] in that he declines to see the soul aspect of the wine. The Baal Shem Tov is quoted as observing that even a Gentile can release the 'holy sparks' when he eats and then uses the fresh energy he has acquired in order to help a Jew(!) who will then, in turn, serve God. But the Gentile himself is incapable of achieving the degree of elevation achieved by the Jew who eats his food with special intention. But what of of that other saying of the Rabbis[27] that one who fasts is a holy man? This is perfectly true, but only a very few can serve God in this way. The easier way is to know God while enjoying food and drink. In this latter observation we have all the tensions between the more ascetic tendencies in earlier Jewish thought and the new way the Hasidic masters sought to encourage.

R. Levi Yitzhak of Berditchev deals with the theme in his work, very popular among the Hasidim, *Kedushat Levi*.[28] He likewise makes the distinction[29] between eating in order to have strength to serve God and having holy thoughts while eating. The former is also considered to be a form of divine worship, although, in reality, it is only a preparation for such. The second is an act of divine worship in itself. The Rabbinic references to the great feast for the righteous in the world to come are to be understood both literally and metaphorically. Simple folk cannot be expected to have holy thoughts and for them the meal in the hereafter will be a real meal consisting of the choicest foods and the finest wines. But the *tzaddikim*, who even in this life find their delight not in the food itself but in their holy thoughts while eating, will be rewarded with a feast consisting of the divine mysteries, which their souls will then be able to comprehend without let or hindrance.[30] R. Levi Yitzhak, too, makes the distinction between one who eats frugal meals and one who enjoys good food. True, it is more difficult to have holy thoughts in the latter instance, but the reward is greater. The former is called 'bread without battle', the latter 'bread with battle', constant struggle being the price one has to pay if the mind is to dwell on the divine without becoming distracted by the tasty dishes.[31] The Torah permits the clean animal and birds to be eaten so that the 'holy sparks' they contain may be elevated. The 'holy sparks' which inhere in the unclean animals and birds can also be elevated, but this is achieved not by direct assimilation, forbidden by the Torah, but by their rejection, i.e. by observance of the dietary laws. By abstaining from forbidden food the Jew elevates the 'holy sparks' in that food.[32]

These basic ideas are found in similar form in the reports regarding the teachings of the Maggid of Mesirech,[33] who is said to have made the distinction between the simple intention of eating in order to serve God and having holy thoughts at the time of eating. The Maggid quotes the verse: 'And they saw God' but adds that the word *et*, the sign of the direct object, represents the first and last letters of the alphabet – *alef* and *tav* – and hence the whole alphabet. The letters of the Hebrew alphabet are the spiritual forces inherent in all things; they are the 'holy sparks'. The Zaddik 'sees God' when he eats; that is to say, his mind dwells constantly on the letters which are the ever-sustaining power of God in the food that he eats.[34] Moreover, by later using the fresh energy that he has acquired to speak words of Torah and prayer, the Zaddik rescues God's word and restores it to Him. The word of God creates the food and is, as it were, in the food, ready to be rescued. When the food is consumed and man utters a holy word through the power given to him by the food he has eaten, it becomes the word once again and the task of rescuing the 'holy sparks' is continued. The Zaddik serves God even when he goes to the privy, because there he expels the waste which the body cannot assimilate, and he thus repeats on earth the cosmic process in which that which can be used for the holy is so used, while the residue nourishes the *kelipot*. The Maggid, too, refers to the taste of food as a faint reflection of the spiritual forces on high. He adds that the different tastes that man experiences when he eats represent the various spiritual combinations of the supernal powers. Thus, for example, sweet foods derive ultimately from *Hesed* ('lovingkindness'), while sour food derives from *Gevurah*, God's sternness and judgment.

R. Menahem Mendel of Vitebsk[35] adds a further nuance. Man embraces in his being the whole of creation since, according to the Kabbalah, he is mirrored after the divine image and pattern. This is why the Kabbalah speaks of the source of all things as *Adam Kadmon*, Primordial Man. It follows that in his 'animal soul', i.e. the physical side of his nature, he something that pertains not alone to the clean beasts but also to the unclean ones. If man allows his animal soul to gain the mastery over him when he eats, so that his intention is solely for his own pleasure and he has no holy thoughts, he then as it were converts the food he eats into that which pertains to the animal, and this includes the unclean animals. Such a man is not allowed to eat meat and must be a vegetarian. The sole purpose for which the Torah permits meat to be eaten is for the 'holy sparks' in the meat to be elevated. But the gross person, far from elevating the 'holy sparks' in the meat he eats, drags them down, converting, in fact, the meat of the clean animal into that which pertains to the realm of the unclean.

The central idea in all these Hasidic teachings is that of worship not only when praying or studying the Torah but even when enjoying food and drink. It is a moot point whether the early masters would have agreed with a much later master[36] that to eat in a spirit of purity and with holy thoughts is greater than prayer. But they all seem to agree with the sentiment expressed by R. Hayyim Haikel of Amdur[37] who quotes the verse:' How fair and how pleasant is love in delights' (Song of Songs 7:7) to yield the thought that love of God is especially fair and pleasant when it is expressed while enjoying physical delights.

Some of the descriptions in Hasidic literature of the doctrine we are considering are, it must be admitted, occult in nature, with the mythological elements strongly pronounced. Occasionally, the doctrine is described in almost totemistic terms, suggesting a kind of eating of the divine by man. Adapting a Scriptural verse for the purpose (Deuteronomy 2:28) the Maggid is said to have noted that the desire for food can be 'broken' for the love of God by abstaining from food one is enjoying in the middle of a meal. But his disciple, Issachar Dov of Zlotchov, remarks that this is only for the majority of folks. There can be found one who has been a Zaddik from his youth or one who has reached the highest rank in repenting of his sins; such a one can eat without hindrance because all his thoughts are on the divine inherent in the food he eats. The Hebrew word for food, referred to in the verse, is *okhel*, and this, spelled *plene*, has the same numerical value (77) as the two divine names, the Tetragrammaton (26) + *El* (51). Consequently, the thought that he is eating so much holiness that it represents two divine names is sufficient to enable such a Zaddik to break his desire for the food itself without him having to stop in the middle of a meal as a lesser person is required to do.[38] There are references in Hasidic literature to the notion that a wandering soul may have been condemned for its sins to become exiled in food. There it must remain until a good man eats in a spirit of holiness the food that is the soul's prison in order to bring about that soul's rectification (*tikkun*). This is why eating at table without saying words of Torah is compared by the rabbis (*Avot* 3:3) to eating 'sacrifices of the dead'. The dead soul is 'eaten' without finding its *tikkun*.[39]

A more 'rationalistic' and more realistic view of the whole doctrine is given by R. Shneur Zalman of Liady.[40] The word for 'read', *lehem*. is associated with the word for 'war', *milhamah*. At every meal battle is enjoined between the holy and the unholy. R. Shneur Zalman explains it in this way:

> We see that when a man eats in order to satisfy his greed for food and to fill his belly, he becomes exceedingly coarse, so that he falls from the state of worship in holiness until he becomes really animal-like in gross insensitivity and the indulgence of the strange desires of the animal soul ... But if man eats in order to become strong for the service of God and does not have in mind so much his own pleasure ... then the food he eats in this manner strengthens his mind, his power of discernment, and his heart, to the extent that when he later contemplates the unity of God, and when he offers his prayers and studies the Torah, all his concentration in depth is due to the food he has eaten ... so that the evil in the food is converted into good.

Another Hasidic author[41] acknowledges that man is incapable of fathoming the mystery of the elevation of the 'holy sparks', yet he should eat, nevertheless, with the thought in mind, just as a faithful servant of the king will deliver a letter as instructed by his sovereign even though he is ignorant of the contents.

Associated in Hasidism with the doctrine of eating as an act of divine worship is the sacred meal[42] in which, especially on the Sabbath and the Festivals, and with particular emphasis on the third Sabbath meal, when the Hasidim sit at the table ('*tish*') of the Zaddik. The Zaddik, who is alone capable of having the proper holy intentions, tastes a little of each dish, the remainder (*shirayim*) being distributed among the Hasidim. In this way the Zaddik assists his followers in their much weaker efforts at elevating the 'holy sparks'. Moreover, the Zaddik gives a Hasidic discourse on the portion of the Torah read at the time. The Torah of the Zaddik further consecrates the meal. Most of the classical Hasidic texts are based on the *torah* originally delivered by the Zaddik at the sacred meal.

NOTES

1. See e.g. *Avot* 6:4; *Berakhot* 63b; *Hagigah* 5b; *Nedarim* 20b.
2. See JT *Kiddushin* 4:12 (66b).
3. *Oneg shabbat* and *simhat yom tov*. For the details see *Shabbat* 118a–119b and *Betzah* 15b.
4. See especially the whole of the sixth chapter of tractate *Berakhot* in the Jerusalem and Babylonian Talmud.
5. *Emunot ve-deot*, Book 10, Chapter 6.

6. *Guide* II, 36 and III, 49.
7. For example in the *Sefer Hasidim* and the *Rokeah*; see J. Dan, *The Esoteric Theology of Ashkenazi Hasidism* (Hebrew), Jerusalem, 1986.
8. See e.g. Schechter's essay on Safed in his *Studies in Judaism*, Second Series, Philadelphia, 1945, pp. 202–306.
9. For example in Bahya Ibn Pakudah's *Hovot Ha-Levavot, Shaar Ha-Perishut*; M.H. Luzzatto's *Mesillat Yesharim*, Chapters 13–15; Jonah of Gerona's Commentary to *Avot* 2:10; *Tur, Orah Hayyim*, para. 231.
10. See *Sefer Baal Shem Tov*, Sotmar, 1943, Vol. 2, to *mishpatim*, end, pp. 68–70, especially the quotation from R. Baruch, grandson of the Baal Shem Tov (*Botzina de-Nehora*, p. 17) that the Baal Shem Tov introduced a new way, without mortification of the flesh, in which the three essentials are love of God, love of Israel and love of the Torah. Cf. the sources quoted here on the danger of the ascetic life. For all that, ascetic tendencies are to be observed among some of the Hasidic masters such as Elimelech of Lizansk and Nahman of Bratzlav. The latter (*Likkutey Moharan*, no. 47) speaks especially of breaking the desire for food, i.e. by eating frugally, though he also speaks of the Zaddik eating well but for the sake of Heaven. Cf. no. 39 for both food and sex. Even some of the more recent masters have been ascetics, for instance, R. Aaron Rokeah of Belz (d. 1957), who is reported to have defended his ascetic life by declaring that one who serves God through eating does so only during his meals, but one who serves God by fasting does so all the time; see B. Landau and N. Urtner, *Ha-Rav Ha-Kadosh mi-Belza*, Jerusalem, 1867, p. 18.
11. Scholem's critique of Buber in this connection is very well founded; see his essay 'Martin Buber's Interpretation of Hasidism' in *The Messianic Idea in Judaism*, New York, 1971, pp. 227–50 and R. Schatz-Uffenheimer:' Man's Relation to God and the World in Buber's Rendering of the Hasidic Teaching', in *The Philosophy of Martin Buber*, ed. Schilpp and Friedman, La Salle, 1967, pp. 403–34.
12. See *Leshon Hasidim* by Nahman of Tcherin, Lemberg, 1876, new ed. Bene Berak, n.d., *s.v. akhilah*, pp. 18–19; the same author's *Derekh Hasidim*, Lemberg 1876, new edn. Jerusalem, 1962, *s.v. akhilah*, pp. 27–34; *Kunteros et ha-okhel* in *Peri Tzaddik* by Zadok Ha-Kohen of Lublin, Lublin, 1901, new edn. Israel, pp. 235–40; R. Aaron Roth, *Shulhan ha-tahor*, Jerusalem, 1966 (a huge book devoted entirely to this theme).
13. For a good account of the basic Lurianic doctrine see I. Tishby, *Torat ha-ra ve-ha-kelipah be-kabbalat ha-ari*, Jerusalem, 1965.
14. *Shaar ha-otiot, s.v. kedushah, be-feh u-ve-veshet*, f. 53b.
15. ed. Warsaw. 1875, *s.v. akhilah*, ff. 50b–51a.
16. *Shulhan shel arba* in Bahya's writings, ed. B. Chavel, Jerusalem, 1969, pp. 496–7. The source of the quotation of Exodus 24:12 in this connection is *Avot de-rabbi natan* I, 1 of the righteous in Paradise but there the meaning is not that of seeing God while eating but of being sustained by the beatific vision. Cf. Onkelos to Exodus 24:12 and Leviticus Rabbah 20:10 (Rabbi Joshua) *she-zanu eyneyhem min ha-shekhinah*.
17. Genesis Rabbah 14:9.
18. *Toledot Yaakov Yosef, tazria*, ed. Koretz, 1780, p. 84b. It would appear that the institution of the 'tish had not yet developed at this early stage of the movement, but see *Toledot*, p. 10b.
19. *Toledot, emor*, pp. 101 a–b.
20. Ibid., pp. 102 c–d.
21. Leshon Hasidim, *s.v. Akhilah*, No. 6, pp. 18–19.
22. To sidra, toledot, *s.v. va-yomer esav*, ed. Jerusalem, 1963, p. 36, following the thought of R. Nahman of Horedenka.
23. See *Derekh Hasidim* on 'Taste and see that the Lord is good' (Psalms 34:9), pp. 33–4; *Kedushat* Levi, Jerusalem, 1964, *Likkutim*, p. 287; R. Nahman of Bratzlav, *Sefer Ha-Middot*, Warsaw, 1912, *s.v. akhilah* 2:6, p. 24: 'If one experiences no taste in his food he should know that God has departed from him.' R. Elimelech of Lizansk (*Zettel Katan*, printed at end of his *Noam Elimelekh*, No. 15, ed. G. Nigal, Jerusalem, 1978, p. 517) writes:

> Before washing the hands to a meal, one should recite the penitential prayer of the Ari of blessed memory. After eating the piece of bread over which grace before meals has been recited, one should say the following: 'For the sake of of the unification of the Holy One, blessed be He, and His Shekhinah. I do not eat, God forbid, for my

bodily pleasure, but only that my body be strong for God's service. Let not any sin, transgression, evil thought or physical pleasure prevent the unification of the Holy One, blessed be He, by means of the holy sparks in the food and drink.' Whenever he eats or drinks anything, he should have in mind that the taste he experiences in his mouth when he swallows the food or sips the drink is the inward part of that food or drink; and that by means of his eating, chewing with his teeth and digesting in his stomach, the inward part of the food becomes refined so that does not become a surplus through which the outside ones are nourished. His soul then benefits from the inward part of the food, the residue becoming waste to be, expelled for the outside ones. He should then have in mind that as soon as he will experience a need to evacuate his bowels he will not, God forbid, retain the waste matter inside him to contaminate his mind and abominate his soul by retaining inside him the excrement and urine for even a single moment. And, as he eats, he should depict to himself the letters of the word *maakhol* ['food'] in their Assyrian form [i.e. in the square Hebrew script] and should have in mind that numerically they have a total of ninety-one, the numerical value of the Tetragrammaton plus *Adonai*.

24. To *sidra, mattot*, pp. 27–9.
25. *Taanit* 11a.
26. Against the *nefesh*; see Numbers 6:11.
27. *Taanit* 11a–b.
28. *Kedushat Levi, s.v. va-yeshev*, Jerusalem, p. 61.
29. *Kedushat Levi, Likkutim*, p. 288.
30. Ibid.
31. *Kedushat Levi, Likkutim*, p. 318.
32. Ibid., p. 314.
33. *Or Ha-Meir* by R. Zeev Wolf of Zabarazh, *derush sefirat ha-omer*, quoted in *Derekh Hasidim*, No. 8, p. 30. *Cf.* the quotations in *Torat Ha-Maggid*, ed. Israel Klepholtz, Tel Aviv, 1969, pp. 149–151.
34. On this theme of the sustaining power of the letters and its significance in Hasidism, see R. Shneur Zalman of Liady, in the name of the Baal Shem Tov, in his *Tanya*, Vilna, 1930, *Shaar ha-Yihud*, Chapter 1, p. 152.
35. *Peri ha-aretz*, to *sidra behar*, ed. Jerusalem, 1965, p. 44.
36. R. Zadok Ha-Kohen of Lublin, *Kunteros et ha-okhel*, No. 6.
37. *Derekh Hasidim*, p. 31.
38. *Derekh Hasidim*, pp. 31–2, quoting *Mevasser Tov* to *terumah*.
39. *Derekh Hasidim*, p. 34.
40. *Siddur Ha-Rav*, ed. New York, 1965, *Shaar Netilat Yadayim*, pp. 200–2.
41. *Derekh Hasidim*, p. 32.
42. See Dubnow, *Toledot Ha-Hasidut*, Tel Aviv, pp. 362–4; S. A. Horodetsky, *Ha-Hasidut Ve-Ha-Hasidim*, iv, pp. 81–2; A. Wertheim, *halakhot Ve-Halikhot be-hasidut*, Jerusalem, 1960, pp. 165–9.

14

The Zaddik as a Source of Danger

Examined here so far as Judaism is concerned is the phenomenon, to be observed in several other religions as well, of the holy man's spiritual powers exercised, even in relation to his followers, not only to benefit others but, at times, to cause harm. Naturally, it is normally assumed that the holy man will bring his baneful powers into play only in exceptional circumstances, but at times he is unable to control the powers he possesses and they break out spontaneously. The idea that the realm of the sacred has to be approached with great caution and can be threatening precisely because it belongs to what Otto calls the numinous, is found in a number of places in the Bible.[1] Our concern is with this power as displayed by holy men.

We can begin with the story of the prophet Elisha, the prototype of the miracle-working Zaddik in Hasidism, of whom we read (2 Kings 23–5):

> And he went up from thence unto Beth-el; and as he was going up, there came forth little children [AV] out of the city, and mocked him, and said unto him: 'Go up, thou baldhead; go up, thou baldhead'. And he looked behind him and saw them, and cursed them in the name of the Lord. And there came forth two she-bears out of the wood, and tore forty-two children of them. And he went forth from thence to Mount Carmel, and from thence he returned to Samaria.

The Talmudic Rabbis (*Sotah* 46b–47a) were bothered by the very questionable ethical implications of the story.[2] First the Rabbis understood the Hebrew *nearim ketanim* not as little children but as young, morally immature lads (or, in one version, as adults who behaved as irresponsibly as little boys). The power of the prophet would not have been exercised, the Rabbis imply, against little children. The puzzle remains, was their offence no more than a bit of harmless high spirits, sufficiently severe to warrant the punishment of being torn by the bears? And what exactly was the offence of calling Elisha 'baldhead'? In the verses immediately preceding the Elisha story of the bears, it is told how Elisha sweetened the bitter waters of Jericho which had previously been too bitter for the people to drink. Rabbinic fancy connects the two stories. Before Elisha had sweetened the waters, these 'youths' had earned their living by taking advantage of the people's plight to whom they sold sweet water at a high price. They were annoyed at Elisha, whose sweetening of the water had deprived them of a good living. According to this, the name they called the prophet did not refer to him being bald-headed but to the 'baldness' he had caused in the rich pickings they had previously had through their profiteering at the expense of the public. All this is obviously apologetic. The fact remains that there was no questioning of the power of the prophet to do harm. In the Talmud passage to which reference has been made, it is noted that the verse says that Elisha looked and then that he 'saw'. What is the significance of 'and he saw'? The answer is that he gazed at them with strong disapproval and his mystic gaze led to their punishment. The saying of Rabban Simeon ben Gamaliel is quoted: 'Wherever the sages set their eyes [in strong disapproval] there is either death or poverty.' Despite the belief in Elisha's powers, the Talmudic passage concludes that Elisha was later punished for stirring up the bears against the 'youths'; as if to say, the holy man exercises his baneful powers at his own peril.

The saying of Rabban Simeon ben Gamaliel is quoted in three other Talmudic passages. In one (*Hagigah* 5b) it is told how his colleagues thought that the fourth-century Amora, Rava, was so well-off that his wealth prevented him from being excluded from evil decree against the Jews. Rava protested: 'If only you knew how much I have to give in bribes to King Shapur.' Nevertheless, the king sent to importune Rava further since the sages, Rava's colleagues, had set their eyes on him, and the saying of Rabban Simeon ben Gamaliel is quoted. In another passage (*Moed Katan* 17b) the saying of Rabban Simeon ben Gamaliel is quoted in connection with a domineering fellow who bullied a scholar and suffered harm through the sages setting their eyes on him. In yet another passage (*Nedarim* 7b) the saying of Rabban Simeon ben Gamaliel is quoted in connection with one who utters a divine name without reason for it, the sages strongly disapproving of such conduct.

In the famous case of the Oven of Akhnai (*Bava Metzia* 59b) the great sage, Rabbi Eliezer, persisted in defying his colleagues, even though they all ruled against his decision, for which he was placed under the ban. When Rabbi Eliezer went away in great distress and anger, at whatever he set his eyes was burned. Rabban Gamaliel who, as the Prince, was ultimately responsible for the banning of Rabbi Eliezer, was in great danger. Rabban Gamaliel's sister was Rabbi Eliezer's wife. She took care not to allow her husband to 'fall on his face' in supplication but one day she was too late to prevent it and she exclaimed: 'Alas, you have slain my brother', whereupon word came to say that Rabban Gamaliel had just passed away.

It is hardly coincidental that the saying (*Avot* 3:19) is attributed to Rabbi Eliezer: 'Warm thyself before fire of the sages, but be heedful of their glowing coals, lest thou be burned; for their bite is the bite of a jackal and their sting is the sting of a scorpion and their hiss is the hiss of a serpent, and all their words are like coals of fire.' In his Prayer Book,[3] the Rev. Simeon Singer seeks to soften this harsh saying by adding the note: 'The highest gifts, if abused, may prove the source of suffering to those they are designed to benefit.' This very mealy-mouthed interpretation overlooks entirely the whole point, to which attention has been called above, that the sage or saint is believed to possess miraculous powers and these can be exercised in a harmful way. The great medieval commentator, Menahem Meiri of Perpignan (1249–1316), also embarrassed evidently by the magical elements if the saying is understood literally, interprets the saying in rational vein.[4] It is good to be friendly with the sages, Meiri understands the teaching of Rabbi Eliezer to be saying, but not by the familiarity that breeds contempt. In the light of the many instances in the Talmudic literature of the harm the sage can cause by supernatural means, only the more rationalistic of the medieval thinkers have overlooked the supernatural elements.

Another Talmudic story (*Bava Metzia* 84a) tells of the early fourth-century Palestinian teacher, R. Johanan and his colleague, Resh Lakish, who had been a bandit chief before being persuaded by Rabbi Johanan to become a student of the Torah. The tale begins with Resh Lakish, a powerful man, who saw R. Johanan across a river and imagined he was a woman. In his desire to accost the woman he swam swiftly across a mighty river, recognizing when he came nearer that R. Johanan was a man. R. Johanan promised that if Resh Lakish would become a student of the Torah, as befits a man with his strength, he would give to him as his wife his very beautiful sister. Resh Lakish agreed but was unable to go back across the river since the Torah is a source of weakness to its dedicated students, Some of Resh Lakish's strength, as a potential student of the Torah, had gone from him. It once happened, after Resh Lakish had acquired fame as a scholar and had become a colleague of R. Johanan, that the two were debating a question about the susceptibility to contamination of such weapons as a sword or a javelin. In the heat of the debate R. Johanan burst out: 'You know all about such things,' referring to his nefarious past. Resh Lakish replied: 'What good has it done me? Before they called me a master and now they call me a master.' R. Johanan was deeply offended with the result that Resh Lakish fell ill. Resh Lakish's wife, R. Johanan's sister, pleaded with her brother to pardon Resh Lakish but all to no avail and Resh Lakish passed away. In this story the harm brought about was indirect but effective none-the-less. Possibly the attempted intervention by a woman in this story and the story of Eliezer is meant to imply that a tender-hearted woman cannot see the justice in a sage condemning others in this way.

The association between the baneful gaze of the holy man and fire is also found in the well-known legend (*Shabbat* 33b–34a) about R. Simeon ben Yohai and his son, Eleazar. A man reported them to the Romans and they were obliged to flee for their lives. They hid in a cave for 12 years. When they emerged from the cave all immersed in holiness, they could not bear to see ordinary folk engaging in their normal worldly occupations, and wherever they gazed there was burning. A heavenly voice proceeded to protest: Have you come out of your cave to destroy My world? Go back to your cave. They went back and stayed in the cave for another year and no longer, since the wicked are punished in hell only for 12 months. (It is implied here, too, that although the holy man is allowed to use his powers even to cause harm to others, yet, if he does use them, he has to be punished.) The tale concludes, nevertheless, that when R. Simeon saw the man who informed against him to the Roman authorities he gazed at the man, who 'became a heap of bones'.[5]

Reservations about the use by the holy man of his power to do harm is found in the curious tale (*Berakhot* 7a) of R. Joshua ben Levi and the *min* ('sectarian') who used to annoy R. Joshua by hurling Scriptural verses at him to prove a heretical point. It was believed that the exact moment when a cockscomb develops a certain red colour more than usual is the moment of God's anger, at which time a curse is bound to be effective. R. Joshua put a cock at the foot of his bed and stayed awake until the appropriate moment arrived, but he fell asleep. He concluded that it was not right to curse the wicked. The Talmud quotes the verse in Proverbs 17:2, which is rendered differently from the usual understanding of the verse, as: 'To punish is not good even for the righteous'.[6]

Another Talmudic story (*Sukkah* 28a) is relevant to our theme. The great teacher Hillel had 80 disciples. The greatest of these was Jonathan ben Uziel. The least of these was Johanan ben Zakkai, whose many attainments are listed. The Talmud asks: If the least of Hillel's disciples was so great how great was Jonathan ben Uziel, the greatest of them all? In reply the Talmud states that Jonathan ben Uziel was so great that when he studied the Torah a bird flying over his head would be burned. Rashi explains that the burning of the bird happened because of the angels who gathered round to hear Jonathan's exquisitely sweet interpretations. The Tosafists understand it as a re-enactment of the giving of the Torah, which was attended by fire. Here the *motif* is of burning by the holy man, but it is quite different from the other instances quoted above since here it had to do with his learning and it was his Torah that caused the bird to be burned. The Jerusalem Talmud[7] asks: If such was the greatness of the disciple, how great was the master, Hillel himself? The reply is given that in the case of Jonathan ben Uziel the bird was burned only if it came within four cubits, whereas in Hillel's case the bird was burned even if it flew higher than four cubits.

The Lithuanian school from the nineteenth century down to the present day differed profoundly from the Hasidic approach. In this school, while the powers of holy men were not denied, the emphasis on the study of Torah was on matter-of-fact, down-to-earth study, which, for this school, was higher than the supernatural effects. In this connection two anecdotes deserve to be mentioned. One is told of Rabbi Meir Shapiro of Lublin. Rabbi Shapiro noted the difference between the Hasid and the Litvak when reading this Talmudic passage. The Hasid waxes eloquent on the high stage of sanctity reached by Jonathan ben Uziel. 'How wonderful', the Hasid exclaims, 'to be so holy.' The Litvak, on the other hand, when he reads the story, first wants to know whether Jonathan would be obliged to compensate the owner for the loss of his bird. The other anecdote concerns the Lithuanian saint, the Hafetz Hayyim. This saintly man offers his own reply to the question of the Jerusalem Talmud. The greatness of the master, Hillel, was that when he studied the Torah the bird was not burned!

Not only is it dangerous to arouse the holy man's intentional anger. Danger can result from a casual remark made by him without intention to harm, which, having made it, neither he himself nor any other holy man can withdraw. This notion is based on the verse (Ecclesiastes 10:5): 'like an error which proceedeth from a ruler', the ruler being the sage or holy man who has been given control over the government of the world through his spiritual powers. The ruler's baneful word, even if is in 'error', cannot be cancelled or revoked. The case is treated in the Talmud (*Ketubot* 23a) of women captured by heathen bandits who, if they had been defiled by the bandits, become forbidden to marry a priest. Some women had been captured but on their release were placed under a guard by the father of the third-century Amora, Samuel. The son, Samuel, protested: 'Who has watched over them until now?' Samuel's father objected: 'If they had been your own daughters would you have spoken of them in such a manner?' As a result of the father's casual remark it happened that Samuel's daughters were captured by bandits. The verse in Ecclesiastes is quoted in support of the daughters' fate.[8] The point of the story is that the father of Samuel would surely have wished to withdraw his baneful remarks, since Samuel's daughters were his own granddaughters, yet he was powerless to withdraw the word once it had been uttered.

In Hasidism tales of the supernatural powers of the Zaddik abound.[9] The Zaddik is the channel through which the divine grace flows so that he is of benefit to others and to the world at large. Here is considered particularly the notion of the Zaddik's powers to cause harm, occasionally even to his loyal followers and others near to him. This aspect of Zaddikism has largely been ignored by modern students of Hasidism. The passages mentioned above were, of course, known to many Jews and came to occupy a place in Jewish folklore before the rise of Hasidism but were used by the Hasidim in order to demonstrate the powers of their own holy men, the Zaddikim. In referring to Hasidic tales about the Zaddikim, it is not suggested that all or even some them actually happened. Even the tellers of these tales were often sceptical concerning their reliability. But the Hasidim believed that they could have happened, and that is sufficient for an investigation into Hasidic attitudes.

We can begin with two accounts, the first[10] about the early Hasidic master, associate of the Baal Shem Tov, Meir the Great of

Premislani, the second about the Belzer Rebbe, R. Aaron (1880–1957).[11] Of Reb Meir the Great the legend tells that he gazed at each of his infant sons soon after birth and would exclaim: 'This is not what I had in mind', i.e. at the moment of conception his holy intentions ought to have brought down a much higher soul of which there was no indication when he looked at the infant. Each time, the infant died soon afterwards. Reb Meir's wife, fearing the harm that her husband would do, did not allow him to come near to her newly born child (who grew up to be Reb Aaron the Great of Premislani) until the child was three years of age. When eventually Reb Meir saw the child, he exclaimed, 'The ones I let go were better than he' and the child became very sick, his life being saved only by the Baal Shem Tov on a visit to the home.

The other story, purporting to be more factual than legendary, concerns R. Mechele Lackman, one of the two *gabbaim* ('attendants') of the Belzer Rebbe; the other *gabbai* being R. Uri Lackman, R. Mechele's father. At the Court of Belz a number of choice Hasidim lived a hermit-like existence, praying and studying the Torah. This elitist group, known as the *yoshevim* ('sitters', 'those who stayed there') adopted a special Hasidic, old-fashioned style of dress different from all the other Belzer Hasidim, whose mode of dress was comparatively more 'modern'. There were a number of youths (*bakhurim*) who studied Torah in Belz. Some of these youths, of whom Reb Mechele's son was one, began to have 'modernizing' tendencies and, instead of adopting the mode of dress of the *yoshevim*, began to dress like the other Hasidim. A fierce battle was joined between the *yoshevim* and the *bakhurim*, but Reb Mechele, anxious to keep his young son within the fold, decided to intervene with the Rebbe. During his talk with the Rebbe, Reb Mechele let slip a critical remark about the *yoshevim*, a group enjoying the special favour of the Rebbe. The Rebbe exclaimed angrily: 'I can get along with only one gabbai.' As soon as Reb Mechele heard this he considered himself to be under the ban and removed his shoes and begged tearfully that the Rebbe should pardon him. The Rebbe said: 'Although I am very upset at what I said, since I have said it I cannot now withdraw it.' Reb Mechele went home, took to his bed and died soon afterwards. Reb Mechele's father and the Hasidim wept bitterly at Reb Mechele's fate, saying: 'Reb Mechele had been burned by our Master's coals.' It is interesting to find that the belief, in Talmudic times, in the power of the saint's word that cannot be revoked persisted among the Hasidim until well into the twentieth century. The narrator of this tale prefaces his remarks by saying: 'Some say', so it is not too categorical, yet the possibility of such a thing happening is never challenged.

A twentieth-century Hasidic author, Zevi Moskovitz, compiled a collection of stories, some new but mostly old, about the Zaddikim called *Otzar Sippurim* ('Treasury of Tales'). This work was originally published in twenty parts between the years 1951–59 but was later published in a special volume.[12] Some of Moskovitz's parts have an alphabetical table of contents, under which he lists the theme of the Zaddik's power to cause harm under the word *onesh* ('punishment'). Moskovitz's work is a bit of a hotchpotch and he is very credulous and superstitious, yet it is worth dwelling at some length on one of his tales and his comment on this as another illustration of how our theme has persisted in Hasidic lore.[13]

The tale is of two disciples of the great teacher, Elimelech of Lizansk. These were Mordecai of Neshkhiz (1752–1800) and the famous scribe, Moshe of Przeworsk (d. 1805). Reb Mordecai had some skins from which parchment had been made ready on which to write a Sefer Torah. Anxious to have the Sefer Torah written by the skilful and holy Reb Moshe, he sent to him to come to his home to write the Sefer, but Reb Moshe declined. Reb Mordecai repeated the entreaty, saying that Reb Moshe would suffer if he did not pay heed to it. When Reb Moshe's son fell ill he became frightened and set off on his journey to Reb Mordecai. On his way he stayed overnight in a hostel where his master, Reb Elimelech, came to him in a dream. 'You should not have set out on the journey,' declared Reb Elimelech, 'on account of the dream. As for your child's illness, this would have been taken care of had you prayed at my grave. But now that you are on the way you must, under no circumstances, stay with Reb Mordecai to write the Sefer Torah there since he wants to capture you in his net as his Hasid. At the most you may agree to take the parchment back home and write the Sefer Torah there.' In due course Reb Mordecai agreed to let Reb Moshe do the work at home. Eventually, Reb Moshe sent Reb Mordecai the finished Sefer Torah, saying that although it is customary for a scribe to go over a Sefer Torah he has written three times in order to check for errors, this was not necessary since this Sefer Torah was so meticulously written that he is confident no errors will be found. Reb Mordecai boasted that he now had a Sefer Torah completely free from error.

The story continues that a certain scribe said to Reb Mordecai

that if he looed it over he would find some errors. Reb Mordecai
gave the Sefer to the scribe to check but, finding no errors, the
scribe poured ink over the word *nega* ('plague') and said to Reb
Mordecai that there was an error. R. Mordecai sent word of this at
once to Reb Moshe, who roundly declared that it was impossible.
Someone else must have been responsible and whoever it was
would be plagued. The scribe began to suffer and when the scribe
confessed his sin to Reb Mordecai he was told to go to Reb Moshe,
who would offer him amulets to heal him. At first Reb Moshe gave
him the amulets but later withdrew them because they would be
of no avail. The scribe died and was buried there.

Moskovitz, after telling the gruesome tale, observes:

> From all this we see that when a person offends against the honour of one
> Zaddik, who punishes him as a result, it is impossible for even the true
> Zaddikim of the generation to help him. Many such things are well-
> known. Therefore even if you are attached to a true Zaddik and do not
> journey to other Zaddikim of the time you must still take great care not to
> offend against their honour. And even if you see that there is a division of
> heart and you see your own Master opposes and speaks ill of another
> Zaddik, you must not take sides since their power and comprehension is
> great. It is possible that on occasion your Master disagrees with another
> Zaddik, it is still possible that he thinks of the other as a great man.

There are echoes here of the fierce controversies among the
Hasidic masters, each with his own follower loyal to him come what
may. Once again the *motif* is found that once a Zaddik has issued a
baneful decree against someone nothing can prevent the evil decree
from taking effect. Moskovitz adds that an offender of this nature is
'bitten by the serpent of the Rabbis for which there is no cure'. This
is based on the Talmudic interpretation (*Shabbat* 119a) of the verse
(Ecclesiastes 10:8): 'And who breaketh through a hedge a serpent
shall bite him.' In the context the reference is to an actual snake bite
suffered by one who offends against Rabbinic law, but, long before
Moskovitz, the reference had been applied to the notion of an
offender suffering the harm caused by the holy man who had been
offended. Such a man will be 'bitten' by the 'snake of the Rabbis'.
Moskovitz also refers to the saying (*Avot* 2:10), mentioned earlier,
that the hissing of the sages is like the hissing of a snake.

It is clear that the conventional image of the Hasidic holy men
as solely benevolent to all is based on a misconception. The idea of
the terrible side of the holy man's activities is found, as we have

seen, much earlier than the rise of Hasidism in the eighteenth century. Yet, once Hasidism had invested the Zaddik with powers far
above those granted in former times[14] it became inevitable that
baneful powers should have been embraced by the Zaddik as well
as beneficent powers

NOTES

1. For the numinous in the Hebrew Bible see Rudolf Otto, *The Idea of the Holy*, trans. G. W.
   Harvey, OUP, pp. 72–81. For other biblical texts implying the potential danger of the
   sacred, see the story of Uzzah, who died when he touched the Holy Ark (2 Samuel
   6:6–9); Numbers 3:10 on the death of those not Levites who draw near; Moses hiding
   his face because he was afraid to look at the burning bush (Exodus 3:6); the death of
   man and beast if they wandered on to Mount Sinai (Exodus 19:12–13); the death of
   Nadab and Abihu (Leviticus 10:1–7); the people afraid to approach Moses when his face
   was shining (Exodus 34:27–35). Cf. M. Haran, 'The Priestly Image of the Tabernacle', in
   HUCA, Vol. 36 (1965), pp. 216f. on the danger inherent in approaching or being affected by the contagious sacred.
2. See, too, the standard commentators to the story, Rashi, Kimhi and Gersonides and
   Louis Ginzberg, *Legends of the Jews*, Philadelphia, 1942, vol.IV, p. 240 and notes; Vol. VI,
   p. 344 for further sources.
3. *The Authorised Daily Prayer Book* (many edns) p. 258. Singer does not usually provide
   footnotes to his translation but evidently believed his note here necessary because of the
   harsh tone of the saying.
4. *Bet Ha-Behirah* to *Avot*, ed. Prag, Jerusalem, 1964, pp. 36–7. Cf. the story of Rabbi Eliezer
   in tractate *Hagigah* 3b. The sage, vexed by a disciple's error, blinded him for a time but
   later restored his sight.
5. The victim of the holy man's gaze becoming a 'heap of bones' is also found in Berakhot
   58a; *Bava Batra* 95a *Sanhedrin* 100a.
6. This *motif* and the adaptation of the verse in Proverbs is also found in *Shabbat* 149b;
   Avodah Zarah 5b (a parallel passage to that of R. Joshua ben Levi) Cf. my article. 'Praying
   for the Downfall of the Wicked, in *Modern Judaism*, Vol. 2, Johns Hopkins University
   Press, 1962, pp. 297–310. Relevant, too, is the saying (*Berakhot* 56a ; *Makkot* 11a; *Sanhedrin*
   90b) that the curse of a sage takes effect even when it is undeserved. *Cf.* the miracle tales
   about sages and other holy men whose gaze was harmful (*Taanit* 23b–24a), especially the
   story of R. Jose of Yokeret, who cursed his own son and daughter.
7. This passage is not found in current editions of the JT but is quoted as such by the *Ritba*
   to *Sukkah*, ed. E. Lichtenstein, Jerusalem, 1968, p. 258.
8. Other stories to this effect as well as the quote from Ecclesiastes are found in *Moed* Katan
   18a; *Ketubot* 62b; *Bava Metzia* 68a. Cf. *Berakhot* 19a: 'Let a man not open his mouth to Satan'
   on which see Joshua Tractenberg, *Jewish Magic and Superstition*, New York, 1970, pp. 56–7.
9. The supernatural aspects of Hasidism have recently been studied by Gedalyah Nigal
   Magic, Mysticism and Hasidism, Northvale, New Jersey and London, 1994, and by Moshe
   Idel, *Hasidism Between Ecstasy* and *Magic*, State University of New York Press, 1995.
10. In *Raza De-Uvda* on R. Eleazar Zeev of Cretchnif, Brooklyn, New York, 1976, Part II, pp. 4–5.
11. In Israel Klepholtz, *Gedoley Hasidey Belz*, Bene Berak, 1977,p.360.
12. Jerusalem 1951–57 and published as a single volume in the collection *Sefarim Kedoshim*,
    Vol. 28, New York, 1985.
13. Moskovitz, Part 3, No. 14, pp. 21–4. Other instances in Moskovitz are, Part 2, Nos 6 and
    and 16; Part 4, Nos 12–14; Part 6, No. 13; Part 15. No. 11; Part 16, No. 10.
14. See my article 'Hasidism and the Dogma of the Decline of the Generations', in *Hasidism
    Reappraised*, ed. Ada Rapoport-Albert, Littman Library of Jewish Civilization, London
    and Portland, 1996, pp. 208–13. Cf. Jerome R. Mintz, *Legends of the Hasidim*, Chicago and
    London, 1968, p. 115: 'On rare occasions the power of the Rebbe may be viewed in a
    negative and even fearful light for if the Rebbe has the power to bless then he also pos-
    sesses the power, rarely seen to be sure, to curse.' Maybe so, but it was believed to be
    not quite so rare, as this investigation has shown.

15

The Munkacer Rebbe
on Christianity

Rabbi Hayyim Eleazar Shapira (1872–1937) succeeded his father, Rabbi Zevi Hirsch, both as Rabbi of Munkacs (Mukachevo) in Hungary (later Czechoslovakia) and as master of the Hasidic dynasty of that name.[1] He is consequently known as the Munkacer Rebbe but more especially as the Munkacer Rov. The Munkacer was a fiery personality in his public life (though, in his private life, even his opponents agree that he was a man of great charm and cordiality), attacking, with blithe impartiality, the Haskalah, political Zionism, and the Mizrachi. Even the Agudat Israel invoked his anger. His vast erudition in all branches of traditional Jewish learning is beyond question. A prolific author, with a number of widely acclaimed works to his credit,[2] he often displays in these a critical, historical sense very unusual in a Rabbi of the old school. What has not hitherto been adequately noted is this Hasidic master's attitude towards Christianity. It is extremely rare to find a notable Hasidic Rebbe considering not alone Halakhic opinions on Christianity but also the theological differences between Judaism and Christianity and the challenges presented by the latter faith to the former.

The Munkacer's originality and acute critical awareness are brought into play in his correspondence with Rabbi Menahem Menchin Heilpern (1844–1924) of Jerusalem, author of *Kevod Hakhamim* ('Respect for Sages'), a defence of the Kabbalistic work *Hemdat Yamim* ('Desirable of Days'), a work suspected by Jacob Emden, David Kahana and others[3] of leanings towards the Sabbatean heresy. Heilpern maintains that the *Hemdat Yamim* is a holy work and he seeks to refute the view that it contains references to Shabbetai Zevi or his heresies. Heilpern had sent his book *Kevod Hakhamim* to Rabbi Zevi Hirsch, Rabbi Hayyim Eleazar's father, for comment but the father delegated the responsibility of a reply to his son, whose essay *Meshiv Mipney Ha-Kavod* ('Reply out of Respect' or 'Reply against the Respect')[4] is a critique of Heilpern. Rabbi Hayyim Eleazar does not necessarily deny that the anonymous author of *Hemdat Yamim* may have been a holy man but argues it is obvious that heretical opinions have been added to the original manuscript as this was circulated.

One of the passages in *Hemdat Yamim* Heilpern attempts to justify is the one in which it is stated: 'On the eve of Passover the first-born son of the modest one [*bekhor ben ha-tzenuah*, a pun on *bekhor ben ha-senuah* in Deuteronomy 21:17] of whom it is said: "I also will appoint him first-born, the highest of the kings of the earth [Psalms 89:28]."' The prayer recorded in this connection in *Hemdat Yamim* reads: 'And now, O Lord our God, we give thanks unto Thee and we praise the name of Thy glory [*tifartekha*] for unto us a child is born, a son is given unto us; and the government is upon his shoulder [Isaiah 9:5].' Critics of the *Hemdat Yamim* had purported to see in all this a clear reference to the false Messiah, Shabbetai Zevi, whose followers believed in him even after he had been converted to Islam. Not so, declares Heilpern. The passage has nothing to do with Shabbetai Zevi but is based on the Lurianic Kabbalah, which speaks of the conception, birth, nursing and growth of *Zeer Anpin* ('Lesser Countenance'), corresponding to the Sefirah *Tiferet*, and is thus a prayer on Passover, the festival of Redemption, for the realization of harmony in the Sefirotic realm so that the divine grace should flow through all creation. Rabbi Hayyim Eleazar protests[5] that Heilpern's interpretation is quite impossible. A prayer in which *Tiferet* is singled out from the other Sefirot just at this time of the year makes no sense at al, and neither does the quotation of the verse in Isaiah. *Zeer Anpin* (corresponding to *Tiferet*) is an aspect of the Deity in manifestation, its birth and nurture, of which the Kabbalah speaks, takes place in the divine realm. How then can the verse be applied: 'unto *us* a child is born'?

It is obvious, remarks Rabbi Hayyim Eleazar, that the whole passage is an interpolation by a Jewish Christian heretic (*min notzri*) who used Kabbalistic terminology to denote the resurrection of Jesus who, the Talmud (*Sanhedrin* 43a in the uncensored versions) tells us, was crucified on the eve of Passover. The reference to 'the son of the modest one' is to the virgin birth. The prayer is obviously an invocation for Jesus to rise from the grave to redeem his followers. The reference to *Tiferet* is, indeed, to the

Sefirah of that name. *Tiferet*, third in the first triad of the 'lower' Sefirot, identified as Jesus to hint at the Christian dogma of the Trinity. It is well known, continues the Munkacer, that the verse in Isaiah is applied to Jesus in this sense in Christian writings. Embarrassed by referring to Christian doctrine, the Munkacer justifies this only because such is implied in the Talmudic statement (*Sanhedrin* 17a) that the members of the Sanhedrin are required to have a knowledge of witchcraft and idolatry in order for them to be capable of rendering decisions when such matters come before them. The only problem is why there should be a Christological interpolation in a work with Sabbatean tendencies, at least in the later additions to the original. What connection is there between Christianity and Sabbateanism? But it is notorious, says the Munkacer, that the followers of Jacob Frank, the Polish successor to Shabbetai Zevi, interpreted the Kabbalah so as to make it yield Christian doctrines. Many of the Frankists were, in fact, converted to Christianity.[6]

> They formed a single bond – 'whatever is attached to the unclean is itself unclean'[7] – with the heretics in our land and in Turkey, with those who preceded them and with those who succeeded them, and who knows which of them made insertions into the *Hemdat Yamim* after it had reached the first manuscript stage. The great scholars of the Sephardi community, of blessed memory, did not investigate the matter thoroughly (in addition, they had no expertise regarding Christian beliefs so as to realize how far-reaching the interpolation actually was) and they had the work printed *in toto* since, in general, they found it to be a sound work, one of high ethical work with laws and mystical intentions etc. Who knows what else is found therein? The work has never been in my possession.

The above is an incidental reference to Christianity. Elsewhere the Munkacer is even more specific. On the basis of a passage in the Zohar,[8] he believes[9] that arrangement of the weekly readings from the Torah (the *sedarim*) to fall when they do is, though late, divinely inspired so that there is a close connection between the events that happened in the past at a particular time of the year and the *sidra* read at that time. Now the *sidra va-yehi* has been arranged to be read towards the end of the month of December when the reading is from the portion, *va-yehi*, which contains the verse (Genesis 48:7): 'And as for me, when I came from Padan, Rachel died unto me in the land of Canaan in the way, when there was still some way to come unto Ephrath, and I buried her there in

the way to Ephrath – the same is Bethlehem.' What is the significance of the final clause: 'the same is Bethlehem'? The significance
is, says the Munkacer, that Rachel's tomb in Bethlehem acts as a
constant protest against Christian worship at the Church of the
Nativity, also in Bethlehem! Thus this verse is appropriately read
in the synagogue near to the season of the year when Christians
celebrate the birth of Jesus. An astonishing observation,[10] implying
that the Torah foretells the rise of Christianity and hints at a
constant protest against this religion and that those responsible for
the arrangement of the *sedarim* were inspired to have the protest
read at Christmas time.

The Munkacer took very seriously the custom of refraining
from the study of the Torah on Christmas eve – *Nittel*.[11] A reliable
report[12] has it that he ignored the date on which Christmas is celebrated by the Western Churches (December 25) but on the date
when it is celebrated by the Russian Orthodox Church he would
refrain from study of the Torah until midnight nor would he accept
a petition (the *kvitel*) before midnight on this date. There is also a
reference to husband and wife abstaining from marital relations on
this night.[13] The Munkacer has a mystical interpretation of all this
based on the late Kabbalistic book, *Sefer Karnayyim*, an extremely
difficult, cryptic work, with a Commentary, *Dan Yadin*, by Samson
Ostropoler, considered by many scholars to be not only the commentator of the book but its actual author.[14] The *Sefer Karnayyim*
devotes a section of the work to each of the months of the year. The
sixth section is on the month of Tevet. The name Tevet is here associated with the word *tovah* ('goodness'). Whoever dies in this
month becomes attached to the Shekhinah. According to the
Kabbalists the patriarch Abraham died in this month since the
initial letters of *tikkaver be-sevah tovah*, 'thou will be buried at a good
old age' (Genesis 15:15) form the word Tevet. Both the book itself
and the Commentary are very circumspect, the latter stating that
the full mystery cannot be disclosed because of 'danger to life', i.e.
because of Gentile objections, which may endanger the Jewish
community. But, reading between the lines, it is very probable that
the *Sefer Karnayyim* is saying in so many words that the death of
Abraham in the month of Tevet offsets the corresponding *kelipah*
('shell' or 'husk', the Kabbalistic term for the demonic side of
existence) of Baal Tzafon, known as the Dog. The *Sefer Karnayyim*
concludes this section with the statement: 'And I have received a
German tradition in a whisper, that here lies the mystery of *reshet*

dam.' The words *reshet dam* mean literally 'blood trap', obviously a hint at the 'blood libel'. Abraham's death in Tevet offsets the death of Jesus whose birth is celebrated by Christians in the month corresponding to Tevet. The Munkacer quotes with approval[15] the hints of the *Sefer Karnayyim* and applies these to *Nittel*, adding that the *kelipah* of the Dog belongs to Edom, who is Esau, and 'we are in the exile of Edom', i.e. in Christian lands. This is why, says the Munkacer in an aside, Christian noblemen are so fond of dogs.[16]

It is well-known that in Gershom Scholem's opinion there took place in early Hasidism what Scholem calls a 'neutralization of Messianism', that is to say, although the early Hasidim, as Orthodox Jews, believed in the coming of the Messiah, this belief was not in the forefront of their endeavours at living the saintly life in the here and now. Without entering here into this involved question except to note that other scholars take issue with Scholem, there is no doubt that in later Hasidism, certainly in the time of the Munkacer, the hope for Messianic redemption loomed very large. The Munkacer's opposition to Zionism, for example, was largely due to his strong conviction that a political movement with the aim of settling Jews in the Land of Israel was an impious attempt to anticipate the only true redemption of the Jewish people, namely, through God's direct intervention when the time had come. During the First World War, the Munkacer used to urge his followers not to be content to pray only for peace among the nations but to pin their hopes on the coming of the Messiah, seeing the war as but a prelude to the final redemption. World peace without the advent of the Messiah was seen by the Munkacer as a catastrophe.

The sermons of the Munkacer contain meditations on the sufferings of the personal Messiah as described in the Midrashic literature, especially in the *Pesikta Rabbati*.[17] The Munkacer[18] asking his congregation to participate in the sufferings of the Messiah is certainly untypical in Jewish thought. The resemblances with Christian meditation on the passion of Jesus is quite extraordinary. (Needless to say, such ideas as the meditation on the passion of Jesus were entirely foreign to the Munkacer and, on the conscious level at least, he was unaware of any resemblances.) A disciple of the Munkacer, Y. M. Gold,[19] gives the following paraphrase of a New Year sermon delivered by the Munkacer when Gold was present:

Dear brethren. On this day the world was created. On this day all the world's creatures stand in judgment. The main thing for which we and for which our eyes yearn and long is the complete redemption, the advent of the Messiah. For this the decision is made each Rosh Ha-Shanah and yet until now we have not been saved. It all depends, without doubt, on our efforts. If only we would direct our hearts to it, returning with longing and with our determined will to the King of Glory, blessed be His name, casting aside all our personal interests and material needs, setting our face to supplicate and entreat solely for the coming of the son of David, may he come to redeem us speedily and in our days. But you might perhaps object: How can living flesh return? How are we able to relinquish our own personal troubles, our lack of sustenance and our inability to earn a proper living? How can we give up asking for these and have the redemption as our sole aim? Brethren, close to my heart, you must know, as stated in the *Pesikta Rabbati*, that the Messiah son of David took upon himself pain and torture, suffering for the sins of Israel. Iron bars have been placed on his neck until his figure is brought low and he cries out and sobs in pain. Now, my beloved brethren, who is he, what kind of a man is he, who can be so cruel to allow this holy one, Messiah of the God of Jacob, to suffer on his behalf? Therefore, I, and I alone, stand here with heart and soul, placing my head under the iron bars of our righteous Messiah in order to take the sufferings away from him and my soul is given in the stead of his pure soul. Who is for the Lord? Let him come nigh to me. All of you stand ready to bring our heads under the aforementioned iron bars, refusing to allow the holy Messiah to suffer on our behalf. To this we give our hearts. We shall weep and cry out in bitterness and return unto the Lord. Through such a meditation we shall be capable of removing from our hearts the personal interests and the desire for worldly things, offering our supplications solely for our salvation and the redemption of our souls and to save the righteous Messiah from suffering for our transgressions. Then we shall reach the true goal, to have the merit of a year of redemption and be inscribed for good life in the book of life, with David King of Israel alive and established, speedily and in our days.

Both the language and the content of this remarkable sermon have no parallel in Jewish preaching, ancient or modern.

Unlike in Russia, there were no laws in Hungary forbidding Jews to accept proselytes. The Munkacer,[20] in an unpublished Commentary to Yoreh Deah, goes so far as to rule that if a Gentile minor expresses a desire to become a Jew the Beth Din is obliged to accept him for conversion. The source for this ruling is the Talmudic statement[21] that the Bet Din can accept a minor as a convert even though, as a minor, he has no legal powers of consent. It is true that Rashi comments that the Talmudic ruling applies only to a minor who has no father and whose mother brings him to be converted. The Munkacer maintains that this comment is not really Rashi's but a later interpolation out of fear of the censor in order for it not to appear as if Jews were like those Christians eager to win souls by baptizing little children before they had become adults.[22]

Gold[23] quotes a curious tale from the same unpublished Commentary. The Munkacer stated that he had heard the tale from his forebears. An ancestor of the Munkacer, R. Moshe Laib of Sassov, once travelled from Sassov with his friend, the renowned R. Levi Yitzhak of Berditchev. The two saints went into a forest, ostensibly to enjoy the scenery, taking with them another man. This man gave the appearance of a mere retainer but, in reality, he was taken along in order to constitute together with the two saints the quorum of three judges for a Court presiding over conversions to Judaism. They had with them a circumcision knife, some wine and other requirements for the circumcision ceremony. In the forest they came upon a sleeping infant in swaddling clothes who had been left there by his mother when she went off to pick grain. They circumcised the infant in stealth and took him away to be brought up in a Jewish orphanage in Brody, leaving there a document stating that the infant was a righteous proselyte and directing that as soon as he becomes of age he should be immersed in the *mikveh* in order to complete the circumcision rite. The boy grew up to be a great scholar. R. Moshe Laib was present at the young scholar's wedding when R. Moshe Laib let others into the secret 'and they rejoiced with great merriment'. People knew of the identity of the young man and knew of his children. The reason why the two holy men had risked their lives to convert the child was because they had seen by the power of the holy spirit that his was a lofty soul. This story also shows, observes the Munkacer, that it is permitted to convert a minor to Judaism even without the consent of the parents since the two were famous scholars, thoroughly conversant with the law. Gold says that he himself had heard the Munkacer tell the story on the anniversary of R. Moshe Laib's death, adding that the playing of the musicians at the young man's wedding was so sweet that R. Moshe Laib expressed the wish that the musicians should play the same sweet melody when he died. On the day of R. Moshe Laib's death, the musicians heard of it and they played the sweet melody.[24]

As an outstanding Halakhist, the Munkacer also discusses Christianity in a Halakhic context.[25] Among the practical questions he was asked is whether it is permitted to tell the time by a clock on a church tower. His questioner had heard that the Munkacer permits it on the grounds that Christians are not idolaters. The Munkacer vehemently rejects such an opinion. If Christianity is not considered to be an idolatrous faith, he argues, why did the martyrs give their lives when faced with the alternatives of embracing Christianity or death? He quotes authorities who declare categorically that Christianity is an idolatrous faith and he refers his readers to two further Responsa on the subject in the same volume.[26] It is true, he goes on to say, that he allows people to tell the time by a clock on a church tower (though he remarks in an aside that it still better to avoid it) but the reason is because the clock is not an object of worship but has simply been placed on the high tower for the convenience of the public.

Of the two Responsa to which the Munkacer has directed his readers, one[27] deals with the question whether it is permitted for a Jew to sell portraits of Jesus and Mary to Christians. Essentially he frowns on the practice but first seeks to analyse the issue from the legal side. The question involves considering whether these portraits are for purely decorative purposes or objects to be worshipped, yet, it can be argued, even if they are for decorative purposes, they are still given a place of honour in the Christian home and this in itself constitutes an act of worship for which a Jew must not be even indirectly responsible. For all that, if a Jewish merchant had unknowingly purchased a large quantity of these portraits in the belief that it is permitted to sell them, he may sell them rather than suffer heavy financial loss since the majority of the artists paint solely for financial gain without any thought of Christian worship. It is likely that the artists are not even believers in Christianity. The Responsum concludes: 'I have written as seemed right to my humble mind and with the help of God, blessed be He. May He help us to cause idols to pass away from off earth and put into us a spirit of purity to serve Him together in truth. May it speedily come to pass.'

The other Responsum[28] to which the Munkacer refers considers the case of a Jewish merchant who possessed a large quantity of medallions he was unable to sell. May he have them recast so as to portray the Pope with his triple crown, which he can then sell to Catholics? The Munkacer refers to the other Responsum, but in that case the portraits are of Jesus and Mary whereas here they are of the Pope. True, Catholics revere the Pope but they never worship

him. As for the cross on the crown, a cross of this kind is like that
on a medallion and is not an object of worship, otherwise we
would never be allowed to use coins since these have the figure of
the king wearing a crown with a cross. Against this it can be
argued that coins are handled daily and hardly treated with rever-
ence, whereas a medallion is so treated. It is also possible that the
craftsman who made the medallion did, indeed, intend the cross
he fashioned to be an object of worship. The Munkacer concludes
that he cannot discover any reason for permissiveness.

Finally, reference should be made to what the Munkacer has to
say on the Magen David.[29] Scholem,[30] in a famous essay, has traced
the history of this mysterious symbol, now so prominent in Jewish
life and art. Both Scholem and the Munkacer point out that in the
earliest medieval sources it was the Menorah that featured as the
escutcheon on David's shield. Both also quote the work *Eretz Ha-
Hayyim* on the book of Psalms by Abraham Hayyim Cohen of
Nikolsburg, a Moravian Kabbalist of the first half of the eighteenth
century. (Scholem notes incidentally that this author's father was
an influential Sabbatean preacher.) In his Commentary to Psalm
18, Cohen states that the kings of the Northern Kingdom of Israel
had a simple triangle on their shields, whereas the kings of the
Davidic house had a hexagram, that is, the Magen David. This was
to denote that the royal house of David was closely associated with
the Sefirah *Malkhut* ('Sovereignty'), the lowest of the Sefirot, which
is why the point of the hexagram is in a downward direction. The
Munkacer finds all this extremely dubious since it is not based on
any authentic tradition. Yet, he continues, even if it were true that
originally the Magen David was a worthy symbol, now that it has
been adopted by the Zionists it should be taboo to have such a
symbol on a sacred object such as the mantle for a Sefer Torah. It
is certainly forbidden to have a Magen David on the roof of a synagogue because, when seen from a distance, it looks like an eight-
pointed cross. Were he not afraid to say so, he concludes, he would
dare to suggest that the Magen David is really a Christian symbol
'and this is sufficient for the discerning'.

From his writings, the Munkacer emerges as a resolute opponent of Christianity, which he considers to be an idolatrous faith.
But, possibly because of this, he evinces a strong interest in
Christian doctrine the better to expose it. Moreover, unlike most of
his contemporary Rabbis, the Munkacer, it is well-known, had
acquired the necessary education in general subjects to enable him

to matriculate in order to serve as a Rabbi and, no doubt, as a result of his studies, he acquired some knowledge of Christianity and Christian texts. Not for the Munkacer are any dialogues with Christians. He would have been horrified at such things. He welcomes Christian converts to Judaism and sees no basic objection to winning these even to the extent of converting minors, though here, naturally, a good deal of circumspection is required if Jewish–Christian relations are not to be impaired. The rise of Christianity has been foretold in Scripture, according to the Munkacer, and this religion belongs to the side of 'Esau', the power of the *kelipot*, which have dominion until the true Messiah comes to redeem mankind. To offset Judaism and Christianity in this way inevitably leads, in all probability quite unconsciously, to a Jewish Messianic fervour expressed in a vocabulary that really belongs to the faith to which it is opposed. And a further reason for the Munkacer's strong attacks on Christianity is due to the need to combat Jewish assimilation, especially rife in a Hungary with cultural associations with Western thought and culture. Thus, instead of merely ignoring Christianity, as did the majority of Hasidic masters and traditional Rabbis of his time, he sees Christianity as a faith to be fought against, a participant in a cosmic struggle, the outcome of which, however, is divinely ordained by the God of Israel.

NOTES

1. On R. Hayyim Eleazar see *Encyclopedia Judaica*, Vol. 14, pp. 1295–6; my *Theology in the Responsa*, London, 1975, pp. 288–90; my *Hasidic Prayer*, London and Washington, 1993, p. 39, S. Weingarten in *Shanah be-Shanah*, Jerusalem, 1980, pp. 440–9; Y. E. Gold: *Darkhey Hayyim ve-Shalom*, Jerusalem, 1974; Herman Dicker, *Piety and Perseverance: Jews from the Carpathian Mountains*, New York, 1981, Index, 'Spira, Chaim Eleazar'; A. A. Muller (ed. P. Muller), *Olamo Shel Abba*, Jerusalem, 1984, pp. 219–28.
2. *Minhat Eleazar*, Brooklyn, 1976; *Nimukey Orah Hayyim*, Jerusalem, 1968; *Ot Hayyim ve-Shalom*, Jerusalem, 1965; *Divrey Torah* (in nine parts), Jerusalem, 1974; *Shaar Yisakhar*, Jerusalem, 1968; *Hamishah Maamarot*, Jerusalem, 1952.
3. On the *Hemdat Yamim* and its alleged Sabbatean sympathies see; A. Yaari, *Taalumot Sefer*, Jerusalem, 1954 and R. Carmilly-Weinberger, *Censorship and Freedom of Expression in Jewish History*, New York, 1977, pp. 97–9 and notes. R. Hayyim Eleazar refers to the work as *Hemdat Ha-Yamim* (the title as given in the Zolkiev edition of 1753), but the original title is *Hemdat Yamim* (without the definite article) as in the Constantinople edition of 1731, published in facsimile by Mekor, Jerusalem, 1970.
4. *Hamishah Maamarot*, pp. 152–6.
5. Ibid., pp. 253–4. R. Hayyim Eleazar's detection of Christological elements in Hemdat Yamim was anticipated in the nineteenth century by A. B. Gottlober, *Zikhronot u-Masaot*, ed. E. Goldberg, Jerusalem, 1976, p.138. Gottlober remarks that not only is the book Sabbatean but there are hints that it is *shomeret yabam*, a pun on the term for a woman bound to a *yabam* (a levir), but here the word denotes *yeshu u ben miriam*, 'Jesus son of Mary'; see Goldberg's note.
6. On the Frankists see the article by Scholem, 'Frank, Jacob and the Frankists', in *Encyclopedia Judaica*, vol. 7, pp. 55–72.

7. *Bava Kama* 92b.
8. Zohar II, 206b.
9. *Divrey Torah*, part 1, no. 46. On the Munkacer's attitude to Christian countries and their rulers see *Divrey Torah*, part 7, no. 80.
10. For a similar suggestion by a Hasidic master that the Torah foretells the rise of Christianity see R. Yitzhak Eisik Safran of Komarno (1806–74) in his Commentary *Hekhal Ha-Berakhah*, Lemberg, 1869, on the verse which deals with the false prophet who gives a 'sign' (Deuteronomy 13:2). But there are traces of this interpretation in much earlier Jewish sources;, see J. Nahshuni, *Hagut be-Parshiot Ha-Torah*, Bene Berak, 1981, vol. 2, pp. 763–6. Nahshuni refers to the comment of Rabbenu Meyuhas to the verse. *Cf.* the saying of the Munkacer's great-great-grandfather, R. Zevi Elimelech of Dynov, that the initial letters of the word *ve-nokev* in Leviticus 24:16 dealing with the blasphemer hints at *yeshu* ('Jesus'); see Gold, *Darkhey Hayyim ve-Shalom*, p. 308, note 1. *Cf. The Torah: A Modern Commentary*, ed. Rabbi W. Gunther Plaut, New York, 1981, p.1434, for the similar comment of the Baal Ha-Turim. Another nineteenth-century Hasidic master who refers to the month of Tevet in similar vein is Jacob Zevi of Parasov in his *Ateret le-Rosh Tzaddik*, Warsaw, 1895, p.37.
11. On *Nittel* (from the medieval Latin *Natale Domini*) see Eisenstein's *Otzar Dinim u-Minhagim*, pp. 267–8 and *Iggerot Soferim*, ed. B. Sofer, Tel Aviv, 1970, *Letters of the Hatam Sofer*, nos 2 and 3.
12. Gold, *Darkhey Hayyim ve-Shalom*, number 828 on p. 308.
13. Gold remarks that the Munkacer gave strict instructions to those in charge of the *mikveh* to instruct the women who supervised the immersions that they should strongly advise the women who immersed themselves on this night not to have marital relations until after midnight. For the practices of the Hasidic group of Lubavitch see the journal *Noam*, Vol. 20 (Jerusalem 1978), pp. 325–7 regarding refraining from Torah study and marital relations on the night of *Nittel*.
14. See Scholem, *Kabbalah*, Jerusalem, 1974, p. 325 that this work is the last of the Kabbalistic works to invent a new demonology, i.e. new names for the *kelipot*. The first edition of *Sefer Karnayyim* is that of Zolkiev, 1707; ed. Lemberg, 1850.
15. *Divrey Torah*, part two, no. 45; *Shaar Yisakhar, Yemey Orah*, no. 122, p. 471 and *Maamar Hodesh Tevet*, pp. 477–8
16. See Gold, *Darkhey Hayyim ve-Shalom* no. 824, p. 307, note 1, that the Munkacer used to point out that many of the evil decrees against Jews were promulgated at this period of the year and he would eagerly await to proclaim in the synagogue the arrival of the next month, Shevat. And see no. 825, p. 308, note 1 for the story of the holy man (probably Zevi Hirsch of Zydachov) who studied the Torah on the night of *Nittel*, whereupon a savage dog came into his home, from which time he undertook never to study the Torah on this night. For 'Dogs' in this connection see *Jewish Encyclopedia*, Vol. 6 p. 632 (quoting Matthew 15:26 and Phil. 3:2); J. S. Bloch, *Israel and the Nations*, Berlin and Vienna, 1927, pp. 211ff; Zohar (in the uncensored eds), see G. Dalman, *Jesus Christ in the Talmud Midrash and Zohar*, Arno Press, New York, 1973, p. 19; *Otzar Ha-Zohar*, ed. Parish and Bransdorfer, Jerusalem, 1976 *s.v. kelavim Isaac of Acre: Sefer Meirat Enayim*, ed. C.A. Erlanger, Jerusalem, 1975. p. 235 and Erlanger's note.
17. Piska 86:2, translated William G. Braude, Yale University Press, 1968, vol.2. pp. 680–1.
18. *Shaar Yisakhar*, Vol. 1, *Maamar Hodesh Tishri*, no. 12, pp. 239–41.
19. *Darkhey Hayyim ve-Shalom*, p. 254, Letter 2. Cf. *Sefer Hasidim*, ed. R. Margaliot, Jerusalem, 1973, no. 528 (p. 348) for the saint who preferred to suffer himself rather than allow the Messiah to suffer. I am grateful to Professor Raphael Loewe for calling this source to my attention.
20. Gold, *Darkhey Huyyim ve-Shalom*, p. 344.
21. *Ketubot* 11a.
22. *Shitah Mekubetzet* to *Ketubot ad.loc.* that all the early versions have the Rashi as in the current texts but see the Commentary *Tosefot Rid*, printed in the margin of the Vilna Romm ed. who understands the passage in the same way as the Munkacer; see also *Shulhan Arukh Yoreh Deah* 268:7.
23. Note 1, pp. 344–5 in *Darkhey Hayyim ve-Shalom*.
24. Ibid., no. 902, p. 329, that the Munkacer was a Mohel and had circumcised over 3,000 boys 'apart from the proselytes he had converted'.

25. Responsa *Minhat Eleazar*, Vol. 2, no. 73.
26. Vol. 2, nos 27 and 30. On the whole question of whether the Halakhists consider Christianity to be idolatry see Jacob Katz, *Exclusiveness and Tolerance*, Oxford University Press, 1961; my *Theology in the Responsa*, London, 1975, Index 'Christianity' and my article 'Attitudes to Christianity', in *Gevurat Ha-Romah* (studies offered on the eighteeth birthday of M. C. Weiler) ed. Z. Falk, Jerusalem, 1987, pp. xxii–xxxi.
27. Vol. 2, no. 27.
28. Vol. 2, no. 30.
29. *Divrey Torah*, part one, no. 92.
30. Scholem, *The Messianic Idea in Judaism*, New York,1971, pp. 237–81.

Index